T0358770

"*Vulnerable Minds* is a mesmerizing read on an extremely important topic. Marc Hauser lucidly illuminates the science that establishes and explains the physical and psychological consequences of many kinds of adversity endured by millions of children in the US and around the world. Hauser documents in heartbreaking detail the prevalence of extreme neglect and of emotional, physical, and sexual abuse, as well as their devastating effects on children's physical and mental health. But the book also offers hope via evidence that many forms of intervention can ameliorate or even reverse the damage done to bodies and minds by childhood adversity. *Vulnerable Minds* is a call to action: we, as a society, cannot continue failing our children."

—Susan Carey, Morss Professor of Psychology, Harvard University, and author of *The Origin of Concepts*

"It will come as no surprise that childhood adversity can undermine the short- and long-term well-being of children and adolescents, no doubt because developmental scholars have been sharing their knowledge on this subject for more than half a century. But beyond the commonsensical claim that bad exposures lead to bad outcomes, there is much about how early life shapes human development that remains underappreciated, if only because keeping up with this ever-faster-moving field is a full-time job. Fortunately, *Vulnerable Minds* makes eminently accessible to the nonexpert much of what state-of-the-art research has taught us since the turn of the century. Even as so much of this latest work proves disheartening, this book also highlights what is promising, including that mistreated children often develop hidden talents; that children vary immensely in how and whether they are affected by adversity; and what can—and still needs to—be done so that ever more children can experience the developmental fruits of growing up safe and secure."

—Jay Belsky, professor emeritus, University of California, Davis, and author of *The Origins of You*

"The driving force of misery and violence throughout generations is the victimization of children. As a result, individuals and entire societies live on as both victims and perpetrators. In a unique and impressive masterpiece, Marc Hauser has elaborated the full spectrum of childhood adversities and its consequences. This must-read book not only provides the reader with revolutionary insights into the very nature and suffering of humans, but gives hope as it provides the necessary compass toward a better place in this world."

—Thomas Elbert, professor, University of Konstanz;
honorary professor, Université Lumière, Bujumbura;
and author of *Narrative Exposure Therapy*

"We have long known that children exposed to adversity in the early years of life are at risk for experiencing both mental and physical health concerns as they grow older. Sadly, today's youth seem to be confronted with even more challenges than in previous generations. The worldwide coronavirus pandemic, mass shootings, and an unprecedented refugee crisis are but three examples. In Marc Hauser's well-researched, exquisitely written and heartfelt account of the misfortunes and horrors many children face, we learn how some children suffer greatly and a fortunate few are spared. For anyone interested in how early life adversity impacts the course of child development, I strongly encourage them to read *Vulnerable Minds*."

—Charles A. Nelson, professor of pediatrics, neuroscience, and psychiatry,
Harvard Medical School; Richard David Scott Chair in Pediatric
Developmental Medicine Research, Boston Children's Hospital;
and author of *Romania's Abandoned Children*

"With the experience of a caring parent, insights of an experienced teacher, and analytical skills of a scientist, Marc Hauser trains his eyes on adverse childhood events, or ACEs. He describes how children process adversity differently depending on its type, timing, toxicity, how long it lasts, and how much local support they find. Along with clear and succinct explanations of the physical and mental health impacts of early adversity, Hauser provides constructive proposals for dealing with trauma's consequences. Anyone raising, interacting with, supervising, or devising policies that impact children needs to read this book."

—Sarah Blaffer Hrdy, professor emerita, University of California, Davis, and author of *Mother Nature*

vulnerable
minds

THE HARM OF CHILDHOOD TRAUMA
AND THE HOPE OF RESILIENCE

MARC D. HAUSER

AVERY
AN IMPRINT OF PENGUIN RANDOM HOUSE
NEW YORK

AVERY

an imprint of Penguin Random House LLC
penguinrandomhouse.com

Most Avery books are available at special quantity discounts for bulk purchase
for sales promotions, premiums, fundraising, and educational needs.
Special books or book excerpts also can be created to fit specific needs.
For details, write SpecialMarkets@penguinrandomhouse.com.

Library of Congress Cataloging-in-Publication Data

Names: Hauser, Marc D., author.
Title: Vulnerable minds: the harm of childhood trauma and
  the hope of resilience / Marc D. Hauser.
Description: 1 Edition. | New York: Avery, Penguin Random House LLC, [2024] |
  Includes index.
Identifiers: LCCN 2023026669 (print) | LCCN 2023026670 (ebook) |
  ISBN 9780593538692 (hardcover) | ISBN 9780593538715 (epub)
Subjects: LCSH: Abused children—Services for. | Abused children—Rehabilitation. |
  Adult child abuse victims—Rehabilitation.
Classification: LCC HV6626.5.H38 2024 (print) | LCC HV6626.5 (ebook)
LC record available at https://lccn.loc.gov/2023026669
LC ebook record available at https://lccn.loc.gov/2023026670

Printed in the United States of America
1st Printing

Book design by Laura K. Corless

To all who have suffered from childhood adversity,
*and to all who provide roads to recovery.**

*A portion of the proceeds of this book will be given
to charities that help children who have suffered
from adversity.

CONTENTS

Introduction: A Stolen Life ___ xi

part one
DAWNING A NEW UNDERSTANDING OF CHILDHOOD ADVERSITY AND TRAUMA

1 **Adversity:** Disrupting Childhood ___ 3

2 **Responses:** Traumatic and Resilient ___ 29

3 **Hidden Dimensions:** The Adverse Ts ___ 47

part two
HARM: LETHAL LANDSCAPES OF ADVERSITY

4 **Deprivation:** The Unmotivated Mind ___ 83

5 **Abuse:** The Fearful Mind ___ 103

6 **War:** The Chaotic Mind ___ 123

part three
HOPE: ROADS TO RESILIENCE AND RECOVERY

7 **Immunity:** The Ingredients of Change ___ 145

contents

8 Community: The Caring Cultures — 167

9 Neuroengineering: The Transformation of Maladaptive
Thoughts — 207

Afterword: The Way Forward: A Deserved Life — 239

Acknowledgments — 247

Notes — 249

Index — 291

A Stolen Life

After his grandmother died, five-year-old LJ lived a nomad's life. He wandered with his mother from house to house, sleeping on couches, alarmed by gunshots, raging parties, police sirens, and drug deals. LJ's mother was only sixteen years old when he was born and he never met his father, a part-time boyfriend with a substantial criminal record. Year after year, LJ missed more school days than he attended. By his ninth birthday, LJ had experienced a wealth of adversity: physical neglect, gang violence, poverty, home displacement, and the absence of a father. LJ was robbed of early childhood.

As LJ entered the fourth grade, his life changed. An athletic coach noticed his chaotic home environment and offered a more stable, nurturing alternative. LJ moved in with his coach. LJ thrived, turning chronic absenteeism from school into perfect attendance and absolute domination on the basketball court. This is LJ's story, the story of LeBron James, one of the greatest basketball players of all time.

LeBron's early childhood story is not an uncommon one, albeit surprising for a wealthy nation such as the United States. It is a story of poverty coupled with other types of adversity that children often experience in tandem: exposure to violence, neglect, loss of a parent or caretaker, and displacement from the home. Children across the globe are exposed to these different types of adversities and others. For many children, their experiences turn into trauma, bleeding them of purpose, meaning, and desire. For some children, like LeBron, they meet these experiences with resilience, propped up by their biology and community.

From the beginning of recorded history, and undoubtedly for millennia before, children—male and female, of all races, in developing and developed countries, within democracies or dictatorships, with or without schooling, and with or without religious upbringing—have been scarred by adversity. Some adversities, such as physical and sexual abuse, racial and sexual discrimination, not only damage the victims but provide a pathway for intergenerational trauma. Other types of adversity, such as emotional and physical deprivation, starve the organs of the body and mind, leaving the wilted child without hope or the skills to flourish. And yet other types of adversity, including racism, stigmatization, domestic violence, and disease can burn the fabric of relationships, annihilate self-worth, and unhinge a child's identity. Our children continue to suffer in spite of the mandate from the UN Convention on the Rights of the Child that we protect them from neglect, physical and sexual abuse, sexual and economic exploitation, being used as soldiers, and exposure to torture, cruelty, and inhumane treatment.

Worst of all, when our children suffer, we often fail to provide them with adequate help, sometimes because we lack an understanding, sometimes because our cultural norms fail to acknowledge the injury, and sometimes because policy fails to recognize the distinctive features of childhood trauma.[1] We are failing our children.

In 1998, medical researchers Vincent Felitti, Robert Anda, and their colleagues published a landmark paper on adverse childhood experiences, or ACEs, that sent shock waves throughout the healthcare world: In a population of several thousand American adults, those with more ACEs had more severe mental and physical health problems. Those dealt a hand of ACEs were more likely to fold in life, suffering extreme consequences including higher incidences of substance abuse, suicide, obesity, depression, liver disease, school dropout, and lower life expectancy. These findings, replicated in other countries, signaled the discovery of a global health crisis, one affecting our youngest and most vulnerable.

The World Health Organization estimates that a billion children, annually, on every continent, travel a Kafkaesque journey through a landscape that is potted with abuse, deprivation, war, family dysfunction, discrimination, and disease. Though the simple math of *more ACEs = more health problems* is relatively clear, restricting the focus to only the *number* of ACEs leaves unresolved two problems at the heart of helping children overcome adversity:

1. Do different types of ACEs result in different scars on a child's body and brain, and does their timing, duration, severity, and predictability matter?

2. Why are some individuals more resilient to ACEs and able to avoid negative outcomes?

Over the past two decades, the sciences have assembled an impressive body of evidence addressing the first question, showing that different types of ACEs lead to different physical and mental scars—they create unique signatures of a disrupted development. What we have also learned is that the type of adversity is not the only dimension that shapes the path this disruption takes. Using a novel framework, I show that the dimensions of timing, duration, severity, and predictability provide unique contributions to the transformation of a child's body and brain. Understanding how this transformation works is the only way we can help children build resilience and recover from adversity.

The second question is urgent for understanding the nature and nurture of recovery, including why some individuals are more resilient to adversity, while others are more vulnerable. Here, too, the sciences have profoundly deepened our understanding, allowing us to help those who have been scarred by adversity, identify those who have positively grown from the trauma they've experienced, and strengthen the core of those who may confront adverse experiences in the future.

Every child begins their journey with a story, one that interacts with their environment to develop a plot. But we now know that we can design interventions that help a child who has suffered and impact how her life unfolds. The sciences show that bringing awareness and guided interventions to communities exposed to the ravages of war, discrimination, poverty, and disease, can help individuals heal, often by removing stigma and discrimination. Radically new, and sometimes controversial, studies suggest that stimulating the brain with electrical pulses or psychedelics can effectively erase pathological responses to adversity, allowing individuals to leave behind traumatic stress disorders, anxiety, and depression. Though our bodies keep score of our responses to adverse experiences, an idea beautifully expressed in psychiatrist Bessel van der Kolk's writings[2] is that we can enable recovery, lower the score, and prepare our children for the life ahead.

This is a science of hope, as distinguished pediatrician Jack Shonkoff has articulated: "The time has come to leverage twenty-first-century science to catalyze the design, testing, and scaling of more powerful approaches for reducing lifelong disease by mitigating the effects of early adversity."[3] In the same way that we have celebrated countless moral victories across the globe, including gay rights, animal rights, freedom of expression, and the decline of wars, let us harness our collective knowledge and envision a world where all children can learn, love, laugh, and live long, healthy lives.

My approach brings together insights from a wide range of disciplines, including fields that rarely if ever cross-pollinate—evolutionary biology, psychotherapy, medicine, anthropology, public health, genetics, psychology, education, and neuroscience. I've always been a firm believer in interdisciplinary work, as I discussed in my two earlier books on the mind—*Wild Minds* focused on animal cognition and *Moral Minds* focused on our sense of right and wrong.[4] No single approach holds all the answers, and understanding often comes from trying on different conceptual lenses. Understanding childhood adversity and trauma is a prime arena for cross-pollination given the vast differences in adverse experiences and a child's responses to them. Whether the adversity is packaged as deprivation, abuse, family dysfunction, war, environmental threats, or a combination of these types of adversity, some children respond with bone-shaking pathology, some with petrified immobility, and yet others with confident resilience. Cross-pollination helps us understand what creates vulnerability and strength.

The sciences of childhood adversity, trauma, resilience, and recovery are vast and growing. In my telling of this literature, I have been selective, focusing on topics supported by the strongest evidence to date. As a result, some types of adversity and approaches to recovery may only be given a brief mention. In addition, this book focuses almost exclusively on children as opposed to the many other books that look at trauma in adults who have experienced childhood adversity. Though there is great need to help adults who suffer from trauma, we must also understand traumatic responses as they unfold in development, because the heightened plasticity of the child's developing body and brain offers the greatest opportunity for change.

In Part I, I start with a discussion of typical child development, including both the unfolding of successful competencies and the challenges that can arise from defective nature and nurture. I then turn to a brief history of the discovery of ACEs, including their staggering potential to undermine physical and mental health—deviations from typical development. I next present a new framework for understanding childhood adversity, one that shifts our focus beyond the type of adversity to consider timing, duration, severity, and predictability—dimensions that uniquely contribute to a child's traumatic response.

In Part II: Harm, I focus on three different types of childhood adversity—deprivation, abuse, and war—including how their timing, duration, severity, and predictability uniquely transform the developing body and brain, creating distinctive signatures. Understanding these signatures is essential to formulating interventions that can help children build resilience to and recover from adversity.

In Part III: Hope, I start with our current understanding of resilience, including the role that biology plays in launching individual differences. I then turn to different approaches to building resilience to and recovery from childhood adversity, including the role of community, school, brain stimulation, and psychedelics. These approaches are often accompanied by talk therapy, though the therapeutic style may vary in focus by culture.[5]

I wrote this book listening to different voices of suffering from adversity. I am the son of a father who lived, as a child, in Nazi-occupied France, often away from his parents. I am the father of two extraordinary daughters: my eldest suffered the pain of my divorce, while my youngest was adopted at an early age from an orphanage, where she was deprived of many core needs. I am a husband, married to a wonderful woman who grew up in poverty and lost her father, at an early age, to manic depression. I am a scientist and an educator who has worked with hundreds of children scarred by different types of adversity. As a child I was badly bullied for a period of two years; and as an adult, I experienced an extended period of adversity that some readers may be aware of. I stepped down from my professorship at Harvard University because of research misconduct. This was painful, for myself, my students and colleagues, my family and friends. But I have learned much from this experience, knowledge that has led to the second chapter of my career, dedicated to helping children with trauma and different disabilities learn, grow, and enjoy what life has to offer. Working with these children, as well as with their teachers, therapists, and doctors, has certainly been the most meaningful and rewarding work of my life.

All these voices of suffering harmonize into a crescendo that is an urgent call to action, to ameliorate the lives of our most vulnerable. As psychiatrist Bruce Perry and actor-host-philanthropist Oprah Winfrey write in their powerful book,[6] we must not only listen to these voices but understand what happened to them if our shared goal is to help them move forward and thrive.

I love the joy, wonder, innocence, and curiosity of childhood. My heart aches when I think of the millions of children, of all cultures, deprived of these experiences. This sinking feeling is buoyed, however, by revolutionary discoveries in the sciences that not only help us understand how adversity transforms the bodies and brains of our most vulnerable but directly contributes to solutions that enhance recovery at the individual and community level. This is a message of hope, one that I want to share with victims, parents, teachers, clinicians, doctors, policymakers, and entrepreneurs so that we can collaboratively contribute to greater human flourishing.

part one

DAWNING A NEW UNDERSTANDING OF CHILDHOOD ADVERSITY AND TRAUMA

I know when a storm is coming.
I can feel the invisible stirrings in the air.
—EVE ENSLER[1]

Adversity: Disrupting Childhood

During World War II, brilliant polymath Alan Turing helped crack the Nazis' Enigma machine for sending secret messages by inventing a program that was both general and generative. Because the Nazis changed details of the specific messages each day, a general framework that would work for every coded correspondence was necessary, since a program designed to translate only a specific message would fail every time the message changed. The generative or iterative piece was able to come up with a novel solution to break each unique encryption. This way of thinking, modeled explicitly by Turing to simulate the human brain's general intelligence, ultimately led to his development of the Automatic Computing Engine, the foundation of modern computing.[1]

Millions of years before Turing, animals evolved general and generative developmental programs to survive in a complex landscape. Whether it is a bee, bird, bonobo, or baby sapiens, every developing organism within a certain species starts this journey with shared, biologically engineered goals and timelines for achieving them. If the developmental program is damaged, due to mutations, significant problems can arise and it can be very hard to get a child back on course, as we will see later in this chapter in the story of a student I worked with named Sean. If the program is undamaged, then a child has the best possible start in life.

However, within that shared journey, the experiences of life are variable and virtually limitless and so our evolutionary programming is not the only factor in how our life unfolds. Our environments play a massive role and must also follow the expected course. If the timing and nature of our experiences are as expected by our developmental programs, the journey is likely to be good: a fertilized egg develops into a babbling baby, a school-ready child, a teenager ready to take the next step, and a skilled and loving adult who eventually retires having lived a well-adjusted, meaningful life. When the evolutionary programming is working correctly, but adversity interrupts this finely tuned set of biological expectations, a child's ability to navigate the journey of growing up is significantly hindered. These children are the primary focus of this book. We have an obligation to minimize the risks of their bad journeys.

DEVELOPMENTAL SIGNATURES OF SUCCESS

Human babies are engineering marvels. Based on millions of years of R & D, evolution has built these tiny creatures with minds and bodies that are programmed for survival and reproduction. Both of these goals depend on skills for navigating the physical and social world, including the ability to recognize and manipulate objects, count, understand others' beliefs and intentions, acquire and use language, enjoy and move to music, recognize, express and control emotions, and judge what is morally right or wrong. Each developmental program has a signature, essentially a set of unique instructions that specifies what experience is expected and when to achieve particular outcomes.

The notion of expected experience doesn't have to be a conscious one, something that babies are aware of. In fact, the majority of developmental programs run far beneath the radar of consciousness, relying on utterly unconscious and inaccessible processes. Consider magic. When we watch a magician performing their art, we are surprised when some principle of the physical world is violated—a person sawed in half, a rabbit emerging from a hat, two solid rings joined, a ripped-up card spontaneously emerging whole. The surprise or trick is what makes it magical. Our sense of the physical world drives our visual systems to expect things to work or behave in particular ways. This sense, and the expectations that follow, do not come from having taken physics classes. Rather, they come from the evolutionary engineering that created brains that expect truths about the physical world: a human body can't be divided in half and then, without major surgery and a Hail Mary of hope, be made whole and walk away; a fragmented solid object can't spontaneously and instantaneously become solid again without some kind of glue; a large, solid object can't fit inside a smaller solid container without some kind of deformation or transformation. Engineered expectations also guide a baby's sense of the social world.

In studies looking at the nature of baby expectations, the design is largely the same, whether we are probing their understanding of physics, music, mathematics, language, social relationships, or morality. Babies sit in a chair or on their parent's lap while watching an event unfold on a stage. One event is consistent with how the world works and one is inconsistent. If babies have expectations about the world, specifically the ways in which it is predictable, reliable, and trustworthy, then they should be bored by the consistent events, but engaged, wowed, and gobsmacked by the inconsistent ones. Based on hundreds of experiments, tiny human babies—just beginning the journey of life—are, in fact, awed by events that disrupt their early understanding of the world. The situations that garner this reaction vary wildly in type: a solid object rolling or dropping through another solid object; a person helping someone who hurt them; musical sequences that are dissonant; a person speaking ungrammatically or using the wrong word to label an object; addition operations that don't generate the proper sums; people who express sadness or fear to objects they like and joy to objects they dislike; and, among these examples, caretakers who ignore requests for help or act aggressively. These expectations about different features of the world are driven by different programs, each with a unique signature that defines the relevant experience for achieving successful developmental outcomes.

Consider language. The way humans acquire language must be generative and general like Alan Turing's solution to the Nazi Enigma machine, but it is also dependent on a certain set of experiences that are necessary for success. The program must be general because a newborn baby can't know in advance what language—of the hundreds that are possible—it will hear or see (if the child is deaf). It must be generative because, ultimately, humans are able to comprehend and convey a limitless number of possible expressions when they communicate. The experience-specific piece comes into play because children only acquire languages with human sounds or signs.

This is just one example of the way our brains were designed by evolution with experience-expectant developmental programs designed to help us become fully functioning human beings. Some programs—such as our ability to acquire language, learn music or math, or gain a sense of morality—need to happen in partnership with highly specific experiences, during certain periods of development, to generate a successful outcome. Other programs—such as our memory, attention, inhibition—require more general experiences, often within a wider developmental window. Our development, as nature designed, hinges on these great expectations being met. And when they are not met, whether it's because the type, amount, or timing of our experiences are not in line with what this code needs, then parts of our development are thrown off course or even erased.

ERASING THE SIGNATURE OF EMOTIONAL AWARENESS

I first met Sean[2] while he was sitting in a quiet space within an alternative school for children with emotional disabilities—disabilities associated with poor recognition, expression, and control of emotion. Sean was a beautiful fourteen-year-old boy with golden hair down to his shoulders, brilliant green eyes, a dimpled chin, and a stocky athletic build. He was sporting a Lionel Messi soccer jersey—one of my sports idols—and he was calm. He asked me my name and age. I obliged and asked him his name and age. He answered and then continued to ask about my interests, including my favorite sports, ice cream flavor, movies, and hobbies. I felt as if I were being interviewed.

In the midst of my perfectly pleasant conversation with Sean, his teacher, Miss Linda, walked in. Sean transformed, unrecognizable from his previous state, sweat pouring from his forehead, eyes piercing, fury filling his voice. He erupted:

"Linda, you fucking cunt. I bet you're a whore, as you'd have to get money to get fucked. I should have smacked you instead of that dumbshit, Johnny. He's a dumb fuck."

Sean then tore up the room, punching and kicking the walls, spitting at Miss Linda, and continuing his barrage of verbal abuse. Miss Linda was calm throughout, ultimately deciding to leave, as Sean was clearly unprepared to process and return to class. As soon as she left, Sean transformed again, wiping the sweat from his forehead and the blood from his fists, sitting down in the middle of the floor, and looking straight up at me, his voice calm: "Hey, Marc, I like soccer, too. I love Messi. He's a genius with his feet. Maybe we can play sometime." Sean's rapid conversion from calm to fury and back again was frightening to observe and wrenchingly sad.

Sean was placed in an alternative school because of conduct problems, which included stealing from or bullying others to give him their Pokémon cards or snacks, physically fighting on a daily basis, and lighting a fire in the bathroom. Children, such as Sean, with conduct problems exhibit a broad range of social problems including violence, manipulation, lying, and violation of moral rules and social conventions. Those that express these characteristics early in childhood commonly develop poor social relationships later in life, coupled with low odds of employment and high odds of criminal records. Though there are many pathways leading to such conduct problems, for Sean it was what clinicians call *callous-unemotional*, traits that were recognizable as early as preschool—a sign that the expected signature of emotional awareness had been erased. Like many such traits, there is a wide spectrum, and Sean was considered on the high end, lacking any sense of remorse, guilt, or empathy. He had no compassion for others' pain or sadness, and felt no joy in others' successes. Without these fundamental emotions and moral anchors, there is little to guide actions in the moment or to learn from the consequences of violating moral and social conventions. Sean didn't feel bad about the barrage of verbal abuse he heaped on top of Miss Linda. He didn't feel bad about his often violent attacks on his loving parents or siblings. He didn't feel much at all, except violent rage.

In the latest edition of the *Diagnostic and Statistical Manual of Mental Disorders (DSM-5)*, the spectrum of traits associated with callous-unemotional is classified as *limited prosocial emotions*. Studies carried out by cognitive neuroscientist Essi Viding[3] and her colleagues of identical and fraternal twins show that callous-unemotional is a highly heritable trait, with a substantial genetic contribution. Sean grew up in a loving family environment, his parents were happily married, though they were stressed and concerned by their inability to help their oldest son, and yet this support could not ameliorate his built-in wiring—a defective developmental program. Remarkably, the callous-unemotional phenotype can be observed as early as three and a half years, remains stable throughout development, and often results in a clinical diagnosis of psychopathy in adulthood, the latter associated with extreme conduct problems and a failure to thrive within the moral, social, and legal norms of society. A child with callous-unemotional traits has been handed a species-*atypical* program for emotional development. The likelihood of a healthy outcome is poor. The likelihood of Sean turning out okay was poor.

Sean's story shows what happens when our evolved developmental program malfunctions. It is the story of a developmental program falling off the rails, and it has an unhappy ending. But unfortunate endings can occur even when a child's developmental program works to perfection.

ERASING THE SIGNATURE OF ATTACHMENT

Our earliest and most critical environmental influence is the bond we share with our mothers, which starts before we are born and extends for many years into our lives. In a secure attachment, a child feels safe, and expects her nutritional, cognitive, emotional, and protective needs to be met at the right time. The child also feels empowered to independently explore and cultivate trusting social relationships with others, both inside and out of her immediate family. But when this essential bond is frayed, a child loses this fundamental sense of security.

Ellie illustrates what can happen when a child fails to develop a healthy attachment signature. Ellie was six when I first met her, but she appeared much younger in many ways. She often moved abruptly, as if controlled by intermittent static electric shocks. She seemed uncomfortable in her own skin. Ellie was raised by her mother, her father having left when she was only a year old. When I met her mother, she seemed detached, rarely looking at, touching, or talking to Ellie. When she did speak to her, it tended to be in command form, variants of *Don't do that!* and *Stop it!* When Ellie was surprised or alarmed by seeing someone she didn't know, she would initially move toward her mom or another caretaker, but then often moved away. Ellie seemed invisible to her mother, who was off the radar when it comes to the kind of parenting that a child is biologically built to expect. Ellie appeared to inhabit a turbulent universe in which maternal love was unpredictable and the threat of abandonment was palpable.

Several decades of exquisite research on human infants by developmental psychologist Karlen Lyons-Ruth, together with observations of children separated from their parents in the process of immigration and detailed experiments on rodents, shows that the threat of abandonment has devastating effects on the developing child and pup, leading to a clinical diagnosis of disorganized attachment.[4]

For newborn human infants and rodent pups, mothers are the only source of nutrition, comfort, and calming. Infants and pups are biologically engineered to expect milk on demand, warmth and protection from the environment, soothing at times of stress, and clear, coordinated communication. Without these ingredients, the healthy attachment signature is erased with devastating consequences. Rodent pups developing in an impoverished maternal environment have more than one thousand genes linked to brain development and stress regulation that are deficient with respect to expression. These pups have a hyper-active amygdala, a brain area involved in the fear response and, more generally, in assigning a valence of roughly good or bad to emotions. Within the amygdala, they have a lower density of benzodiazepine receptors—critical for regulating or inhibiting anxiety—and a higher output of stress hormones. All of these physiological changes lead to life-changing behaviors: they reach puberty at an earlier age and have heightened sexual activity; once they have babies, they show less of an investment in their own pups; even three generations later, this family of mice have pups who are more stressed, which suggests that the stress is passed through the generations.

We now know that these features of abandoned pups have direct parallels with abandoned human infants. An infant with disorganized attachment shows behaviors that are distinct from the signature reper-toire of an infant with organized attachment, including:

- fearful, uncertain expressions and depressed or lethargic behavior
- freezing and spontaneous arrest of previously initiated actions
- wandering and mixed-message expressions (e.g., crying and laughing)
- lack of consistent or appropriate strategies for care (e.g., calling for help, moving away)

These behavioral indicators of poor attachment are, unfortunately, maintained by a mother who may mock or tease her infant, communicate an invitation to approach while moving away, express confused or frightened emotions, interact at a distance or in silence, and show little coordinated communication. By the age of eighteen months, infants who have experienced this type of abandonment in the form of moth-ers withdrawing from their responsibility are more likely to have borderline personality disorder by the age of fifteen years. In the *DSM-5*, borderline personality disorder is defined as "a pervasive pattern of instability of interpersonal relationships, self-image, and affects, and marked impulsivity beginning by early adulthood and present in a variety of contexts." The impact on these individuals, as well as society, is massive, with evidence of heightened suicidal ideation, sexual promiscuity, eating disorders, substance abuse, bullying, and reactive violence.

It's important to note that disorganized attachment has sometimes been misinterpreted by doctors, clinicians, and policymakers as inextricably linked to maltreatment. Though some children with disorganized attachment have been maltreated, not all have. Some children with disorganized attachment have biologically rooted impairments of emotion, communication, and sensory systems. And some children who *have* been maltreated or neglected don't show disorganized attachment at all.

What Lyons-Ruth's work shows is that deprivation early in life is a massive risk factor, predictive of bad things to come. Ellie, as well as all other children who have been abandoned or deprived by their parents of expectations of care, are likely to suffer later in life.

THE ORIGINS OF ACES

In 1985, the adverse experiences that Ellie and other children confront early in life were codified by a chance conversation between a preventive medicine doctor and his patient. This small moment launched a seismic shift in our understanding of the risk factors impacting human physical and mental health across the globe.

Dr. Vincent Felitti was in charge of an obesity clinic in Southern California. One of his patients, Patty, weighed 408 pounds when she entered the clinic. By means of a novel and safe fasting procedure, Felitti helped Patty drop down to 132 pounds within fifty-two weeks. But within less than a month of this profound transformation, Patty regained 37 pounds. When Felitti asked her what was going on, she noted that she lived alone, but felt that she must be sleep-eating, as she would come downstairs in the morning and notice open boxes or cans of food, pots and pans—evidence that someone had been cooking and eating. She had no recollection of doing this. When Felitti probed further, he learned that she had recently been sexually involved with an older coworker. When he asked why, she revealed a long history of incest, and that she had been sexually abused by her grandfather. She felt that this abuse opened her up to heightened promiscuity, which led to lowered self-worth, which led to uncontrollable eating to reduce the associated anxiety. Sex with her coworker was a trigger. Eating was her response.

Felitti proceeded to ask dozens of additional patients in his obesity clinic about their history, and repeatedly, the majority indicated a history of sexual abuse. When he presented his findings at a professional conference on eating disorders, he was mocked by the audience of experts, considered naive for not seeing that his patients were creating fabricated versions of reality to hide their failures. Fortunately, that night at the conference dinner, he sat next to Dr. David Williamson, who worked for the Centers for Disease Control and Prevention (CDC). Williamson told him that if he was right about the link between childhood sexual abuse and later-life health, it had immense implications for medicine and policy. But to prove his point, he would need a large-scale study of thousands of individuals, including from a more general and representative group, and assessing other types of childhood adversity than just sexual abuse.

Felitti and his CDC medical collaborator, Robert Anda, were fortunate in that about fifty thousand individuals came through the Kaiser

Permanente clinic each year for highly comprehensive medical examinations, including details of physical and mental health problems. Of these, they were able to recruit 8,056 in the first wave of the study, evenly split among women and men, all older than eighteen years with an average age of fifty-six years. The majority were White, all with high-end medical insurance, and slightly less than half with a college degree. Though this was a largely middle-class American population, it was a start in broadening the population.

To broaden the range of potential risk factors beyond sexual abuse, Felitti's team created a questionnaire that included other potential adverse childhood experiences, or ACEs, within the family environment—experiences that seemed atypical, unexpected, and potentially harmful to a child's developmental programs.[5] The ACEs were clustered into two broad **domains**, each with their own specific *types*[6]: **Abuse** included *physical, sexual,* and *emotional.* **Household dysfunction** included *substance abuse, mental illness, incarceration,* and *mother treated violently.*

The questionnaire asked subjects to identify whether they had experienced these seven different types of adversity before the age of eighteen years—a broad swath of time, all linked to what Felitti, Anda, and their colleagues considered "childhood." Felitti's team tallied up the number of ACEs for each participant to create an ACE score. This was not a measure of when or how often or for how long or with what intensity an ACE occurred. It was simply a measure of the number of ACE types, yielding a score from zero to seven.

The initial results, published in 1998,[7] were mind-blowing in three different ways. First, half of the population had one or more ACEs. Second, a majority of people with one ACE had other ACEs, showing that ACEs pile up in the lives of many. Third, those with more ACEs had more mental and physical health problems.

Following the original publication, Felitti, Anda, and their team carried out a second study, adding several thousand more people, a third domain of adversity—**neglect**—as well as an additional type of household dysfunction—*parent separation* or *divorce*. Thus, in addition to answering questions about different types of abuse and household dysfunction, participants also addressed whether they had been *emotionally* or *physically* neglected, or experienced a marriage breakup. With these three additional ACE types, the potential score increased to ten.

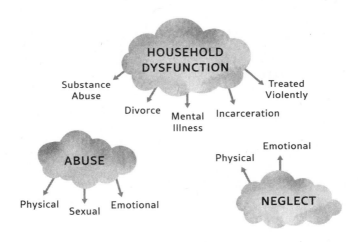

With a total sample of 17,337 individuals, and comparable demographics to the first half of the study, the results were clear: 64 percent had at least one ACE and 12.5 percent had four or more ACEs. And paralleling the first study, the higher the number of ACEs, the more severe the mental and physical health problems: compared to individuals with zero ACES, those with four ACEs were ten times more likely to be substance abusers, twelve times more likely to attempt suicide, and 240 percent more likely to get hepatitis or a sexually transmitted disease; individuals with six or more ACEs had a shorter life expectancy of almost twenty years and a 4,600 percent greater likelihood of attempting suicide than those without ACEs. As ACEs pile up in a population, so, too, do the cumulative health risks of this population.

Felitti and Anda's findings sent a shock wave through the medical community. Given the millions of children across the continents that were likely exposed to such adversity, as well as the number of individuals who, as adults, were already suffering the consequences, there was little doubt that this discovery would have far-reaching implications for medicine, healthcare, education, policy, social work, parenting, and human rights, perhaps signaling a global health crisis. For individuals exposed to ACEs, it might help them make sense of their maladies—what happened to them.

While Felitti and Anda's original work was impressive, the study population was largely middle-class, educated, White Americans from Southern California. Few suspected that ACEs would observe either state or national borders, but an army of researchers soon got to work to consider potential sources of variation.

In the United States, there is little evidence that certain states are prone to have residents with more ACEs than others. There is also no difference between urban and rural areas, though some studies report different percentages for those with only one ACE and those with four or more.[8] Differences arise because of income, education, and race: people of color, those without a high school degree, and individuals with annual incomes less than fifteen thousand dollars have more ACEs than White, college-educated individuals with annual incomes above fifteen thousand dollars. Across all states, poverty appears as the most significant correlate of the number of ACEs, a dimension of society that ought to be fixable. But what if poverty was an intermediary marker, not a primary cause? We will dig into this more in Part III, where I tackle how society can help reduce the burden of childhood adversity.

ACEs also disrespect national borders. Using an international translation of the original ACEs survey, the World Health Organization and Centers for Disease Control launched a global initiative that reveals the universality of childhood exposure to adversity, as well as its costs. In both Eastern and Western Europe, the prevalence rates of

ACEs are similar to the United States, with 50 to 60 percent of the population reporting at least one ACE, and about 10 to 15 percent reporting four or more ACEs. In China, studies report that between 40 and 70 percent of people have at least one ACE. In studies of middle-lower income countries, prevalence rates are often higher. For example, in a study in South Africa, 88 percent had one or more ACEs and 33 percent had four or more; in Botswana, 73 percent had at least one ACE, whereas 15 percent had five or more ACEs.[9]

ACEs have acquired frequent-flier status, globe-trotting with a universal access passport. But what about their cost to the human condition? Is one ACE sufficient to derail the developmental signatures or are multiple ACEs required?

THE CUMULATIVE BURDEN OF ACES

The number of ACEs matter, in part, because of how our bodies and brains respond to repeated experiences. Think of heavyweight championship boxers like Mike Tyson or Floyd Mayweather who took repeated blows to the head and upper body during their careers. Studies of professional fighters reveal a high percentage who are punch-drunk or, more technically, have chronic traumatic encephalopathy (CTE), a form of brain damage first identified by Dr. Bennet Omalu in National Football League players. Among boxers, repeated hits to the head are often associated with shrinkage in key areas of the brain, which is linked to Parkinson's disease, neurological disorders, and even early death. Importantly, the higher the Fight Exposure score—a measure of the duration and intensity of fights—the smaller the brain volume. In the same way that repeated hits to the head lead to lasting damage in boxing, repeated experiences with stressful adversity also injures us, undermining the process of allostasis, or the essential adaptive process through which we regulate short-lived stressors and keep our body and brain in balance. A heavy load of ACEs will likely undermine our allostasis. The three essential players in allostasis are our nervous, immune, and endocrine systems, which all evolved to be most sensitive and flexible to changes in our environment. But staying in balance is a tightrope walk, as there are limits to the amount of flexibility these systems can handle.

Think of our body's core temperature. Most of us hover, most of the time, at about 98.6°F. But if the temperature dips below 95°F or rises above 103°F, there is severe risk of body and brain damage. These are the body's guardrails. When stress accumulates, as in the case of repeated exposure to adversity, we build up what biologist Bruce McEwen called *allostatic load*—leading to potentially irreversible changes in our regulatory tool kit.[10] Allostatic load is our body and brain's fingerprint— a unique marking of our individual history of adversity.

In a lecture to the National Congress of American Indians,[11] Felitti described a particularly striking example of allostatic load in a woman who, as a child, was sexually abused by her father and often brought along to local saloons, pimped out to drunken men who wanted sex for the night. Despite her repeated childhood experience of sexual abuse, she somehow made it through grade school, college, and law school, and onto the bench as a federal judge. On the surface, she appeared a model of resiliency, immune to the abuse she endured as a child. But her résumé concealed adversity's toll. Her allostatic load was high (though, as I will discuss in the next section, her ACE score was one) and the consequences severe, as she had battled five different types of cancer, multiple sclerosis, rheumatoid arthritis, and lupus. Her immune system was destroyed. Sexual abuse left an imprint on her body that was, in some sense, concealed by her professional achievements.

To appreciate the impact of allostatic load, let me translate to some population-level health measures. In a 2019 analysis of 20,654,832 individuals, early childhood adversity accounted for 439,072 deaths and 15 percent of all mortalities, with heart rate, cancer, and suicide being the primary mediators. Another study, by public health researchers Karen Hughes, Mark Bellis, and their colleagues, analyzed the impact of ACEs using data from thirty-seven studies and approximately 240,000 individuals looking at a key statistical measure called an *odds ratio*, which shows how strong the association is between an exposure to some experience and some outcome. In this case, they were looking at the strength of association between exposure to some number of ACEs and a suite of health outcomes. Odds ratios that are equal to one indicate no association, whereas values greater than one indicate an association; the bigger the odds ratio, the stronger the association. Comparing individuals with zero ACEs to those with four or more, Hughes and Bellis found that the weakest odds ratio (<2) was for physical inactivity, obesity, and diabetes; a strong odds ratio (3–6) for sexual risk-taking, mental illness, and alcohol abuse; and the strongest odds ratio (7+) for substance abuse and physical violence toward self and others. These results show that cumulative adversity during childhood has significant health risks, and some health risks are more likely than others.[12]

The cumulative burden of ACEs plays out in another arena: economics. ACEs leave us with an impressive financial tab, linked to costs of healthcare and expenses associated with crimes. In a 2019 paper by Bellis and colleagues, analyses showed that the annual cost of ACEs was $748 billion in North America and $581 billion in Europe.[13] For North America, this represents 2.67 percent of the gross domestic product, 3.55 percent for Europe. In North America, this percentage of the GDP is comparable to other big-ticket items: Transportation and the combination of Arts, Entertainment, Recreation, Accommodation, and Food Services. Strikingly, more than 75 percent of this amount in North America and Europe is due to individuals with two or more ACEs.

Economic analyses such as these have, in part, inspired government policies around screening and treatment, often linked to insurance coverage—a topic I will talk about more in the next chapter.

Numbers matter, but is the number of ACE types the only relevant dimension?

SEEING BEYOND NUMBERS TO EPIGENETICS

As we have seen, for any given group of people, a higher ACE score is associated with a higher physical and mental health risk. But this is only one sense of what the number can tell us, and it is based on the number of ACE types. Two populations, A and B, could have the same average ACE score, say four, but with life experiences that were extremely different. Population A experienced emotional abuse, physical abuse, sexual abuse, and domestic violence, whereas Population B lived with emotional neglect, physical neglect, incarceration, and mental illness. A population could also have the same average ACE score of one, but perhaps some of this population experienced repeated occurrences over a long time, such as children who are beaten by an abusive father over many years or the woman we met in the last section who was repeatedly sexually abused. As another example, two populations could have the same ACE score, but one population includes sexual abuse and the other doesn't. As I will discuss further in chapter 5, sexual abuse disproportionately contributes to psychopathology relative to all other ACEs—a relationship that is described as synergistic.[14] A total ACE score does not account for any of these nuances or dimensions.

There are also characteristics of the adversity a child has suffered that may vary greatly, including when the adverse experience occurred, for how long, and with what kind of intensity and predictability. The "when" of adversity not only includes the timing of events during childhood, but what happens in utero as well as the experiences of previous generations, what I referred to earlier as intergenerational trauma.[15] When one generation's suffering is handed down to the next as some type of adversity, a child starts out life as an older soul even in the womb, in a process of aging that results from the process of epigenetics.[16] These are dimensions of adversity that extend far beyond the mere number of types.

To understand epigenetics, think about a piece of music that you are familiar with. I'm queuing up Bruce Springsteen's "Rosalita (Come Out Tonight)" from his second album, *The Wild, the Innocent & the E Street Shuffle*. The patterns of notes are like the sequences of nucleotides making up DNA. Though there are many more notes than nucleotides, which have only four (adenine, guanine, cytosine, thymine), the sequence is what determines the musical score and genetic function. Changing the note sequence, either leaving notes out or reordering them, would be equivalent to a mutation. In "Rosalita (Come Out Tonight)," Springsteen wails, "I just want to be your lover, ain't no liar / Rosalita, you're my stone desire." What if he flipped the lyrics, singing, "Rosalita, you're my stone desire / I just want to be your lover, ain't no liar"? It would feel like a completely different song. But if he keeps the lyrics in their original order and plays with the timing of different instruments and voices, the length of different notes, and how loudly they are played, then the music is still recognizable as the original "Rosalita (Come Out Tonight)." Likewise, epigenetic changes leave DNA sequencing the same, but alter the expression of genes, that is, whether they are turned on or off. We now know that epigenetic changes show up as a response to early life adversity, accelerate aging and, often, contribute to poor health later in life.

A compelling example of the impact of epigenetics comes from World War II. In the winter of 1944–45, Germany occupied the Netherlands and, for a period of time, they cut off access to food and fuel to towns in the west. This caused a famine that impacted some 4.5 million people, including many women who were pregnant. Fast-forward several decades to when those individuals gestating during the famine reached adulthood and we find the epigenetic branding on this new generation.[17] Babies whose mothers experienced famine during any stage of gestation developed into adults who were glucose intolerant, while famine during the early stages of gestation resulted in adults who were more likely to suffer from obesity, blood coagulation problems, breast cancer, schizophrenia, and impairments in attention. If a woman's mother was malnourished during the middle of gestation, the adult women were shorter in height and had obstructive airway disease in adulthood. Famine is an ACE type—physical neglect—but its impact on health outcomes depends on timing. As much as the womb provides safety and nutrition for the developing fetus, mom's stress leaves a mark, one that may set up her child's destiny even before she is born.

One of the most easily measured biological markers of epigenetics is DNA methylation, which regulates gene expression. During DNA methylation, a small molecule called a methyl group—that is, one carbon and three hydrogens—is added to part of the DNA creating a kind of chemical cap that functions like an on-off switch for that gene. DNA methylation changes reliably as an individual ages, but environmental experiences can also affect the process. In this way, DNA methylation is like a clock that keeps track of aging, parallel in many ways to the rings of a tree. Just as adversity in nature such as a drought or extreme cold creates thinner rings in the trunk of a tree, the adversity a child experiences early can be seen as a change in their DNA methylation rate. Essentially, a child's chronological age no longer matches her biological age. If you read the short story or saw the movie *The Curious Case of Benjamin Button*, you know the oddity of such a mismatch: Ben was born an old man.

For women who were born during the Dutch famine, their DNA methylation rates were higher when their own mothers lacked food early in gestation. No changes were observed if famine occurred later in gestation, or in same-sex siblings who were born after the famine. The fact that siblings didn't show any differences in biological aging reveals the transformative impact of adversity above and beyond shared genetic makeup. The results from the Dutch famine study show that the adversity a mother experiences impacts her fetus. These findings remind us that the number of ACE types don't give us the full picture of a child's life, and prompt us to think more carefully about what we mean by adversity, childhood, and experience.

DEFINING ADVERSITY, CHILDHOOD, AND EXPERIENCE

In 1964, the Supreme Court deliberated over a case involving a theater in Ohio showing *The Lovers*, a movie by French director Louis Malle. Many Ohioans reacted badly, put off by what they considered pornography. The theater's manager, Nico Jacobellis, disagreed. The case, *Jacobellis v. Ohio*, ultimately rested on an interpretation of what counts as pornography by the nine sitting justices of the Supreme Court. Is it certain kinds of sex acts or how most people react to certain kinds of sex? The majority of the justices argued in favor of Jacobellis, ruling that the movie did not push prurient buttons. The most striking statement about the nature of pornography came from Justice Potter Stewart, who stated: "I shall not today attempt further to define the kinds of material I understand to be embraced within that shorthand description; and perhaps I could never succeed in intelligibly doing so. But I know it when I see it, and the motion picture involved in this case is not that."[18]

Research on ACEs raises similar questions of definition. But in the sciences, there are at least two reasons why we can't be satisfied with *I know it when I see it*: One, what we know is based on more than what we can see, especially since seeing can be biased or distorted based on what we know. Two, we can't do science if we don't define what we are trying to measure, observe, or understand. We need to specify what counts as *adverse, childhood,* and an *experience*, especially since the ACE score depends on a count.

Let's start with childhood as defined by Felitti and his colleagues as birth to eighteen years. This time frame has been used in other domains, including policy documents concerning the rights of the child and, as I will discuss in chapter 6, what defines a *child soldier*. But it's problematic, as it blurs together all the developmental changes that occur within these years, as well as before, in utero, including the exceptional dependency of a fetus, newborn, and infant on its caretakers, the unfolding of skills around language, emotional regulation, social relationships, and moral decisions, the onset of puberty, sexuality, and education. As I will discuss more in chapter 3, the timing of when a child experiences adversity might critically disrupt some of these changes, but not others. Further, though an eighteen-year-old is legally considered to be an adult in different parts of the world, it takes another five to seven years for a child's brain to fully mature, particularly the frontal lobes, which are critical to self-regulation, working memory, planning, and attention.

Felitti and colleagues also didn't define experience, and certainly didn't specify a duration for an adverse event. Within their own list of adverse types, however, some, such as those of abuse and neglect, can occur over long periods of time, potentially for the entirety of childhood. Other types of adverse experiences may occur over a short period of time, such as loss of a parent or a divorce, though the consequences—

such as neglect—may be long in duration. Defining experience in terms of its duration places adversity on a continuum of stress from acute to chronic, as well as showing how adversity overlaps with the emergence and development of different abilities.

Adversity is the most problematic of terms. Recall that in the first wave of the original ACE study, there were only seven *types* of adversity, separated into two broad **domains—abuse** and **household dysfunction**. In the second wave, the questionnaire included three more types, two associated with the third domain of **neglect**. Felitti, Anda, and their colleagues considered these types to be adverse in the sense of atypical, outside the normal range of experiences for a developing child. But this lens on the types of adversity wasn't developed by finding the best predictors of poor health outcomes in ways that are sensitive to potential cross-cultural differences.[19] As a result, at least in part, the original list of types ignored what happens to children outside the household and in other cultures, as well as the possibility of cross-cultural differences in the perception of adversity. An ACE in one culture may not be an ACE in other cultures. For example, within the United States, there are nineteen states that allow corporal punishment, including hitting children, and within the majority of these, physical aggression can be used from nursery school to high school.[20] This is an extraordinary fact, especially given that 196 countries have signed on to Article 19 of the United Nations Committee on the Rights of the Child, stating that all measures should be taken "to protect the child from all forms of physical or mental violence." In the nineteen states that support punishing children by means of physical violence, including spanking by parents and teachers, physical abuse might not even be included in an ACE score, whether retrospectively reported by adults or prospectively reported by parents and their children as they occur during development.

To push further on the definition of adversity, consider the original survey question associated with sexual abuse, which effectively breaks down into four different subtypes:

Did an adult or person at least five years older ever . . .

> *touch or fondle you in a sexual way?*
> *have you touch their body in a sexual way?*
> *attempt oral, anal, or vaginal intercourse with you?*
> *actually have oral, anal, or vaginal intercourse with you?*

A "Yes" answer to any one of these options scored a one for the sexual abuse ACE, irrespective of the individual's age, the frequency or severity of sexual contact, the number of abusers, and so on. But sexual touching and intercourse are two entirely different experiences, and presumably the age difference and culture matter a great deal. A five-year-old girl who was sexually touched by a ten-year-old boy doesn't seem at all equivalent to a fifteen-year-old teenager who had inter-course with her twenty-two-year-old uncle, though in some cultures, this fifteen-year-old could be married to her uncle through an arrange-ment set up when she was five. Almost all of the other ACE items are associated with a spectrum of experiences, but a "Yes" response is al-ways coded as one ACE.

Clinical neuroscientist Katie McLaughlin defines adversity in a way that makes clear that we are talking about experiences that are atypical for most members of our species—certainly not expected by the developmental programs that evolved—and are long-lasting or re-peated:

> *Adversity is an environmental event that must be serious*
> *(i.e., severe) or a series of events that continue over time (i.e.,*
> *chronic).*[21]

The seriousness and chronic components are key. We are not discussing parents who sometimes *neglect* to cuddle or provide snacks to their children. We are talking about children who are *deprived* of basic nutritional needs, shelter, nurturing attachment, supportive communication, and more for extended periods of time. Adverse experiences in this sense are chronic, extreme, and highly atypical with respect to our developmental programs. And critically, we are talking about what happens to the child, and not yet about her response to these experiences, which might be traumatic or resilient. Being clear about these distinctions is necessary if we are to understand the nature of vulnerability and resilience to adversity.

Responses: Traumatic and Resilient

n the opening introduction to this book, I suggested that the question of why some children are more resilient to adversity is a central piece toward helping those who are not. Though we care deeply about the kinds of experiences that children face during development, it is the response to these experiences that lives on in their bodies and brains. How can some children suffer greatly, while others escape the terrible impact on their mental and physical health that would seem to be their destiny? Relatedly, why does the same adverse experience give rise to different kinds of pathology in some children, whereas in other situations, different types of adversity lead to the same negative outcome? For example, some children dissociate from reality in response to what happened to them, while others experience debilitating memories or act out behaviorally when they are triggered by certain people and places associated with abuse. Other children shut down emotionally, and some react by making risky decisions, often accompanied by violence. And yet other children are exposed to different types of abuse or domestic violence or war, and all end up with a shared response profile—emotionally dysregulated and out of control.[1]

Traumatic reactions to adverse childhood experiences are what I will refer to as **TRACEs**, while resilient responses are RACEs. TRACEs and RACEs are the two fundamental pathways departing from ACEs. Which journey an individual child takes is determined by the unique and blended contributions of both their nature and the nurture they receive, a recipe that defines their individual histories.

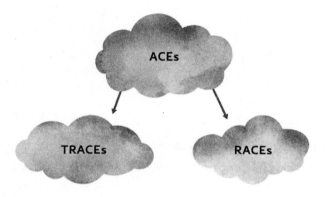

To understand TRACEs, we must understand the nature of children's responses to adversity, including how they are triggered and encoded in the body and brain, and how they change during their development. To understand RACEs, we must understand resilience, including why nature and nurture allow some individuals to deflect the destructive impact of adverse experiences. I will dig into these issues over the course of the next two parts of the book.

To illustrate the difference between TRACEs and RACEs, consider a study by the cognitive neuroscientist Rasmus Birn and colleagues involving young adults who, as children, were either exposed to no stress, or exposed to one or more highly stressful experiences including multiple foster care placements, parent mental illness, parent incarceration, and severe marital conflict.[2] The two groups played a gambling game while Birn and colleagues scanned their brains, in particular focusing on brain areas critically involved in learning about rewarding or costly decisions. The results were stunning. Those with highly stressful childhoods showed little response in the brain areas responsible for processing rewards and losses, and they engaged in much higher levels of risky behaviors as adolescents. These children had a high allostatic load that impacted their ability to learn from their decisions, engaging in beneficial decisions and avoiding the costly ones. This general result shows that there is a powerful relationship between early life stressors—the kinds of items on the ACE questionnaire—and changes in the brain, linked to unhealthy decisions.

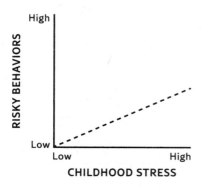
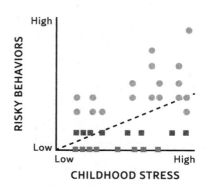

Lurking behind Birn's overall pattern of results were individual differences: some of the subjects showed TRACEs, others RACEs, revealing the incredible variation observed when we drill down to consider a particular at-risk child. Have a look at the chart above on the left, showing the relationship between the severity of childhood stress and risky behaviors. The dashed line indicates the nature of this relationship or correlation, which is linear: as childhood stress increases, so, too, do risky behaviors. Now look at the chart on the right. This is the same chart, but you can now see the individual data points, and there is considerable variation around the dashed line. But there's something else that is even more striking. Look at the data points toward the bottom of the chart that are squares. These are individuals who, despite a broad range of childhood stress from low to high, showed either no risky behaviors (bottom row of squares) or the lowest level (the row of squares above the baseline). Individuals at the highest end of the stress scale all had several ACEs. Some had TRACEs (circles with high risky behavior scores) and some had RACEs.

The individual differences that show up in Rasmus Birn's study are by no means exceptional. Seeing this pattern of variation is the norm in research on childhood adversity, and it should be expected given the handiwork of nature and nurture in creating complicated creatures such as ourselves. Some individual differences result in greater vulnerability to adversity and others in greater resilience. Interestingly, some children respond in ways that go beyond resilience and can be thought of as being equipped with what developmental psychologist Bruce Ellis calls *hidden talents*.[3] Ellis has defined these talents as superpowers or hyperdeveloped skills that enable a child to cope with a specific adverse situation, such as being hypervigilant to danger following exposure to physical violence or being highly resourceful in finding food and shelter when living with poverty. Resourcefulness in finding food and shelter can be a hidden talent that empowers greater problem-solving and grit in the face of difficult challenges. These strengths can be hidden if we don't understand how to look for them.

When we see the different ways that children respond to adversity, it tells us that we must be clear about how we define trauma. While some children come through adversity unscathed, for others the impact shapes the course of their entire life, and in specific ways we can isolate and study.

WHAT IS TRAUMA?

Colloquially, people often use the word *trauma* to describe anything emotionally upsetting. But unfortunately, this shorthand effectively undermines the careful work that scientists and medical practitioners carry out to both identify and help people who have responded to adversity with traumatic reactions. In the *DSM-5*, trauma is used in the more restricted sense of responses to violence, including physical and sexual abuse, as well as witnessing domestic and community violence.[4] This specificity is important for both treatment and policy, as it provides the criteria for the diagnosis of post-traumatic stress disorder (PTSD). As noted by a number of clinical scientists and doctors, this definition of trauma enabled victims to be recognized and treated for their internal wounds, perhaps especially military combat veterans and sexual abuse survivors.[5]

Added to the colloquial and *DSM-5* definitions of trauma is one provided by the National Child Traumatic Stress Network.[6] This remarkable organization functions as a warehouse for resources and scientific evidence to help parents, schools, and communities gain awareness of childhood trauma, specifically the distinction between traumatic *events* and traumatic *stress*. A traumatic event is "a frightening, dangerous, or violent event that poses a threat to a child's life or bodily integrity." A traumatic stress is when a child experiences "one or more traumas over the course of their lives and develop[s] reactions that persist and affect their daily lives after the events have ended. Traumatic stress reactions can include a variety of responses, such as intense and ongoing emotional upset, depressive symptoms or anxiety, behavioral changes, difficulties with self-regulation, problems relating to others or forming attachments, regression or loss of previously acquired skills, attention and academic difficulties, nightmares, difficulty sleeping and eating, and physical symptoms, such as aches and pains."

The definition of traumatic events is quite narrow, focusing primarily on violence and threats to a child's life. A child growing up with a parent who comes and goes or inconsistently engages in nurturing, or a family that is often displaced to a new home, or a child who experiences a parent with mental illness, or a child who repeatedly experiences racial or gender discrimination, may never experience any of these events as life threatening or dangerous, but they are nonetheless adverse and can impact their development in ways that are significant, as I will show in Part II. Traumatic stress, on the other hand, relates to the impact of adversity on stress, which may not be the only way that a child reacts. Children may shut down, take risks, or lose motivation, which are not reactions that typically engage the stress response, but show the powerful ways trauma can continue to reverberate over time.

What is broadly problematic about current definitions of traumatic responses is that they fail to capture the spectrum of signatures of a child's response to chronic adversity, that is, the many ways in which trauma imprints biologically to affect our health.

TRAUMATIC SIGNATURES

At the beginning of chapter 1, I discussed the idea that developmental programs have distinctive signatures of success, a biological blueprint that is built into us, but also requires us to have specific experiences to reach developmental milestones. Developmental programs also have distinctive signatures of failures. Traditionally, these failures are often identified by neurologists working with brain-damaged patients or individuals with specific developmental disorders. In a neurologist's office, when a person shows up who can't recognize faces, but can recognize other parts of the body and all other objects, this is not be-cause of some general insult to the brain. Rather, a face recognition deficit—known as *prosopagnosia*—is a signature of damage often involv-ing the fusiform gyrus, a region of the brain that is dedicated to face recognition. When a child avoids looking at another's face and finds it difficult or impossible to understand what others believe or intend, this is not a general intellectual impairment, but rather a common feature of autism, a developmental disorder with increasingly well-specified molecular causes.

What we are now beginning to understand is that ACEs can lead to unique traumatic signatures. A lot rides on how we define these trau-matic signatures as it drives education and healthcare policies, includ-ing who receives insurance coverage for a mental disorder. Philosopher Jerome Wakefield has described these issues as the clinician's dilemma: "On the one hand, mislabeling normal conditions as mental disorders is intellectually dishonest, stigmatizing, undermining of research, and can lead to inappropriate treatment, especially in an era emphasiz-ing pharmacological treatment for all manner of psychological dis-turbance. On the other hand, broader diagnostic categories—even if invalid—do allow the clinician to obtain reimbursement and thus to help more people who need and deserve help but who would be denied support from our shortsighted, self-defeating, and frankly cruel reim-bursement system. In confronting this ethical dilemma, it would be useful to clarify the situations in which public reimbursement for treat-ment of psychological conditions other than mental disorders might be most plausibly defended on moral grounds."[7]

The *DSM* is perpetually stuck in this dilemma, criticized for both excessive inclusion as well as exclusion. It took until 1980 for PTSD to be recognized by the American Psychological Association and included in the third edition of the *DSM*. That was a major breakthrough for people suffering from such trauma. Over the past decade, a group of

clinical psychologists led by Julian Ford and Joseph Spinazzola, together with psychiatrist Bessel van der Kolk, have attempted to add
developmental trauma disorder (DTD) to the *DSM*.[8] Their motivation:
because many children with adverse experiences and traumatic responses to them don't meet the *DSM* criteria for PTSD, their symptoms
are often misdiagnosed or missed altogether, and as a result, they are
not eligible for treatment. These would seem like essential symptomatic criteria for inclusion in the *DSM*, and to some extent they fit with
the *DSM*'s criteria. But the price of admission to the *DSM* is much
higher given the economic, political, educational, and sociological implications of accepting a new, *certified* disorder. To gain entrance to the
DSM, the evidence must show that the proposed disorder is common
and associated with significant mental and physical health problems
that are distinctive from other disorders already included in the *DSM*.
And it must also be clear that the diagnostic label is useful to clinicians
in treatment.

Ford and his colleagues dutifully followed the *DSM* admission
script, mapping out five criteria, each with several mandatory elements.
The first criterion focuses on chronic exposure to violence or disruption
of caretaking, the second on emotional dysregulation, the third on attentional and behavioral dysregulation, the fourth on relational challenges including self-loathing, attachment insecurity, and low empathy,
and the fifth on impairments in daily functioning including school,
family, and social relationships. Ford and colleagues also carried out
studies with psychiatrists, assessing both the usefulness and uniqueness of the criteria, finding that DTD was consistently seen as distinctive, especially in comparison with PTSD. They then deployed trained
traumatic stress experts to assess parents and children living in urban,
suburban, and rural areas of the United States. Results of these assessments showed that DTD, in contrast with PTSD, was uniquely associ-

ated with the experiences of emotional abuse, family violence, and significant, frequent separation from the caregiver. Though DTD appears to carry a unique traumatic signature, some children also exhibit pathologies that are characteristic of PTSD, including being emotionally out of control or dysregulated, having intrusive memories, and living with crushingly low self-esteem. What this research shows, supported by studies carried out by other psychiatrists and clinical scientists, is that DTD has all the hallmarks of mental disorders that are currently accepted into the *DSM-5*, the latest version.

And yet, the overseers of the *DSM* have soundly rejected DTD. This is surprising, especially since a number of psychiatrists have worried that the current definition of *mental disorder* is too broad and, as a result, threatens to pathologize developmentally typical mental issues. This concern was voiced by distinguished psychiatrist Allen Frances in anticipation of the fifth version of the *DSM*: "Many millions of people with normal grief, gluttony, distractibility, worries, reactions to stress, the temper tantrums of childhood, the forgetting of old age, and 'behavioral addictions' will soon be mislabeled as psychiatrically sick."[9]

Despite the fact that children who show the pathologies of DTD are not eligible for services that fall under the *DSM* list of disorders, it is important that the features of DTD are understood and recognized by professionals such as clinicians, therapists, doctors, and teachers so that they may design appropriately targeted interventions to help children grow into healthy adults with meaningful lives. Ultimately, only professionals such as psychiatrists or trained clinical scientists can administer the screening tools and assessments for trauma. What the sciences suggest is that these professionals must not only be equipped with the most effective tools but a wide variety of tools that acknowledge the diversity of adverse experiences and responses that children have including both traumatic and resilient responses.

RESILIENCE SIGNATURES

Unlike the word *trauma*, which is defined in the *DSM*, *resilience* is not. But like trauma, resilience has also entered into the colloquial mainstream, meaning to "roll with the punches" or "bounce back." As for trauma, this has muddied the waters for practitioners.[10] For some experts, resilience is about an individual's ability to actively recover from an adverse event, returning to a healthy physical and mental state, or to show no traumatic reactions despite the experience of adversity. Here, resilience is an outcome of actively attaining equilibrium, staying on the balance beam even when something tries to knock you off. For others, resilience is about the capacity of multiple systems, including the individual, community, and government to adapt to adversity that challenges functioning. Here, resilience is a team sport that includes the balance beam, uneven bars, horse, and floor experts, coaches, trainers, local and national organizations, all pulling to achieve an outcome that is more than the sum of its parts. For all experts, resilience entails a capacity, built by nature and nurture, to recover in some way from either acute or chronic adversity.[11]

Understanding of how our biology pens a signature of resilience comes from experimental studies of mice and humans. Neuroscientist Lindsay Willmore and her colleagues showed that when mice are repeatedly defeated by a dominant aggressor over several days—a form of chronic physical abuse—some sink into a depressive state as evidenced by their lack of movement and eating, whereas others remain alert and active. The vulnerable traumatized mice tend to cower throughout the repeated aggression, whereas the resilient ones tend to fight back and remain vigilant. The resilient mice also have greater activity in brain regions responsible for the neurochemical dopamine. Dopamine in mice, as well as other mammals including humans, is involved in the anticipation and experience of reward, and is critical to learning and decision-making. To determine whether heightened dopamine activity causes resilience, Willmore experimentally stimulated dopamine neurons to increase their output, while victim mice were repeatedly attacked by a dominant aggressor. With higher levels of dopamine, these victims were more resilient to the adversity of physical abuse.[12]

In studies of children and adolescents exposed to chronic physical abuse, a significant proportion—between 10 and 20 percent of the population—manage to avoid, in some way, the stressful consequences, equipped with a signature of resilience that includes the ability to think about their experiences in a less negative way, take advantage of caretaker supports, and engage in positive social interactions with peers. But like the mice that Willmore and her colleagues studied, this backbone also includes important contributions from nature including genes associated with reward and self-regulation.

Anthropologist Connie Mulligan and colleagues looked for the signatures of resilience in teenage Syrian refugees, a population previously exposed to the adversities of war and presently living with the adversities of a refugee camp—a pileup of chronic ACEs. Using a simple mouth swab to extract DNA samples, it was possible to look at genetic variants associated with different levels of serotonin and dopamine—critical to self-regulation and reward, respectively. Results showed that teenagers with genes associated with higher levels of serotonin and dopamine were more resilient to the stressors of war and life in a refugee camp, showing less insecurity and fewer symptoms of PTSD. A mix of genes associated with self-regulation and reward, linked to a supportive community, protected these children from the cumulative burden of severe, long-lasting, unpredictable adversity. For these children, a fortuitous combination of nature's and nurture's ingredients placed them on a resilient path to recovery. Many of their brothers and sisters were less fortunate.

WHICH PATH, TRAUMATIC OR RESILIENT?

One way to think about the variation in responses to adversity is by considering different trajectories or paths, as psychologists Stevan Hobfoll and George Bonanno have elegantly discussed.[13] These paths can either be considered in response to an acute adverse experience or to chronic adversity that may arise during child development. In the figure below, focused on chronic adversity, I define the space of possible paths with two dimensions, one reflecting age, the other allostatic load. Where a given individual lands within this space is relevant to the cumulative burden of adversity—how long it lasts—and what systems of the body and brain are developing. Individuals on the *resistant* path show low allostatic load despite the adversity they confront during development. Individuals on the *resilient* path start with a significant allostatic load burden due to adversity early in life, but then recover from it. Individuals on the *delayed pathology* path start life without any allostatic load burden, but then accumulate a higher and higher load. Individuals on the *chronic pathology* path live with a high allostatic load from birth onward.

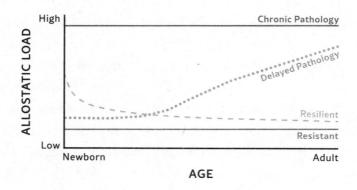

In a study by Hobfoll, looking at adult Jews and Arabs living in Israel during a particularly intense period of war involving rocket bombings, 22 percent were on the resistant path, 14 percent resilient, 10 percent delayed pathology, and 54 percent chronic pathology. Chronic pathology was the most common response to a long tenure of adversity, an enduring experience for many living in Israel and Palestine. What this shows is that we can see, at a population level, groups of individuals that follow distinctive paths in response to the adversity of war, and that the majority showed traumatic, pathological responses.

A study by Bonanno and his colleagues explored the potential contribution of genetic factors to whether adults, fifty years or older, were more likely to appear on a resilient or vulnerable path of depression following the experience of an acute traumatic event—divorce, death of a loved one, job loss. Of the approximately two thousand subjects, close to 80 percent were resistant, with the remaining 20 percent equally distributed among the three other path types of resilient, delayed depression, and chronic depression. There were also significant genetic correlates to each path. The resilient group had fewer genetic variants associated with mental and physical health problems, and a higher number of variants associated with educational achievements. In contrast, the delayed and chronic depression groups had higher numbers of genetic variants associated with depression and anxiety. These results show that certain genetic constellations are predictive of vulnerability and resilience to health risk, with some more likely to have TRACEs and others, RACEs.

What we can't see or predict in either the studies of war or acute traumatic experiences is who will walk onto a particular path. In the same way that an ACE score doesn't predict an individual's health risks, we don't yet have a way of predicting who will be more resistant and who will be more vulnerable to adverse experiences, be they acute or chronic. But as we will learn in Part III, a growing body of knowledge is beginning to sharpen our understanding of how nature hands some individuals a gift of greater neural, immunological, and psychological resilience and how different experiences can nurture individuals onto the resilient path.

MOVING BEYOND
THE ORIGINAL ACES FRAMEWORK

While the original framework for understanding childhood adversity was utterly groundbreaking, it must evolve, as I hope I've shown clearly in this chapter. First of all, an ACE score is a score of experience, not the response to the experience, that is, whether a person reacts with TRACEs or RACEs. Second, there are other dimensions of adversity than type, including when the experience occurred, for how long, with what level of severity and predictability. Third, the sheer number of ACEs does not map neatly to potential traumatic reactions. This has not been fully appreciated by healthcare providers and policymakers. As Robert Anda, one of the lead medical researchers on the original papers with Felitti, noted in 2020: "Inferences about an individual's risk for health or social problems should not be made based on an ACE score, and no arbitrary ACE score or range of scores should be designated as a cut point for decision-making or used to infer knowledge about individual risk for health outcomes."[14]

Anda's comment highlights both that the ACE score isn't set up as a screener and, critically, a screener for individuals. An analogy to heritability is helpful here. When we determine the heritability of a trait, as I noted earlier in my discussion of the callous-unemotional trait, we are referring to a population measure, not a diagnostic of an individual, such as Sean. So it is for the ACE score. When Felitti, Anda, and their colleagues reported that individuals with ACE scores of seven or higher have a threefold higher risk of lung cancer, they were not referring to Jane Doe's risk. In a study of women, individuals with two or more ACEs were twice as likely to develop cancer by the age of fifty as individuals with no ACEs, but of those with two or more ACEs, approximately 80 percent never developed cancer.

Another concern with the ACE questionnaire is that it asks adults—older than eighteen years—to reflect back on the adversity they have experienced. Depending on the age of the individual responding, the adversity might have been recent (e.g., a nineteen-year-old answering "Yes" to sexual abuse that occurred at age sixteen) or in the distant past (e.g., a fifty-year-old reflecting on when he was six and his father was incarcerated). The ACE questionnaire is retrospective. We now know, however, that the evidence from retrospective studies doesn't line up well with prospective studies—collected as the adversity unfolds in a child's life.[15] In studies comparing retrospective and prospective evidence, there is a large percentage of individuals who, based on court records, were maltreated but don't report it, and an equally large number of people who report maltreatment with no corroborating evidence. These mismatches are a clear sign that we must tread carefully with the retrospective ACE questionnaire, as well as other survey tools that have spun off from this approach. It is also a clear sign that we need multiple eyes on children to maximize the odds of picking up on childhood adversity as it occurs, to diminish exposure to future adversity, and to remediate the damage as early as possible when the body and brain are most malleable.

There is an urgency to understanding and recognizing the limitations of ACE scores because they risk undermining policy initiatives. In many American states, ACE scores are being used in healthcare policy and insurance. Consider California, a highly progressive American state that is commonly ahead of the curve when it comes to policies around physical and mental health. In January of 2020, California's surgeon general, Nadine Burke Harris,[16] in collaboration with Medi-Cal—an insurance company for low-income families in California—launched a $160 million screening initiative using the ACE survey. Medi-Cal provided codes for reimbursement that were based on results from the ACE screening questionnaire:[17]

- G9919—High risk, patient score of four or greater
- G9920—Lower risk, patient score of zero to three

What is clear from the billing codes is that the number of ACEs is tied to a designation of risk. As Medi-Cal's website indicates, and as further developed by Burke Harris and her more recent initiative with the University of California called Aces Aware,[18] an individual's score is meant to guide treatment. The logic here is clear: if we can obtain an accurate record of childhood adversity, and if we can tie the number of adverse types to treatment, then individuals with ACEs benefit from enhanced and more targeted care, insurance companies benefit by avoiding the high costs of treating older individuals with more resistant pathology, and society wins by having healthier adults. That seems like airtight logic with wins at the level of individuals, society, and healthcare. But as I noted at the start of this section, the ACE questionnaire is not an accurate screening tool for individuals. As distinguished sociologist David Finkelhor noted in 2019: "If general ACE screening were to result in a big increase in unnecessary and inherently expensive child welfare referrals and investigations as one of its main outcomes, we might look back on the ACE mobilization as a disastrous distraction to the development of evidence-based child welfare policy. Such concerns merit very serious consideration."[19]

The time is ripe to build from the knowledge we have gained about the impact of ACEs on the bodies and brains of children. We can learn more about how different dimensions of adversity transform the child's body and brain. We can use this knowledge to drive powerful interventions, customized to the diversity of children and their experiences. Though adverse experiences are part of the human condition, no one should be committed to a life sentence of suffering from the pathology of their responses.

Hidden Dimensions: The Adverse Ts

eah walked straight up to me, blue eyes beaming, smiling, and giggling. She told me her name, her age—eight years old—asked me mine, and then asked if we could make something out of Play-Doh. We sat down at the table, and she scooched her chair right next to mine. As we played with the Play-Doh, Leah reached out to hold my hand. Since the school had a no-physical-contact policy, I reluctantly moved a bit farther away, recognizing the desire in her eyes. This didn't turn out well. Leah transformed into an inconsolable puddle of tears, on the floor, full-blown tantrum.

All that we knew of Leah at the time was that her parents had died in a terrible accident when she was three and since then she was living with her grandparents. Two years after I met Leah, her grandparents had passed away and she was living with an uncle and aunt. During this period, Leah struggled in school with emotional outbursts, little sense of personal boundaries, and few meaningful or stable social relationships with peers. Any new adult who entered the classroom became an obsessive focus of interest, as she enthusiastically stated, "You're my best friend."

Just around her eleventh birthday, and coinciding with the onset of puberty, Leah's life took a turn for the worse. She was angry and often violent. Male staff in the school triggered emotional outbursts, often associated with attempts to run away. We soon learned that Leah had been sexually abused by her uncle and most likely by her grandfather as well. She was soon displaced out of her third home into a government-run residential facility for children without parents or other guardians.

My heart ached for Leah. Not only had she accumulated a lifetime's worth of adversity, but her behavior appeared to provide a signature of the underlying pathology. Her two ACEs—emotional neglect and sexual abuse—appeared to be associated with the traumatic responses. But there are two problems with this interpretation, which I was well aware of at the time. First, this interpretation falls into the pitfall of using an ACE score for an individual, as opposed to its original intent as a population measure. Second, some of Leah's adversity wouldn't show up in her ACE score, as it wasn't considered one of the original ten types. Leah's parents and grandparents died, and then due to sexual abuse by her uncle, she lost a third set of familial caretakers when she moved to the government-run facility. Death or loss of a caretaker was not considered one of the original ACE types, and nor was it seen as a direct cause of emotional neglect, possibly physical neglect as well. When Leah went to live with her grandparents, not only were they in their seventies, but her grandmother had Alzheimer's; their ability to emotionally nurture a three-year-old was far below her level of need. Leah was also displaced several times from her home, another form of adversity that imposes a high level of stress. But that was not included in the original ACE typology. Adding these two different types of adversity into the rather cold formulation of an ACE score, and mindful of the fact that Leah had repeated experiences with some of these—

multiple caretaker losses, home displacements, and sexual abuses—we obtain a score of four rather than two.

Leah's modified ACE score of four is certainly more representative of her experiences. But from an understanding of her experiences, we learn little about how such experiences result in traumatic responses, if they do. What we saw in Leah was a child who had trouble controlling her emotions, her later hatred of men, her anger, violence, and fleeing from situations. Was one ACE type more responsible for these behaviors than the others, or was it some combination or synergistic relationship among the different ACE types? Did the timing of each ACE type—loss of parents at age three years, emotional neglect from ages three to five, sexual abuse between the ages of three to eleven—make a difference in terms of how her body and brain were affected? Did the possibility of repeated sexual abuse—frequency within one ACE type—create a different signature of pathology? Did loss of parents and then grandparents, each associated with emotional neglect, cause different signatures from sexual abuse? Did Leah's inability to control any of the adversity lead to a sense of helplessness, a lack of voice in her own journey? Was she resilient to some types of adversity?

If we are to help children build resilience, overcome their traumatic responses, or avert it altogether, we need answers to these questions. We need a new way of understanding how different dimensions of adversity impact the bodies and brains of our most vulnerable, leaving behind definitive signatures. The good news is that decades of research on our own and other species makes it possible to answer these questions, using a new framework I call the **Adverse Ts**, an approach that separates out the experience of adversity into its underlying dimensions.[1]

You can think of the Adverse Ts framework like a prism. When white light enters a prism, different colors emerge from the other side. The reason for the transformation is because different colors of light travel at different speeds. When the different colors hit the glass of the prism, they are bent to different degrees, red the least and violet the most. When the light leaves the prism, each color leaves in its own lane, a distinctive dimension. Put a second prism in front of the rainbow of light that emerges, and you get white back. The prism shows us the different colors that are within white light.

The Adverse Ts framework, represented as a hand above, has five separate dimensions, each associated with a finger, each dimension starting with the letter *T*: **Type**, **Timing**, **Tenure**, **Turbulence**, and **Toxicity**.[2] Like our hands that allow various functions when all fingers are working in concert, it is also possible to consider the unique contributions of each finger. Such is the case for the Adverse Ts, with each of the five dimensions occupying its own role in shaping human development:

- **Type** refers to the kind of ACE.
- **Timing** refers to when an ACE occurs in child development.
- **Tenure** refers to an ACE's duration.
- **Turbulence** refers to an ACE's predictability and uncontrollability.
- **Toxicity** refers to an ACE's severity.

Like the varying colors that exist within a prism, we can assemble each of these five dimensions into one coherent picture or grasp of adversity. This will equip us with a deeper understanding of how to enhance a vulnerable child's resilience and recovery, including children like Leah.

TYPE

The original ACE questionnaire was sensitive to *types* of adversity, though it was limited to ten general types thought to occur within a family, clustered within three **domains**: **abuse** (*sexual, physical, emotional*), **neglect** (*emotional, physical*), and **household dysfunction** (*incarceration, mental illness, separation/divorce, substance abuse, mother treated violently*). As time and more research has shown, these domains don't fully encompass the types of adversity that can arise within and beyond the family that may cause chronic stress for the developing child, some with uniquely traumatic effects. Let's first have a look at what is understood to be the diversity of types as it stretches our understanding of potential adversity both globally and cross-culturally.

Let's start with the domain of neglect and the two types designated in the original ACEs questionnaire: emotional and physical. Though lack of emotional (e.g., love, kindness, support) and physical (e.g., food, shelter, water, clothes) experiences are detrimental to child development, there are other dimensions of neglect that also play a role. As we learned in chapter 1, there are developmental programs underlying our cognitive capacities as well as our social relationships. These programs require specific kinds of experience, during certain periods of time, to ensure the proper outcomes.

Cognitive and social neglect can have a profound impact on a child. A child who is socially isolated, for whatever reasons, does not have the interactions that guide the development of dedicated brain mechanisms for navigating the social world, including understanding others' beliefs, intentions, goals, norms, conventions, and moral rules. A child who is cognitively deprived misses out on experiences that shape the development of dedicated brain mechanisms for acquiring an understanding of objects, language, decision-making, and all of the competences taught in schools such as reading and formal math. Both cognitive and social competences are linked to critical and sensitive periods of development (I will discuss this further on in this chapter) in which specific experiences are required to avoid delays or unrecoverable developmental failure. Children born with cataracts on their eyes don't have the critical experience of seeing faces, and thus show significant delays in recognizing the faces of friends and foes. Teenagers deprived of social interactions during the first two years of the COVID-19 pandemic showed significant mental health challenges including depression and anxiety.[3]

Let's move on to the domain of household dysfunction. I noted in discussing Leah's case that the original types associated with the domain of household dysfunction missed out on at least two striking and common adversities within the family: *caretaker loss* and *home displacement*. It is estimated that 1.5 million children in the United States will lose one parent before the age of eighteen, and approximately two million will lose both parents. Global statistics vary greatly, with factors such as war, poverty, and disease magnifying the problem. As of May 2022, global estimates suggest that 10.5 million children lost parents or caretakers, and 750,000 were orphaned. Of these losses, several countries reported a disproportionate percentage among minority groups. A recent survey of 137 countries revealed that there are 5 to 6 million children living in institutional facilities and, thus, without parents. Children who lose a parent are at significantly higher risk for depression, poor educational outcomes, suicide attempts, and death.[4]

Statistics for US children being displaced from their original homes indicate that about 20 percent will move at least once before their eighteenth birthday, with several moving multiple times, thus losing the support of friends and creating stress around finding new ones. Displacement, in both the United States and elsewhere, may be driven by poverty, war, or ecological disasters. In the case of war or disasters, the home may be destroyed, and along with it, all of a child's possessions and memories. The International Organization for Migration's *World Migration Report 2020* indicated that the number of people, globally, who were forcibly displaced as a result of violence and conflict was a staggering 41.3 million, the highest number on record since 1998—the year such statistics were first gathered. As of February 2023, the UN reports that there have been eight million Ukrainian refugees displaced as a result of the war with Russia.[5] Refugee crises are unlikely to abate anytime soon.

Restricting our focus to a child's household fails to take into account the culture around her—including the local community, school, social-political-religious groups, and government. **Cultural dysfunction** can include *war, gang violence, poverty, oppression-discrimination,* and *bullying,* all of which can result in trauma. The limited category of a child's household also fails to recognize the surrounding ecology and potential threats—including the climate and available resources for survival. **Ecological threat** includes *severe weather* (e.g., hurricanes, monsoons, droughts, earthquakes) and *disease* (e.g., viruses, parasites). Cultural dysfunction and ecological threat are two omnipresent domains of adversity with distinctive types that can impact a child greatly.

This new typology for ACEs is not meant to be comprehensive, but it highlights the importance of stretching beyond the original ACE questionnaire to encompass a greater diversity of adversities that children across the globe are likely to confront.

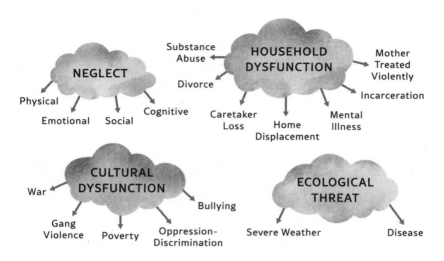

To appreciate the importance of these different ACE domains and types, consider a young Sudanese girl named Aliya, who I met in a therapeutic residential school. At snack or lunchtime, she devoured her food and asked her peers for their portion. At recess, Aliya was often rebuffed as she either butted in or grabbed toys without asking. When asked to read or do math, she screamed or threw objects at her teachers.

Aliya was adopted in her teens by White, wealthy American parents who adored her. But beforehand, Aliya and her brother had been forced to trek thousands of miles from her home in Southern Sudan to Ethiopia without food, clothes, water, shelter, or her parents—ACEs of physical, emotional, and cognitive neglect; poverty (cultural dysfunction); home displacement and caretaker loss (household dysfunction); and severe weather (ecological threat). Aliya was forced to leave home because Islamic forces were systematically torturing and killing families; they got to her parents and older siblings—cultural dysfunction ACE of war. While Aliya was in a refugee camp in Ethiopia, she was physically abused—abuse ACE. Under the original ACE questionnaire, Aliya would have three ACEs—physical neglect, emotional neglect, and physical abuse. With a broader taxonomy of ACE types, compiled in the figure below, Aliya had nine ACEs.

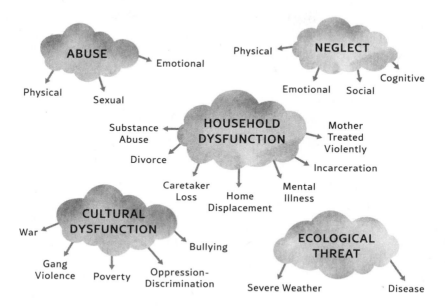

We already know that numbers matter in a dose-dependent sense, at least at a population level. But enhancing the number of types still doesn't tell us about the relationship between adverse experiences and traumatic responses to them. The odds are high that different types of adversity will result in different alterations of a child's developmental programs. For example, lack of essential resources—deprivation—and the presence of danger—abuse and violence—are evolutionarily ancient experiences that have shaped the life history responses of all invertebrates and vertebrates. If you grow up in an environment that is impoverished, whether due to climatic or social conditions, then natural selection favors slowed or delayed development, effectively waiting for a richer set of offerings. In our own species, this slowed, patient, future-oriented perspective is associated with lower levels of aggression and violence.[6] If you grow up in a harsh environment, where direct threats to survival from predation, violence by tribe members, and the climate are high, then selection favors speeded up development, less self-control, and more present-oriented action, effectively giving young the competences of their chronologically older peers. We would therefore expect, contrary to the cumulative number of ACEs approach, that depriving children greatly delays or permanently impairs their developmental competencies, whereas abuse and exposure to violence should speed up their maturation. In Part II, I explore the idea that different types of adversity leave different signatures on the developing child, and in Part III, I discuss why these ideas matter for developing roads to recovery from adversity.

TIMING

Here's a fact, backed up by considerable evidence:[7] ACEs, irrespective of type or type combinations, have more detrimental effects on the physical and mental health of children if they arise during the first five years of life than later in development. These early-occurring experiences of adversity can have long-term, intergenerational consequences, with evidence that pregnant women who experienced one or more ACEs as children are more likely to have pregnancy complications (e.g., preterm births) as well as children with mental and physical health problems.[8]

We first met our youngest daughter, Sofia, when she was twenty months old. She had lived most of her life in a Russian orphanage. As she sat on a caretaker's lap, my wife, Lilan, handed her an apple, which she devoured. I tried to make Sofia laugh with funny faces and sounds. At first she quizzically stared at me and then she giggled. We then said goodbye, knowing that we would have to wait for our official adoption papers before fully welcoming her into our family.

After two months of stressful waiting, we boarded a plane and headed back to Russia. With adoption documents in hand, Sofia in our arms, we headed back to Boston with a stop in Zurich. We decided to go for lunch and ordered spaghetti and meatballs—a first for Sofia. If she could have jumped into the bowl, she would have. All of a sudden they announced that our flight was boarding. With urgency, we put all the remaining food, including much of Sofia's pasta, onto our trays and headed to the garbage bin. Bad move. Sofia let out a scream that I will never forget. We had no idea what was wrong at the time, and then realized that we were taking her food away, a precious commodity for a child whose nutritional needs had been neglected. We soon learned to appreciate the significance of food in her life, along with the other expected experiences that Sofia had been deprived of, including love, consistent caretakers, physical contact, toys, and social play.

It is estimated that there are 140 million abandoned or orphaned children around the world, close to a third in sub-Saharan Africa, and many of these children live in destitute orphanages or on the streets, in slums. We now understand, thanks to detailed scientific studies at the level of genes, neurons, hormones, psychology, and behavior, the devastating consequences of such deprivation, and the importance of timing.[9]

Months after Sofia was at home with us, we invited a social worker to provide an assessment. I watched with great interest, especially since many of the little activities she did with Sofia were straight out of the developmental psychology textbook: fine motor control of grasping objects, finding hidden objects, play, humor, responding to verbal instructions and facial expressions. At the end of her time, the social worker gave us an assessment: Sofia was emotionally attached to us, had strong motor, emotional, and cognitive skills, but was language delayed. The language assessment didn't sit well with me. It conflicted with what is known about the developmental programming of language acquisition, and in particular the role of experience in this process. Somewhat annoyed, I asked the social worker, "What do you mean by language delay? Sofia is chattering away in Russian because this has been her only language experience, until recently." The social worker then said, putting her arm on my shoulder, "Don't worry, Marc, many fathers often get upset when we say that their child is language delayed. We can teach Sofia English." At this point, my wife could see that I was about to blow a fuse and intervened: "This may be a topic we want to skip, as Marc works on language acquisition professionally." That calmed me down as I replied in a more reasonable, if not professorial tone: "There's no need to teach Sofia. Like all children, Sofia was born with the ability to acquire any language and now that she is hearing English, she will quickly, on her own, become an English speaker." I then turned to my bookshelf and handed her a copy of *The Language Instinct* by my friend, psycholinguist Steven Pinker. Well, maybe that was a bit too much!

Sofia wasn't language delayed. Within months she was chattering away in English, telling us stories, asking for her favorite foods, and commenting on her storybooks. Within less than a year, most of her Russian was, sadly, gone, as we had no ability to continue the Russian input. But as we know from dozens of studies by psycholinguists, Sofia's memory held on to her Russian, ready to be sparked into action if she wanted to reacquire it, which she readily would eighteen years later in college. And as many of you will know from trying to learn a second language, some parts are harder to learn later in life, including the proper accent, and in Romance languages, those grammatical genders— a female sock (*la chaussette*) but male notebook (*le cahier*). There are windows of opportunity for acquiring language, including specific windows for the sound system (phonology), vocabulary (semantics), and grammar (syntax).

Timing and windows of opportunity are defined by the developmental programs we learned about in the first chapter. Because such windows of opportunity appear in millions of species, it is fair to say that evolution has designed them for the function of survival.[10] Miss the opportunity or encounter adverse experiences during this period, and the individual may show either significant delays in acquiring a skill or may not acquire them at all.

Developmental programs establish one of two different kinds of opportunity windows for experience known as *sensitive* and *critical periods*. Sensitive and critical periods are defined by starting and ending times for growing body parts, acquiring motor skills, sensory processes, or cognitive capacities. During these periods, there is considerable plasticity to change that is highly dependent on the timing and nature of experience. For sensitive periods, the starting and ending time points tend to be rather loose, whereas they are rigid for critical periods.

Evidence for the importance of these windows of opportunity in animals was first brought to light in the early 1900s. Experiments carried out with a diversity of species showed that exposure to toxic substances early in embryonic development was the most disruptive, whereas later in development, when the form and function of organs had matured, there was little to no effect. This work led to an elegant series of experiments by the late Nobel laureate Konrad Lorenz, who explored imprinting in birds. As soon as precocial birds hatch, they can effectively move and feed themselves. Upon hatching, the chick follows the first object that moves. In most cases, this object is mom, and following her is adaptive with respect to finding food and safety from predators. The chick imprints on mom. But if the first moving object is a red ball, the chick will imprint on the ball. This isn't adaptive, but the imprinting system doesn't count on such low probability events. As Lorenz and others who followed in his footsteps showed, once the birds imprint incorrectly there may be no going back, revealing a critical period for attachment. The process of imprinting is like stamping or branding a tattoo, a permanent mark of attachment.

Human infants also imprint, though because they rely on a care-taker to move and eat, there is less of a branding effect than in birds who are independently moving and eating soon after hatching. Within minutes of birth, human neonates are much more likely to follow face-like images than non-face-like, despite the fact that their vision is blurry at this age. And once they see mom's face—which, in many situations, they will experience a lot as they nurse and stare into her eyes—they obsessively follow her face over any other face, a process that can be disconcerting to fathers. Unlike the rolling balls presented to chicks, we don't know if human infants would imprint on any old object that loomed close by, as it would be unethical to raise babies who only saw rolling balls. But there are, sadly, many naturally occurring situations—discussed in Part II—that have removed infants from their mothers, or reduced their access, or exposed them to other types of adversity, and these illuminate our understanding of sensitive and critical periods for attachment and much more. Miss the timing window for cuddling, care, and communication, and the bonds of attachment may be irreparably broken in the child. Neglect, as a type of adversity, has left its signature imprint.

Such is the fate of children who, as we will learn in chapter 4, live their lives in austere orphanages. Unlike Sofia, who left her orphanage before her second birthday, children who spend more time in the de-prived conditions of many orphanages often have dysfunctional relationships and damaged competences for learning more generally.[11] And not only do these children suffer the consequences, but if they have children later in life, they, too, may suffer. Here, the trauma that parents experience as a result of adversity can get under the skin of their chil-dren, altering their bodies, brains, and even their genetic expression—as I noted in the discussion of the Dutch famine in chapter 1.

Epidemiologist Erin Dunn and her colleagues further advanced our understanding of the timing dimension by testing three different ideas or models of how adversity might impact aging, using the DNA methylation marker as her biological clock.[12] The first model they investigated was the *numbers* game, or dose-dependency, of Felitti and Anda's original research: the more ACEs, the greater the impact on DNA methylation. Though it's of course possible that more ACEs accumulate over longer periods of time, a high ACE score could occur within a short or protracted period of time, and either early or late in development. The numbers model doesn't take these aspects of time into account. The second model is that the more *recent* the adversity, the greater the impact. And the third model is that there is a *sensitive period* for the impact of adversity, with some developmental periods linked to greater vulnerability.

Dunn's results were clear, supporting the third idea focused on sensitive periods: only timing had an impact on DNA methylation as a biomarker of damage, and the effect was strongest when the adverse experiences occurred before the age of three years, pinpointing a sensitive period for vulnerability. We are back to the opening sentence of this section: ACEs occurring within the first five years of life are associated with the most detrimental outcomes for the body and brain.

We have now briefly covered two dimensions of adversity: type and timing. We will have much more to say about each of these Adverse Ts, including how timing interacts with type, as when the COVID-19 pandemic, which launched in 2019, deprived teenagers of social interactions during a sensitive period of development and, for many, increased their exposure to domestic violence, which rose six- to eightfold in some countries, including the United States.[13] We will also learn how the timing of adversity determines whether and how the body and brain are transformed, sometimes in ways that lead to permanent damage and sometimes in ways that open the door to building resilience, as was the case for my daughter Sofia.

TENURE

"If there is a hell on earth, it is the lives of children in Gaza."[14] This pronouncement about the Israeli-Palestinian conflict could have been made following the horrific civil war of 1947–1948, or the war of 1948–1949, or the nonstop violence between 1950 and 1967, or the Six-Day War that followed. In fact, it was pronounced by UN Secretary General António Guterres following the Israeli military bombing of Gaza during the spring of 2021, which claimed the lives of more than sixty children. Beyond the loss of innocent lives, thousands of Palestinian children living in Gaza have survived, but live with chronic stress, fear, and anxiety. Nadine is one of these children.

Nadine dreams of being a doctor when she grows up. She wants to help people. In her spare time she takes care of her younger brother and posts YouTube videos as an aspiring influencer. Most of her videos capture her life around Gaza, and she shares the screen with her brother. In late May of 2021, she posted a video that went viral, one showing the catastrophic devastation that enveloped her.[15] In the video she speaks, eyes teared up, voice trembling: "I'm always sick. I can't do anything, you see all this. What do you expect me to do? Fix it? I'm only ten. I can't even deal with this anymore. I just want to be a doctor or anything to help my people, but I can't. I'm just a kid." Exactly. Just a kid living under constant stress, the joys of childhood stolen. It's not up to Nadine to fix things. And yet she soldiers on, often rising above her own misery to cheer up her younger brother, shielding him from the daily fears and casualties. Empathizing with her brother's stress, and those that surround her, simply compounds the chronic nature of Nadine's worries. This is the long tenure of adversity.

Nadine's body and brain were not designed to endure a relentless, assaultive attack on her stress system. What it was designed to handle, thanks to millions of years of evolutionary refinements, is more acute stress, the kind that occurs in isolation, giving us more time to recover biologically. *Tenure* refers to the duration of the adverse experience, one that we can map, in some individuals, to a continuum of TRACEs associated with our stress response. This continuum begins with positive stress, shifts to tolerable stress, and ends with toxic stress. Positive stress is associated with short-lived experiences such as bracing for a vaccination shot or seeing a snake. If a young child lives in a supportive world where parents and other caretakers are on standby to help, she will convert this experience into a positive, rising above the temporary emotional distress experienced to celebrate a victory on the other side. Tolerable stress ramps up the level of adversity to situations that are still limited in duration, but are longer lived than positive stress, with the potential to cause damage to the developing child's body and brain. Examples of adverse experiences associated with tolerable stress are seeing parents fighting, repeated bullying or discrimination, and losing a parent in a car accident. What makes these experiences tolerable is, again, having a support network in place to help manage the emotions that arise. These experiences hurt, but when the child refuses to go to school because of bullying or racist discrimination, there are parents and teachers who show compassion and a willingness to intervene. The hurt is tolerable. Take away the support—systems that build resilience and enable recovery—and the tolerable converts to toxic. Toxic stress emerges when the adversity is relentless, uncontrollable, deeply damaging to the child's developing body and brain, and with little sign of hope that someone might relieve the pain and suffering. Such was Nadine's plight, as it was for Leah, who we met earlier.

An important point about the tenure dimension of adversity is that a single ACE type that endures can result in significant trauma. A population of children with ACE scores of one may not hit the radar of those using an ACE questionnaire to determine the need for intervention or insurance coverage, as most policies seem to be focused on children with multiple ACEs—those who, given the dose-dependent response from population-level analyses, are most likely to have significant mental and physical health problems. And yet, children who have been emotionally neglected from birth to adolescence have been deprived of a fundamental need during various sensitive and critical periods of development (**timing**), and the prognosis for their bodies and brains being healthy is poor. As another example, children who have *only* experienced sexual abuse, but during the tenure of adolescence, are likely to be revictimized later in life, often sentencing them to a life with trauma.[16] Tenure is a dimension of adversity that, on its own, can assault our stress systems, cause atrophy in the brain, destroy our immune systems, and result in a life of physical and mental illness.

Like the terms *trauma* and *resilience, stress* is often used colloquially to refer to a subjective experience. Everyone knows stress when they feel it, and each of us has a different threshold for setting this feeling in motion. But underlying this subjective sense are objective facts about how our bodies and brains change, both in the short and long run, when we are stressed.

When we are stressed, we experience—consciously and unconsciously—changes in our breathing, muscle tension, heart rate, salivation, hormones, intestinal and urinary sphincters, attention, memory, facial expressions, and mood. These changes are choreographed by one wandering nerve, the vagus nerve, which connects our brain stem to our guts by way of our heart. The communication flows in both directions, from gut to head and from head to gut, a process eloquently captured by the physiologist Stephen Porges in his *polyvagal theory.*[17]

We can understand polyvagal theory by thinking about our reptilian ancestors. Imagine you're an Anolis lizard, sitting on a rock, looking around, soaking up the sun. Life feels safe—you're having a "greenlight" experience. You start to flex your shocking red dewlap to fend off other guy lizards who may be lurking and to court the gals who might be interested. Danger—a "yellow light"—arises when you spot another guy lizard trying to take over your territory or compete for access to the gals. Life-threatening experiences—"red lights"—arise when a hawk or snake tries to grab you for lunch. To respond to red-light events, either you mobilize all of your resources to flee or fight, or you immobilize your resources and freeze. These are automatic, unconscious responses. The sympathetic nervous system serves fleeing and fighting, whereas the parasympathetic nervous system serves freezing. As an Anolis lizard, you might flee if the guy lizard is much bigger and tougher, or fight if a win looks promising. On the other hand, if the predator is a looming hawk or slithering snake, fleeing or fighting are off the table, leaving you with freezing as the only response to potentially lethal termination.

The evolutionarily ancient, reptilian system of dealing with yellow- and red-light situations is still with us. When we are stressed, we can mobilize our resources to flee or fight, or immobilize them and freeze—what Porges calls the *dorsal (back) vagal state*. But where we, and our mammalian relatives, parted company from the reptiles is in the evolution of a system exquisitely designed to shut down fleeing, fighting, and freezing in the service of enabling social engagement— what Porges calls the *ventral (front) vagal state*. Think of this more recent evolutionary add-on as an automatic brake connected to the signaling taillights of a vehicle. The brake controls the more primitive, impulsive, emotional, and reactive engines of the body and brain, while the taillights communicate the intent to rest, relax, and relate to others. When we perceive that the world is green-light safe—that is, we experience smiling faces, relaxed bodies, calm voices, gentle touches, familiar people—our sympathetic nervous system is dampened, allowing us to be with others, at peace. When we perceive that the world is red-light unsafe, the tenure of adversity wears down our brake pads and rotors due to overuse, turning us into out-of-control, runaway disasters.

For a ten-year-old child like Nadine, whose brain is still maturing, the incessant, uncontrollable stress of war wears down her ability to stay calm and engaged with the people she loves and cares about. War, as I will describe in more detail in chapter 6, has stripped away the safe, healthy, and nurturing conditions that would typically enable Nadine's frontal lobes to provide greater control over her emotions, along with enhanced abilities to reflect, recall, reason, and relate to others.

As a type of adversity, war is on the high end of the toxicity dimension—our fourth Adverse T. We don't, however, have to reach this level of toxicity to see the detrimental impact of a long tenure of adversity. The recession of 2007–2009 in the United States—the largest economic contraction since the Great Depression of 1929–1933—provided a natural experiment of how sustained financial hardship impacts the child's developing body and brain.[18] For rural Black communities in the southeast, who were already financially challenged before the recession, and who commonly suffer from higher rates of morbidity and mortality linked to cardiovascular diseases than rural White communities, this new economic downturn compounded their challenges. Some communities were already below the poverty level before the recession and dropped even further; some were at the poverty level at the start of the recession and dropped further; and some didn't change, remaining as stable low-income communities. Analyses of individuals in their mid-twenties, who were between sixteen and seventeen years old at the time of the recession, showed that the highest rates of metabolic syndromes—a combined measure of health risk that includes obesity, hypertension, high triglycerides linked to hardening of arteries, raised fasting blood glucose associated with diabetes—were seen in individuals who were below the poverty level before the recession— the ones who sustained the longest tenure of adversity.

The tenure dimension of the Adverse Ts may have the most significant impact on child development, as it potentially traverses several critical and sensitive periods of development. A child like Nadine, who was conceived in a world of conflict, did not have the kind of developmental journey that is expected or typical. It was a journey in which her parents were living under stress, and as we know, her mother's stress was likely transmitted to Nadine through changes in hormones and epigenetic expression—remember the girls born during the Dutch famine of World War II that I mentioned in chapter 1. From birth to the age of ten years, when she was acquiring self-control, emotional awareness, language, an understanding of others' beliefs, and moral and conventional rules, she was deprived of typical experiences that are required to nurture the competences of human nature. For Nadine, the odds of a healthy body and brain are poor in the absence of intervention. A long tenure of ACEs will most likely lead to a life of negative outcomes—TRACEs.

TURBULENCE

In reviewing the 1980 French film *Mon Oncle d'Amérique*, or *My American Uncle*, critic Roger Ebert wrote, "One thing's for sure: we have as much free will as lab rats." The film, directed by Alain Resnais, won a special jury prize at the Cannes Film Festival. It's extraordinary in many ways, but what stands out is its seamless integration of a fictional narrative among three characters with the science of learning in rats. The three characters, René, Janine, and Jean, grow up under very different circumstances—a poor farmer's son, a working-class daughter, and a wealthy bourgeois son, respectively—and yet all find themselves as adults in a similarly constrained world where there appear to be few options. All three seem stuck, helpless. There is a fourth character, who tells us about the science of learning in rats and he isn't fictional at all. He is Henri Laborit, a distinguished surgeon, neuroscientist, and philosopher who played a critical role in the development of chlorpromazine, a drug that is used to treat psychotic disorders such as schizophrenia and anxiety. Laborit narrates the scenes with white rats in cages, and quite quickly one realizes that their experiences are intended to be analogous to those experienced by René, Janine, and Jean.

Early on in *Mon Oncle*, we see a rat that has learned to associate the sound of an alarm with an impending foot shock from the floor of the cage and change his behavior in response, moving through a door into an adjacent cage. That's simple learning by association, captured in the 1890s by the classic studies of the Russian physiologist Ivan Pavlov on dogs. But the next sequence shows what happens when the door to the adjacent cage is closed. The rat initially tries to get through the door, but then, realizing the futility of its efforts, stops. This is learned helplessness, a phenomenon well characterized by Laborit as well as the American psychologist Martin Seligman.[19] Rats, and the human characters in the film, realize that some circumstances eliminate free will, the sense of control and agency over the future.

Mon Oncle has the hallmarks of the world many children find themselves in when they are exposed to ACEs. It's a world where adversity is **turbulent**—unpredictable, uncontrollable, and chaotic. It's an environment filled with experiences that are painfully unmanageable, resulting in hopeless depression or revved-up anxiety.[20]

To understand the impact of living in a turbulent world, it's helpful to have a closer look at Laborit's lab rats. Remember that the rat first learns that a tone predicts the upcoming foot shock and so, to avoid the shock, the rat must move through the open door. All of this happens within an environment that has specific features: a white rectangular box with a metallic floor, an escape door in the corner of the shorter wall, and a 200-hertz pure tone of 50 decibels. In thousands of studies of learning by association, we know that rats bind these features to their learning experience. But when the door and option for escape are closed, the rat's sense of helplessness generalizes far beyond the features of the learning environment. The rat's thought bubble isn't "I have no control in this turbulent white rectangular box when a 200-hertz pure tone at 50 decibels is played," but rather "I have no control anywhere, whatever sound I hear, and whatever shaped environment I see." That's overwhelming, relentless stress.

When a rat shuts down because it can't escape shock, it is expressing a response that is evolutionarily ancient, observed in many invertebrates and all vertebrates. It's an adaptive response that has been called animal hypnosis and, less anthropomorphically, tonic immobility. It's adaptive because, in some situations, when prey spot a predator, it pays to be statuesque. Immobility is an adaptive response when fear is triggered by life-threatening danger and flight-or-fight options are impossible or maladaptive—a much bigger and tougher competitor or a swift predator who can pick you off. But what evolved as an adaptive response can turn into a maladaptive, unhealthy response, if it persists over time.

We see the devastating impact of these ongoing unhealthy responses in rats. A rat's experience of helplessness and lack of control is associated with changes that can be observed from the level of behavior down to gene expression, hormone regulation, and brain activation. Helpless rats show inconsistent patterns of eating, drinking, and sleeping. When subsequently exposed to situations where escaping shock is possible, rats fail to learn, or do so with great difficulty. When rats experience inescapable shock, their core body temperature rises, akin to the symptoms of a fever. This feverish state is also accompanied by an immune response, as if their bodies had been attacked by a disease. When a rat is helpless, there is a significant hormonal response (adrenaline, glucocorticoids) regulated by the hypothalamic-pituitary-adrenal (HPA) axis, one that results in ulcers and death to neurons in the hippocampus—a key region for memory and learning. At the level of the brain, rats that are in a state of learned helplessness show a decrease in the neurochemical serotonin, especially in a control region of the brain called the dorsal raphe nucleus, critical for decision-making, memory, learning, and sleep.

When rats perceive the world as turbulent—uncontrollable and unpredictable—they effectively shut down all systems of the body and brain, exhibiting the behavioral and physiological signatures of depression and anxiety. Treating them with SSRIs, or selective serotonin reuptake inhibitors, can help, but they need the experience of control to turn these systems back on, which may take time if the tenure of turbulent stress is long, thus damaging the body and brain significantly.

The learned helplessness that emerges from turbulent environments is not unique to rats—it shows up in wildly different species, from flies to dogs to monkeys. It's therefore reasonable to assume that something similar can happen in humans as well.[21] In chapter 1, we discussed disorganized attachment, which results when an infant frequently experiences inconsistent responses from a mother to his or her needs. Again, in healthy attachment, when a baby has a need, he or she expects a timely and predictable response from mom. For example, when an infant cries, it signals to a mother that her baby needs to be soothed, fed, or otherwise cared for. If a mother is responsive to her baby's actions in a consistent way, her child begins to rely on that result. From a baby's perspective, this serve-and-return relationship teaches her that she has some control over the environment and that her actions are linked to particular outcomes. From a mother's perspective, she learns that when she returns her baby's serve, or need, she can satisfy her baby—something she wants as well. Moms who are in sync with their serve-and-return relationship have higher empathy, which leads, in turn, to babies who develop into more empathetic adults.[22] Though a sensitive, synchronized mom is aware of her child's needs and meets them, she doesn't return all the serves. Some serves are out-of-bounds, beyond what is deemed reasonable for proper development—a four-year-old who asks for a smartphone or an eight-year-old who asks to stay up too late watching a movie. Others are ignored so that the child can struggle with the feeling that they are not always in control—a five-year-old crying for help as she tries to tie her shoes or ride a bicycle, or a fourteen-year-old throwing a tantrum because she's asked to do her house chores. Some level of stress is good for the developing child especially when she has a mother or other caretaker who is there to support and buffer her stress, which makes it positive, or at least tolerable. Over time, mothers return fewer and fewer serves to allow independence to emerge. This is all normal, typical of healthy mother-child relationships.

But when a child's serve is frequently ignored or met with an aggressive response, especially early in life, the child experiences control deprivation just like the helpless rat who can't escape shock. The child doesn't know whether to approach mom when she is alarmed or move away. She feels threatened by abandonment. This turbulent mother-infant relationship can fuel disorganized attachment, which, as I mentioned in chapter 2, greatly heightens the risk later in life for borderline personality disorder, suicidal ideation, sexual promiscuity, and eating disorders.

A dysfunctional mother-child relationship is only one way in which turbulence can manifest in a child's life. Children can experience turbulent environments, such as uncertainty around reliable support in their lives, when they will be able to eat or live in a safe home, or whether and when someone will abuse them. A child with a violent father may not know if he will attack his mother on any given day, while another child who lives in abject poverty may not know whether she will go hungry that day. The effects of the climate crisis can create uncertainty in a child's environment—in vulnerable areas of the world, a child may not know when she will have to abandon her home due to a fire, tornado, hurricane, or monsoon. And in the last few years, children living through the COVID-19 pandemic confronted uncontrollable uncertainty about when they would ever see their friends, be in class with their teacher, and play sports.

Children living in turbulent environments suffer psychologically and physiologically, sometimes well into their adult years. Psychologically, they learn that their actions are rarely connected to intended outcomes. They perceive themselves as helpless, and they focus on the causes of failure rather than on solutions or coping strategies.[23] The intense stress they experience can disrupt sleep, eating, learning, and social interactions. When that kind of stress weighs on a developing brain that hasn't yet acquired a mature frontal lobe to control strong emotions, the perfect storm for anxiety emerges. On a physiological level, uncontrollable stress and anxiety are associated with heightened activity of the HPA, which ultimately releases cortisol, killing off cells in the hippocampus. A smaller hippocampus is associated with a decrease in the ability to learn, store and retrieve information in memory, and make healthy decisions.[24]

A study by epidemiologists Allison Schroeder, Natalie Slopen, and Mona Mittal offers strong evidence of the impact of turbulent adversity on child development.[25] The study looked at what types of ACEs a group of children experienced at three ages—when they were a year old, three years old, and five years old. In addition to the type, they also obtained data on the timing, tenure, and what they called intermittency, or essentially the predictability of each ACE. At each of these three age milestones, as well as at nine years of age, they assessed *internalized* mental health problems (e.g., anxiety, depression) and *externalized* behavioral problems (e.g., aggression, oppositional conduct). What they found was that among the Adverse Ts, turbulence had the most significant impact on internalized and externalized problems. This doesn't mean that type, timing, or tenure are irrelevant. Supporting the consistent evidence that numbers matter, children exposed to six ACEs had three times the magnitude of internalized and externalized problems at age nine compared with children who had zero to one ACE. But in this population of children, with the types of adversity they experienced, for a particular length of time, and linked to certain time periods of development, turbulence was the more important dimension of the Adverse Ts.

Turbulent ACEs add a layer of stress. Leah didn't know when she would be abused by her uncle and certainly had no control over the situation. Aliya didn't know when she would find shelter or food or water and had little control over her ability to access these necessities. Nadine didn't know when the next bomb would hit her beloved Palestine, or whether it would strike her family, and she had little control over the level of safety. Perhaps the only thing children who live through turbulence can control, as Viktor Frankl, the Nazi concentration camp survivor, noted,[26] is their freedom to choose how they will respond to the adversity. As we will learn in Part III, a traumatic response is not a given.

TOXICITY

Victoria was a charming, pudgy, freckle-faced, curly haired redhead. She was eleven years old but looked as if she could have been sixteen. She had just gone through puberty. The class was on a bit of a break from reading a book and Victoria was drawing. She asked me if I wanted to draw with her. When I sat down and looked at the drawing she had started, something wasn't right. Tucked away in the corner was clearly a drawing of Victoria herself: a little girl with freckles and red hair. She had drawn a skirt, but it was hiked up in such a way that you could see her backside. Standing behind her in the picture was a large man and his penis was sticking out.

The large man in Victoria's drawing turned out to be her father. He had started raping her when she was six years old, perhaps earlier. The only reason the raping stopped was because Victoria's mom found out about it and swiftly left to start a new life. But the damage was already embedded in Victoria's body and brain. She was perpetually on high alert, vigilant to every sound and movement. Simple requests to get ready for recess or lunch often resulted in her completely shutting down—flopping onto the floor, head down, as if asleep. Other requests, especially for academic work, were met with throwing books or pencils. Though the school had worked hard to provide her with coping skills to calm down when she was frustrated, her road to recovering from such severe, highly toxic sexual abuse was going to be long.

In the heat of the #MeToo movement, actor Matt Damon offered his thoughts on what he perceived as a spectrum of inappropriate behavior by men toward women: "You know, there's a difference between, you know, patting someone on the butt and rape or child molestation, right? Both of those behaviors need to be confronted and eradicated without question, but they shouldn't be conflated, right?"[27] This comment was immediately attacked for being insensitive to the pain and suffering that women have endured and endure to this day. Damon later apologized for his comment.

Damon's timing was poor. The nation was reeling from the despicable actions of Bill Cosby and Harvey Weinstein, who sexually harassed dozens of women, and raped many. But if we want to understand how adversity negatively impacts our bodies and brains, we should, in fact, be concerned with the relative severity or toxicity of the acts for all different types of adversity. Emotional abuse may have the same or different impact on the developmental programs as being raped or beaten. All three types of maltreatment instill fear. But what we are learning is that the toxicity of the experience may alter the nature of the fear response because it affects what is stored in memory, how readily that memory holds on, and how easily it is triggered. This shapes how we approach building resilience, focused on reducing the pathological fear response.

In the now famous experiments by psychologist Stanley Milgram on obedience, subjects were led to believe that they were shocking others whenever they failed to recall a word from a list. The shock-delivering device involved a scale from 15 to 450 volts of intensity. To help subjects calibrate the intensity of shock, Milgram added a second scale with the words *slight, moderate, strong, very strong, intense, extreme intensity, danger-severe,* and *XXX*. The goal of the experiment wasn't to determine if shock intensity impacted learning, which was clearly unethical, but rather, to see how far subjects would go when a dominant experimenter nudged them to keep increasing the intensity. Though there was considerable variation in how far individuals went on the intensity scale, some went all the way despite feedback that the learner was unresponsive.

What is considered unethical and unlawful in humans—at least for psychological experiments—is considered by many to be ethical and lawful with animals, and in the context of using shocks of varying intensity, rats are the subject of choice. Based on experiments covering at least two decades, we understand how fear is acquired, triggered, stored in memory, retrieved, forgotten, and erased at the level of genetic expression, neural circuitry, and behavior. And we know that toxicity matters.

A common technique used to generate fear in rats is called *fear conditioning.* The method starts by building an association between a conditioned stimulus like a tone and an unconditioned stimulus such as a shock to the foot, much like the experiments in *Mon Oncle* that I discussed earlier in this chapter. Over time, and with repeated presentation of the tone-shock pairing, the rat learns that the tone predicts the shock. Prediction is key to survival, as it enables all organisms to anticipate, plan, and adaptively respond. Predicting a shock launches a cascade of changes in the rat's body and brain, including a flood of hormones, increased heart rate, amygdala activation, and gene expression, as well as premotor and motor cortex activation in preparation for escape. Anticipating pain—and inescapable pain in this case—triggers stress, anxiety, and fear.

To explore the role of toxicity, the fear-conditioning paradigm is subtly tweaked by increasing the intensity of the foot shock—think of the Milgram device. When the intensity is low, rats show minimal defensive behavior. When the intensity is moderate, rats show defensive behavior, but only in response to the specific tone frequency and environmental context in which they learned the association; their response is selective. When intensity is high, rats consistently show defensive behavior, but they do this in response to tones that are a different frequency, as well as in varying environments—their response has generalized beyond the original experience. What this tells us is that the acquisition of a fear response in rats depends upon the toxicity of the experience. If toxicity is low or moderate, then the rat's fear response is only triggered by the specific sound that predicted shock. If toxicity is high, then the rat's fear response generalizes to a wide range of sounds.

Toxicity matters to rats. And the reason it matters comes from the logic of evolution. If something in the environment predicts a potentially lethal outcome, it's better to be safe than sorry: get out of Dodge. If something in the environment predicts a less dangerous outcome, then the cost-benefit analysis suggests that it's better to be sure than to flee unnecessarily.

This evolutionary logic ought to apply to our own species, and a clever experiment by cognitive neuroscientist Joseph Dunsmoor shows that it does, revealing the importance of toxicity as a dimension of adversity.[28] Dunsmoor set up a fear-conditioning experiment for human adults. A 550-hertz tone was associated with a low-intensity shock. A 1,000-hertz tone was associated with a high-intensity shock, white noise, and an aversive image (e.g., a gaping-mouthed snake). The addition of white noise and a scary image was designed to amp up the aversiveness of the high-intensity condition, while staying within the guidelines of human experimentation—though I said using shocks in humans was unethical, it is permissible at intensities far below those used with rodents. To assess fear conditioning, Dunsmoor used the autonomic nervous system measure of skin conductance; basically, sweatiness. This measure has been validated in numerous ways, including by demonstrating that skin conductance is correlated with activation in the fear-processing amygdala and the release of stress hormones.

Like countless studies of rats, Dunsmoor showed that skin conductance in our own species ramped up in response to both tones, showing that they had learned the predictive association between tone and shock. But whereas sweatiness only ramped up in the low-intensity condition when the tone was precisely 550 hertz, it ramped up to tones both lower and higher than 1,000 hertz in the high-intensity condition. Like rats, humans overgeneralize their fear response to a host of potential triggers when the potential threat is in the dangerous zone. This overgeneralization is adaptive in the sense that it's better to be safe than sorry. But overgeneralization to triggers associated with highly toxic experiences is also what leads to post-traumatic stress disorders, hypervigilance, anxiety, and fear of the world. This was the world that Victoria inhabited. It helps us understand why Victoria was hypervigilant around all men, erupted in anger in response to school demands, and why she sometimes shut down entirely because of the unbearable pain of being.

Toxicity, like the four other Adverse Ts, is a dimension that helps us understand how adversity affects us at a biological level. But like the prism experiment that brought the color spectrum together into white light, we must unite the five T fingers of adversity into a unified fist to understand the lethal landscapes of adversity that we have created for our children. This unification, and the understanding it generates, provides the best opportunity to help children cope with the lethal landscapes that may await in their future.

A HAND OF ADVERSE Ts

In 1984, I was carrying out research for my PhD dissertation, living in an idyllic campsite in the middle of Amboseli National Park, Kenya. My Kenyan field assistant and friend, Benard, invited me to his sister's wedding up north. It was going to be a traditional wedding of the Kamba tribe, with a big dinner on the first night, followed by a formal ceremony in the morning, and then an all-night party. At the party, I met Serena, a shy twelve-year-old girl, and her larger-than-life aunt, Auntie Mumbe. Mumbe was sitting with one of her sister's babies in her lap. Mumbe asked me if I wanted the baby. Taken aback, I turned to Benard for clarification. He laughed and walked away. I explained to Mumbe that I was too young to be a father. She laughed.

Mumbe and I talked for much of the night. She recounted stories of her childhood, her family, and her struggles with Serena, who had been living with her for the past year. Serena often refused to go to school and when she was in school, was fighting with other children. Serena was often sick and appeared malnourished. She had only just recovered from an almost lethal bout of malaria, a disease that was rampant in that part of Kenya. Serena's parents were dead, both killed in front of her by a vengeful neighbor when she was only seven years old. Before they were killed, she was often beaten by her drunken father, who also beat her mother and other siblings. Her father was also in and out of jail. Mumbe didn't have much to offer Serena, as she was a poor, frail widow in her late seventies, fighting to make it through the 1983–1984 drought that caused massive famine in Kenya. In just twelve years of life on earth, Serena had hopped onto a field of land mines, a count of at least fourteen ACEs—incarceration, parental loss, domestic violence, physical abuse, emotional abuse, social neglect, physical neglect, emotional neglect, cognitive neglect, displacement, community violence, disease, and poverty.

Serena, like millions of other children across the globe, inhabits multiple peaks of adversity within the lethal landscape. For some, their tenure within each peak is long, impacting multiple sensitive and critical periods of development, and it is often highly toxic and turbulent. By the age of seven, Serena's tenure with abuse, neglect, incarceration, poverty, parental loss, and community violence overlapped with the stages in which she would acquire language, morality, and a theory of mind, and it lined up with the early phases of emotional development and regulation. Though there were no formal medical or psychiatric assessments of Serena's health, much of what she presented to the naked eye appeared to be direct responses to her adversity: she was behaviorally dysregulated, sick and challenged to surmount disease, unfocused and anxious around others. The pathology expressed in her body and brain appeared to be related to the cumulative adversity she had experienced—her allostatic load. And from everything we know about such cumulative adversity, the timing and tenure of such stress most likely resulted in rapid epigenetic aging, decoupling Serena's chronological and biological ages.[29]

This section has brought us full circle to where we started: the greater the accumulation of adversity, the greater the burden on children's physical and mental health. Numbers matter. But the way in which they matter has been greatly expanded from the original ACEs study of Felitti, Anda, and their colleagues. We now know that the typology of adversity is much larger than originally conceived and different types of adversity leave different signatures on the brain and body. Type is only one dimension within the suite of Adverse Ts, accompanied by timing, tenure, turbulence, and toxicity, and they all shape the signature that adversity leaves behind.

part two

HARM: LETHAL LANDSCAPES OF ADVERSITY

Every Night & every Morn
Some to Misery are Born
Every Morn and every Night
Some are Born to sweet delight
Some are Born to sweet delight
Some are Born to Endless Night
We are led to Believe a Lie
When we see not Thro the Eye
Which was Born in a Night to perish in a Night
—WILLIAM BLAKE[1]

Deprivation: The Unmotivated Mind

Beginning in the fourteenth century, governments throughout Europe invested in homes for infants who were often illegitimate, birthed by single mothers who were slaves, prostitutes, or marginalized in other ways that kept them from being sufficient caretakers. In northern Europe, these infants were often referred to as *found* or *discovered*, whereas in southern Europe they were referred to as *abandoned* or *thrown away*. Throughout the eighteenth and nineteenth centuries, Catherine the Great of Russia invested heavily in homes for such children, calling them *foundling homes*. For most Russians, foundling homes were perceived as symbols of enlightenment and humanitarian ideals. This perception was, however, a gloss on top of a dark underbelly, one that was at least in part motivated by the desire to cultivate a working class for the state, while also failing to acknowledge the high mortality rates of the children in their care—estimates of up to 80 percent of those admitted.[1] Though foundling homes were terminated by the twentieth century and replaced with

more health-oriented orphanages, such institutional rearing conditions were, and still are in many parts of the world, insufficient.
Orphanage-reared children are often deprived of basic needs, including the healthy serve-and-return interactions with caretakers we
discussed in chapter 2 that are essential for typical development.
Ethan was one of these children.

Ethan was abandoned by his mother at birth and placed into an
orphanage in Eastern Europe. During the first two years of his life, he
slept in a crib with one to two other babies, along with twenty other
baby-filled cribs. He then graduated to a larger room with perhaps ten
rows of fifteen beds for older children. Neither Ethan nor the other infants were underfed, but the meals typically lacked sufficient nutritional value. Ethan had clothes, but they were not his to keep. Ethan
had toys to play with, but they were also not his possessions. There
were books, but caretakers rarely read to him and the books were not
his to keep. No caretaker was ever consistently with Ethan, and no
caretaker soothed him if he was upset.

Ethan lived in a desolate landscape until he was about six years
old, when he was adopted by Julie, a loving young American mother.
Ethan was her first and only child. For Ethan, a journey of hope had
started. For Julie, a journey of joy, love, devotion, and excitement had
begun. For the two of them, the road ahead would not be easy—six
years of deprivation had left its trademark signature on Ethan's body
and brain.

To understand the impact of the deprivation Ethan experienced,
and what I saw during my interactions with him in the classroom, we
must start with a ground zero question: What kind of experience is sufficient to ensure that a child develops competencies that are fundamental to human flourishing? Because we are not homogeneous lumps of
clay, but highly differentiated individuals, there will not be one answer
to this question. Also, what is sufficient experience for developing our

immune systems, hormonal stress responses, and fine motor control is bound to be different from the experience required to develop attachment, self-regulation, attention, memory, emotional awareness, language, and morality. And because of the unique imprint of our genes, there will also be differences in what each person requires to develop. When we say that someone was deprived—like Ethan or the millions of children who grow up in austere orphanages around the world— we are effectively making the point that their experience was deficient with respect to the needs that most developing humans require. But we must be cautious in how we determine what's minimally needed.

CRITICAL MOMENTS FOR LEARNING

To understand the nature of deprivation, and in particular how a lack of experience can derail development, let's step away from our own species for a moment and consider what we have learned from experimental studies of other animals. Understanding how things work in other animals has at least two advantages: one, we are typically afforded a higher level of experimental control than in studies of humans, thereby allowing for a more detailed level of specificity in our understanding of how things work; second, depending on the species, and its proximity to us in the tree of life, we may learn about how a mechanism evolved, including its origins and adaptive significance.

Let's start with newly hatched songbirds that must learn their songs from hearing others sing, similar in many ways to newborn babies who must learn their language from hearing others speak. Songbird learning progresses in two stages: there is a sensitive period when a nestling listens to and memorizes song material twittered by adults— males in most species—followed by a period when the nestling practices and ultimately refines its own song. It is a process with elements that all songbirds share, but it is still ultimately unique for each individual nestling. We know that for many species, if you deafen a nestling during the sensitive period of song acquisition, the song produced often has little to no resemblance to that of the species. If you provide the young nestling with exposure to songs from another species during the sensitive period, it will also produce degenerate song material. And if you provide the nestling with exposure to species-specific songs during the sensitive period but deafen the bird during the sensorimotor period, the song will also be wrong. These observations tell us that experience with species-specific song—**type**—is necessary during the sensitive period—**timing**—and hearing is required to generate a song that matches essential elements of the species' repertoire.

But how much experience with the song is necessary during the sensitive period? Is there a minimum amount? Studies of songbirds also allow us to answer this *how much* question of experience—a form of **tenure**. Most impressive is a study by my postdoctoral advisor and the father of neuroethology, the late Peter Marler.[2] In this study, one group of four song sparrows listened to thirty different song sparrow songs for a total of five minutes, within one day of the sensitive period of development. For two song sparrows, this exposure was sufficient to produce an accurate version of their species-specific song, while the other two song sparrows failed to produce a species-specific song. This is a beautiful result, as it helps us understand both what is sufficient experience and what constitutes deprivation for some individuals. For two birds, one day and thirty songs was sufficient, but for two other birds, one day and thirty songs was insufficient—a case of deprivation. So while we can't define deprivation for an entire species, we can get very close to saying how little experience is sufficient for some individual birds.

What about deprivation in animals who are closer genetic relatives to us on the evolutionary tree of life? Consider rodents—mice and rats—and the newborn pups' dependency on mom for food, warmth, and getting rid of bodily waste. You can think of pup development as a time-lapsed version of human infant development. For mice, for example, the early postnatal period from birth to twenty-three days is associated with growing fur, opening eyes and ears, producing ultrasonic vocalizations to maintain contact with mom, and suckling mom's milk until they are fourteen days old and can eat solids. During the adolescent-pubescent period, pups are weaned on about day twenty-four, and for females, their vagina opens at around day twenty. Puberty occurs between thirty-four and forty-seven days, followed by sexual maturation and full adulthood at sixty days. In essence, mice do in about two months what we do in anywhere from thirteen to twenty-three years; I'm being generous here with the age range for our species, as much depends on whether you're focused on our anatomy, physiology, behavior, or cultural norms. The key point is that mouse and rat pups have a period of time in which they depend on maternal care, and so do we. This opens the door to using the experimental tools of research on rodents to precisely understand how the time course of deprivation impacts development.

Paralleling the work on songbirds, several rodent research groups have looked at the impact of pups being separated from their mother for different lengths of time, including the effects of just a single day. In some experiments, the mother is removed for a day and the pups are kept together with other littermates, and in other experiments, a pup is left alone in a cage; in each of these experimental approaches, pups are fed so that nutrition isn't a confounding factor. Strikingly, a single day of separation during the early postnatal period wallops the signature of mouse development, resulting in heightened anxiety, increased depression, lowered motivation for rewards, and a weakened immune system.[3] This is mind-blowing. Only a single day of maternal deprivation causes a cascade of changes in brain circuitry, immune response, and behavior, linked to psychopathology that looks a lot like human psychopathology. If we use current estimates of developmental timing where one rodent day is equivalent to thirty human days,[4] one can begin to imagine how much damage a month of maternal deprivation would have on the developing human infant. We can see signs of the possible impact in studies of monkeys, a species more closely related to us.

In 1958, the comparative psychologist Harry Harlow presented a talk titled "The Nature of Love" where he urged scientists to study this "wondrous state, deep, tender, and rewarding." Harlow was quick to lead the pack of scientists investigating love, but somewhat bizarrely, his approach involved depriving infant rhesus monkeys of maternal care—in other words, what happens without love?[5] Over a period of thirty years, Harlow and his team allowed female monkeys to give birth and then, within twelve hours, removed and placed the infant alone in a cage.[6] In Harlow's own terms, infants were "incarcerated" or "sentenced" to complete social isolation. Seeing these infants is excruciating.[7] Deprived of maternal care, and living in a barren metal cage, infant rhesus monkeys resort to compulsive self-clutching, rocking, thumb-sucking, self-injury, and lethargy; the self-clutching and rocking are, as Harlow noted, reminiscent of what has been observed in some autistic people, an indication of a need for self-reinforcing sensory stimulation.

Harlow and others then followed up on these initial experiments, providing critical tests of the Adverse Ts (though this terminology wasn't used at the time): emotional deprivation (**type**), different critical periods of development (**timing**), for different durations of time (**tenure**), with no control given to the infant (**turbulent**), and with different extremes of deprivation (**toxicity**). In one experimental series varying toxicity, infants were either completely isolated, kept alone but in view of other rhesus that they could see and hear but not touch, or were caged only with a wire-sculpted mother. Fake mothers dispensed milk, but some were wrapped in a soft cloth, whereas others were only wire. Only the cloth-wrapped wire mother provided a potential positive benefit, and a weak one at that. The experimenters intentionally frightened this group of infants with a scary-looking mechanical monster, causing them to cling to the cloth. The soft cloth seemed to provide infants with a partial replacement for the mother's fur, a security blanket of sorts, but the infants nonetheless continued to show all the stereotypical, self-clutching, self-harming, and other-harming behaviors.

To test for timing, Harlow kept some infants in complete social isolation for three, six, or twelve months before relocating them to a new environment with peers; another group of infants spent the first six months of life in a nursery with peers and were then relocated to complete social isolation for six more months. The three-month social isolates slowly developed appropriate social interactions when they moved to a normal social group, whereas the six- and twelve-month isolates failed to, maintaining stereotypical, self-injurious behaviors as well as heightened stress. The severity of these behaviors was worse in the twelve-month isolates than in the six-month isolates, revealing a dose response to deprivation, which is akin to the dose response we discussed in chapter 1 for the ACE score. Individuals who were reared with peers for the first six months and then isolated developed some socially appropriate skills but were hyperaggressive both to others and to themselves. Interestingly, and despite the social deficits observed, the six- and twelve-month isolated infants showed no deficits when tested on a battery of learning tasks. This led Harlow to conclude that deprivation impacts the "social mind" but not the "intellectual mind." This important distinction was, however, largely ignored in the decades that followed.

Harlow's findings were immediately adopted by John Bowlby and Mary Ainsworth—the leading developmental psychologists of the time—who argued that infants have an innate need for maternal care.[8] Deprive them of this need and psychological devastation follows, an impairment that is irreparable if it occurs within a critical period of development and for a particular duration of time.

To more precisely explore the role of timing, neuroscientist Judy Cameron carried out a series of experiments in which an infant monkey spent different amounts of time with its mother at the start of life and was then separated.[9] Strikingly, spending one, three, or six months with mom was sufficient to ensure species-typical, appropriate social behavior at six months and for the remainder of their lives. In contrast, spending only one week with mom was insufficient. For rhesus monkeys, therefore, infants require between two and four weeks of time with mom if they are to develop the signature of species-typical social behavior.

Separating rhesus monkey infants from their mothers early in life causes irreparable psychological damage. If this grim prognosis is true for one of our close evolutionary cousins, it does not bode well for our own infants.

HOW TOXIC DEPRIVATION HALTS GROWTH

In the late 1960s, the president of Romania, Nicolae Ceaușescu, implemented three population-growth policies designed to improve the country's power and status on the global stage: women of reproductive age were expected to produce at least five children, those who produced less than five children were hit with a celibacy tax, and abortion as well as contraception were banned. Under Ceaușescu's rule, women were reproductive factories for the glory of Romania.

In 1989, there was a coup and Ceaușescu was deposed. Soon thereafter, he was tried for genocide, found guilty, and put to death. Of those who died during the genocide, many left behind babies and young children who were *found* and placed in fortress-like orphanages that were already home to more than 170,000 children; many of the veteran residents had disabilities and were deemed *irrecoverable* by the government. Newly arriving babies were placed into an assembly line of untrained, emotionless caretakers, wrapped up in cloth, mummy-style, placed in metal cribs, and fed by bottle—much like young calves in a meat factory. For three years, these babies were crib-bound, muscles atrophying, hearts aching, minds dying. Older children were branded as either "productive" or "deficient and unsalvageable." Productive children went on to slightly better orphanages, whereas the deficient and unsalvageable—typically children with some kind of disability— remained in the squalor of the asylum to die. As investigative journalist Tom Jarriel of the show *20/20* reported in "Shame of a Nation," these facilities were akin to Nazi concentration camps, protected and guarded from public awareness.[10] The children in them were no better off than the caged monkeys in Harlow's experiments that I discussed in the first section of this chapter.

Following a flood of international attention, relief, and adoption, the distinguished developmental scientists Charles Nelson, Nathan Fox, and Charles Zeanah were invited by the government of Romania to begin the Bucharest Early Intervention Project (BEIP). The goal was to document how toxic deprivation impacts the developing child and what, if any, interventions might reverse the deficits, including the placement of children in foster care. This research, spanning three decades, has not only transformed our understanding of how toxic deprivation impacts the body and brain but has resulted in fundamental changes in international policies around the needs of developing children.[11]

The BEIP team wanted to compare children who were institutionalized in the Romanian orphanages with Romanian-born children of the same age and sex, living at home with their biological parents since birth. As in any well-designed experiment, if you want to understand the impact of some factor, you need a control group that isn't exposed to this factor but is similar in all other ways. So the BEIP team started with two groups, children who were institutionalized and those who were raised by their own parents. The institutionalized group was then randomly divided into two additional groups: one group of children remained in the institutional setting until their teens and the others were placed in a high-quality foster care home in Romania, between the ages of six to thirty-one months. This allowed the BEIP team to see whether the timing and tenure of highly toxic deprivation make a difference.

At this point, you might wonder about the ethics of this kind of work. After all, if a child benefits from foster care—which may seem like an obvious outcome given the horrid conditions of institutional rearing—how could you further deprive the children who were required to stay in the institution? Why not give everyone foster care? Several things should be kept in mind in thinking about these ethical issues. For one, staying in institutional care was simply keeping children in the kind of care environment that the government of Romania had implemented as an intervention for orphans; and as noted earlier, orphans in many other countries across the globe have been raised in orphanages, and some with success.[12] Second, there was no consensus at the time that foster care would provide a clear benefit. It was possible, in fact, that children living in an orphanage for any amount of time (**tenure**) would be irreparably damaged even if placed into a loving family or that the kind of care provided by a foster family was insufficient or not of the kind needed by such children. Third, consider the nature of a vaccine trial, such as the ones carried out at the onset of

COVID-19. It was not unethical to give some the vaccine and some the placebo, especially when the outcomes were uncertain. But once it was clear that the COVID-19 vaccines were effective and safe compared with the placebo, it was imperative to disseminate them widely. So was the logic of foster care intervention. If foster care worked relative to institutional care, eliminating or reducing some of the early deficits, then foster care programs would be developed as alternatives to institutions, and supported by the Romanian government. At least that was what the BEIP team hoped for.

On the basis of standardized pediatric measures, the institutionalized children had lower weight, height, and head circumference at age two than the parent-reared children. As the *20/20* documentary reported, and as the BEIP team observed, the institutionalized children also exhibited stereotyped behaviors akin to Harlow's rhesus monkeys, self-stimulating and fearful—behaviors that were nonexistent in the parent-reared Romanian children. Keep in mind that the institutionalized children were not reared in solitary confinement, as the monkeys were, but with peers and some contact with adults. These interactions were, however, insufficient to develop healthy attachments.

When the institutionalized children were placed in the context of an adult stranger—a method developed by attachment expert Mary Ainsworth to see how babies respond to unfamiliar people in the absence of their mother—about 60 percent showed *disorganized* attachment (described in chapter 1), expressing fear, uncertainty, and jerky, staccato actions, and about 10 percent showed no attachment at all. The complete lack of attachment in some institutionalized children was deeply shocking, as many developmental scientists—dating back to Bowlby, Ainsworth, and Harlow—felt that our desire to connect, relate, and attach was part of our DNA, no different in many ways from our instinct to drink, eat, and breathe. These children proved that deprivation could leave you marooned, inside the confines of your own mind, uninterested in others.

The institutionalized children also showed significantly lower scores than parent-reared children for broad measures of development, including the ability for pretend play, attending to and naming objects, copying shapes, following instructions, social communication, and self-calming. Critically, for the tenure dimension, the longer a child's time within the institution, the greater the deficits across these measures of cognitive and social-emotional development.

To dig deeper into the potential signature of toxic deprivation, and especially the impact on specific developmental programs, cognitive neuroscientist Margaret Sheridan carried out a study of learning by association with the Romanian orphans. Recall that the Adverse T of turbulence and the research on learned helplessness, in particular, show that typical development relies on making associations between actions and outcomes. When a rat learns that a tone predicts a future shock, and that escape through the open door avoids the shock, an association with a positive outcome has been forged. When the door is closed, helplessness emerges because the predictive power of the association no longer delivers a positive action. Associative learning is the most primitive or basic mechanism of learning and memory, one that we share with our earliest ancestors, even the most basic creatures like the sea slug. Given the ancient origins of associative learning, and its critical role in survival, one would expect it to be robust, protected from adversity.

Sheridan created two computer games of associative learning for twelve-year-old Romanian orphans and a comparison group of Romanian children raised by their parents. The first was a simple shooter game: click a key whenever the crocodile moves into the strike zone. A successfully timed click delivered stars as rewards. The second game involved matching keys to numbers—for example, touch the #1 key when the numeral 1 appears on the monitor; in some cases, the numbers appeared in a pattern—1-2-3-4—and at other times they were random—3-1-4-2.

Compared with parent-reared children, the Romanian orphans had much lower scores on both games, indicative of weakly formed associations. And the longer an orphaned child's tenure within the orphanage, the lower her score. These are shocking results. Despite the ancient origins of associative learning and its foundational role in learning about the positive and negative aspects of the world, toxic deprivation, timed to early in child development, with a long tenure— up to twelve years—undermines its developmental program.

Associative learning is not the only developmental program disrupted by toxic, long-tenured deprivation during early childhood. Compared with children reared by their biological parents, the Romanian orphans—assessed at ages eight, twelve, and sixteen years—showed more psychiatric disorders, more dysfunctional peer relationships, weaker social communication skills, greater deficits in understanding words and sentences, weaker self-control, higher levels of substance abuse and risky sexual behavior, and more signs of reactive attachment and disinhibited social engagement disorders. Given the years of institutionalization (long tenure), the lack of control (turbulence), high toxicity, cutting across multiple sensitive and critical periods of development for different cognitive, social, and emotional competencies, it's difficult to determine when these competencies were impacted, and how much exposure to deprivation was necessary. But the fact that such deficits show up early in adolescence and are maintained for years, shows the devastating and persistent impact of toxic deprivation on the essential elements that allow humans to flourish.

HOW TOXIC DEPRIVATION
ALTERS DEVELOPMENTAL PROGRAMS

As we discussed in chapter 1, over the long haul, wear and tear ages us and leaves epigenetic changes that are signatures of our stressful past, just like the rings on a tree. In 2009, molecular biologists Elizabeth Blackburn, Carol Greider, and Jack Szostak were awarded the Nobel Prize for their discovery of a unique marker of aging: a region at the tip of our chromosomes called the telomeres. Telomeres are evolution-arily ancient molecular structures, appearing hundreds of millions of years ago in single-celled microorganisms such as yeast. You can think of telomeres as akin to the plastic caps at the ends of shoelaces. Intact caps make it easier to both thread the holes of your sneakers and tie your laces. Telomeres allow chromosomes to properly function in cell division. In the same way that the caps of your shoelaces ultimately break and fray after repeated use, the telomeres shorten following ev-ery cell division, eventually resulting in cell death. Individuals who have to fight more to combat adversity have shorter telomeres than those who have to fight less and, as a result, age faster.

Pulling together dozens of studies from a variety of populations shows that shorter telomere length is associated with a higher rate of stress-related psychiatric disorders such as PTSD and anxiety, which in turn are related to the number, tenure, timing, turbulence, and toxicity of adversity.[13] The institutionalized Romanian children fit this pattern to a T: compared with parent-reared children, institutionalized chil-dren showed significantly shorter telomeres, measured between the ages of two to fifteen years, and the longer a child's tenure in the insti-tutional setting the shorter their telomeres.[14] Let this point sink in. By the age of two, the stressors of toxic deprivation have impacted children at the molecular level. For those who continue down this path of toxic deprivation, aging continues, as do the layers of psychopathology.

The signature of toxic deprivation also shows up in the child's stress response, which we can look at through the lens of two body and brain systems: the hypothalamic-pituitary-adrenal axis and the sympathetic nervous system. When we are stressed by a real or imagined experience—no food, lack of a responsive caretaker, an aggressive parent—our HPA typically responds by releasing cortisol and increasing our heart rate. These somewhat invisible changes can show up in our bodies as sweating, muscle stiffening, and flushing of the face. This is a highly adaptive response that evolved long ago and is part of the human phenotype, whether we are living as current-day hunter-gatherers or city-dwellers. But for the Romanian children raised in orphanages, repeated exposure to toxic deprivation effectively puts their stress response into hibernation because it is worn out from overuse. Whereas parent-reared children respond with an increase in cortisol and heart rate when exposed to a stressful situation, orphanage-reared children show a blunted response, a signature that continues until the teenage years. This sensitization to life's stressors is maladaptive.

The Romanian orphanage studies also show that toxic deprivation leaves an actual imprint on the brain. The problems these children experience in cognition, perception, and emotional regulation show up as structural and functional brain differences as early as twenty-two months. We can see this in electroencephalogram (EEG) readings, which provide a readout of different brain frequencies, or waves. Think of these waves like an old-fashioned radio with a knob that lets you tune to different radio frequencies corresponding to stations. For our purposes here, there are three stations: Alpha, Beta, and Theta. Theta waves are at the lower frequency range of the stations, followed by

Alpha and then Beta. Studies of animal and human populations show that deficits of attention, short-term memory, and self-control are associated with low Alpha frequencies. These differences in brain wave frequencies are accompanied by smaller brain regions critical to learning, memory, and self-control—the prefrontal cortex and hippocampus. Institutionalized toddlers have brains that are tuned primarily to the Theta station, and rarely to Alpha and Beta. Toxic deprivation has blunted these children's brains.

Based on the evidence presented, it is clear that children who remain for several years in such austere orphanages experience significant and stubbornly persistent biological effects: damage to their telomeres, brain circuitry, immune system, stress physiology, cognitive and social-emotional competences. This was most likely what was happening to Ethan's body and brain during his six years of institutionalized life, though his mother, Julie, wasn't aware. What Julie and his teachers were aware of was Ethan's behavior, reflections of the underlying damage, including tantrums and an inability to self-soothe, challenges creating and maintaining relationships with peers and adults, and a lack of focus and inability to plan, which resulted in poor grades. These behaviors signaled the need for a different approach to caretaking and teaching.

In contrast, my daughter Sofia, who left the orphanage at twenty-two months and is now twenty-two years old, has a much different story. Our journey with her as parents was familiar. From elementary school to college, her teachers were able to use typical approaches to learning and growth and they worked beautifully. Both Ethan and Sofia were neglected from birth, but Ethan's tenure was much longer and, as a result, several of his developmental systems were damaged over time, making it much more difficult for him to thrive, even once he was in a loving home.

THE IMPACT OF SOCIOECONOMIC STATUS

The research around orphanages shows us the alarming toll that extreme cases of deprivation clearly take on children. But many more children around the world experience a lower level of deprivation that can still create a heavy burden. One way to understand the toxicity dimension of deprivation is by looking at socioeconomic status, or SES,[15] which, like ACEs, is another population measure. A simple way to think of SES is in terms of a scale that starts on the left, with individuals who are worse off, and stretches out to the right with those who are well-off. The worse-well scale is based on a combination of both material (food, water, shelter, money) and nonmaterial (education, safe neighborhood) assets. These elements, in turn, impact the kinds of lives that children have growing up.

Children who are worse off in terms of food and shelter not only experience anxieties around when they will have their next meal and place to sleep, but suffer the physiological consequences of such turbulent environments, especially the impact on hormonal regulation and immune responses. Relative to children with highly educated parents, those with poorly educated parents receive shorter tenure, higher turbulence stimulation in the social, cognitive, and linguistic domains. Children who are worse off generally have caregiver relationships that are less consistently stable, warm, and nurturing. Though it would be ideal to separate out the different contributions of, say, food and shelter from education and neighborhood effects, this is often not possible in studies that use SES as a measure.

The SES score gains its validity from the fact that there is often a strong relationship between the different measures that enter into the score, and it is remarkably predictive of outcomes. Higher SES is, on average, associated with better physical health; longer life span; lower rates of cancer, heart disease, and diabetes; lower rates of depression, anxiety, and psychosis; higher academic achievement; greater school readiness in young children; and up to a fifteen-point IQ difference when compared with the worse off.[16] Children growing up in worse-off SES environments have lower cortical volume and surface area, a smaller hippocampus, weaker connectivity between the frontal lobe and amygdala, higher activity of the amygdala, lower activity of the hippocampus, and smaller volume of the orbitofrontal cortex, which is associated with higher levels of conduct disorders.[17]

On a global level, low SES is often intertwined with war and the displacement that follows.[18] In 2019, UNICEF estimated that there were thirteen million children living in refugee camps—a life of squalor that is on the higher end of the worse-off SES scale, and indicative of a population that is likely to grow as environmental threats and civil strife within countries cause more displacement and economic uncertainty. Added to this population of deprived children are those who may end up separated from their parents—alone, hungry, and frightened. Sometimes such separations are unforeseen consequences of the brutal challenges of migration, as we have witnessed from news broadcasts of overloaded boats attempting to land on the coasts of Europe from the Middle East and Africa. Sometimes, such separations are horrifyingly the result of policies designed to separate children from their parents, as documented by investigative journalist Caitlin Dickerson, who covered the United States' secretive policies during President Trump's tenure in office.[19]

Low SES is also associated with greater vulnerability to the impact of diseases, a phenomenon on full display during the COVID-19 pandemic. Not only was the devastation of social isolation hardest on teenagers growing up in worse-off conditions, but so, too, were the health consequences for this age group and others, both younger and older.[20]

The significant impact of SES doesn't mean that negative outcomes are certain. We all enter the world with a unique biological inheritance that makes some of us more vulnerable to lower SES and others of us more resistant. We must keep this interaction in mind as we think about the impact of SES, and all forms of deprivation. We will dive much deeper into this in Part III.

As we've seen in this chapter, deprivation is very often the result of a child's frayed bond with her caregivers. The consistent serve-and-return synchronized relationship that she expects is not in place, and her physical and psychological needs are not being met. But deprivation can manifest in the environments around a child as well. Some children live in poverty, lack food and shelter, or are forced to work grueling jobs that tax their immature bodies and brains. Some children experience all of these heartbreaking situations.

Depending on the Adverse Ts, deprivation will leave different signatures on the bodies and brains of children, but essentially, all greatly hinder a child's ability to learn. Without a parent or caretaker who reads, plays, and teaches her child, the mind atrophies. Absent secure attachment and loving relationships with other family members and friends, curiosity vanishes. Deprived of food or a stable place to sleep, the energy to attend, learn, and plan dissipates. Without feedback and encouragement, motivation wilts.

Abuse: The Fearful Mind

t was 8:15 a.m., the start of first period, and Kevin was sitting at his desk, hoodie up, head down. Kevin was twelve years old but was so small he could have passed for a six-year-old. His teacher, Greg, asked him to take off his hoodie and pass in his iPhone from his backpack, two rules that the school developed for reasons of safety and distractibility. Kevin didn't budge. Greg walked over, gently put his hand on Kevin's shoulder and asked him again, this time adding that he would have to go to the therapeutic break room if he failed to comply. Kevin picked his head up, looked at Greg, and said, "No way, Greggo. Break room it is." Kevin walked to the break room and curled up in the corner, hood over his head. He was in this position for close to an hour when I asked Laura, a counselor at the school, why they couldn't just take the iPhone from his backpack and allow Kevin to get back to the classroom. My thinking was that it was better to engage Kevin in his academic classes than to engage in a power struggle over his iPhone.

Laura told me about Kevin's past, providing important corrective lenses to my thinking.

Kevin was the youngest of two children. He lived at home with his mom. His father was in jail for domestic violence and child abuse. For much of Kevin and his sister Joani's childhood, they watched as an oft angry father struck his wife, their mother. Witnessing violence, especially within the family, is bad enough for a developing child who needs security, stability, and loving parents. But for Kevin and Joani, the adversity didn't stop there. For entertainment, and to teach them that life is tough, Dad put Kevin and Joani into the outdoor dog cage, threw food in, and forced them to compete for their nightly dinner. If they refused, he beat them until they entered the dinner arena.

We often resort to the expression *unimaginable* when we learn of human cruelty. And yet, over and over again, history teaches us that we are masters of the unimaginable. What is unimaginable is for some of us to conceive of doing what Kevin's father did to his children. Though Kevin's father was removed from the family and put in jail, he had already inflicted years of damage, burned into their memories. In his short life, Kevin had experienced domestic violence, emotional abuse, physical abuse, the incarceration of his father, and the divorce of his parents—five ACEs, all timed to several sensitive and critical periods, each with long tenures, high toxicity, and turbulence.

Kevin's TRACEs were numerous. He was food obsessed, hoarding it at school whenever he could. His food obsession generalized to other objects, his iPhone being a prime example. He wouldn't give up what he owned, worried that he would never get it back. He flinched when new men walked into the room, including me on our first encounter. His growth appeared stunted, his skin translucent. He was frequently sick, missing more school days than he attended. He shut down frequently, often triggered by the slightest academic demand. When he wasn't shut down, he was hypervigilant, scanning the surroundings like a twitchy squirrel checking for hawks. A sudden, unexpected sound, including someone crying or yelling, caused him to jump out of his seat and, sometimes, to bang his head against the desk or wall. Kevin mirrored the fear he perceived in others, automatically and unconsciously putting himself in their shoes.

If we want to help children like Kevin, we need to understand how abuse is embedded in the body and brain. Does emotional, physical, and sexual abuse sign off on the body and brain in different ways? Do we see a different legacy of this abuse when we compare it to deprivation or other types of adversity?

What you will read in this chapter is not easy. For those of you who may have experienced life as Kevin did, reading similar accounts may well be triggering. Though I have not personally shared your experiences, I have worked with hundreds of children who have, each encounter a painful reminder of the horrific impact that parents and other caretakers have on our most vulnerable. I hope you will bear with me as I share this literature with you.

TRIGGERING FEAR

Fear is an evolutionarily ancient emotional response that is triggered when an animal anticipates or detects a threat to their well-being. Because animals can recognize some threats without any prior, negative experience, the capacity for fear is innate, built into a species' genome. For example, rodent pups avoid the urine of predators such as cats, even if they've never had any dangerous interactions with the predators. Other reactions to threats come from making a negative association between a cue and an experience—a creature links a smell, sound, image, or taste that was once neutral to a negative outcome and understands it is bad for its well-being. For example, a hawk's whistle registers as a negative sound to infant monkeys because it predicts danger, just as the low, raspy voice of a drunken father sparks distress in a child because it foreshadows violence. The bad outcome changes the valence of sensation from neutral to negative. This is the process of fear conditioning, a version of Pavlov's experiments with dogs. Fear conditioning is the precursor to learned helplessness that I described in chapter 3, where the rat connects the tone with a shock, learns to fear what happens when the tone goes off, and, ultimately, is stymied when there is no escape. The fear is instilled, but there is no option to avoid danger.

Fear can also be acquired by watching something bad happen to others. This can happen in one of two ways. The first is simple observational learning, or learning by association. For example, rat pups can acquire fear by observing a littermate being attacked and eaten by a predator, in the same way that a child can acquire fear of her father from watching him beat her mother. The second way arises unconsciously and is orchestrated, in part, by a system of neurons located in different parts of the mammalian cortex called mirror neurons. When an individual experiences fear or sees fear in another, these neurons fire, effectively creating fear by contagion in much the same way that yawning and laughter are contagious.[1]

Situations or events that trigger fear are shaped by the five Adverse Ts of type, timing, tenure, turbulence, and toxicity. As I noted in chapter 1, a child who grows up in a harsh environment with frequent exposure to life-threatening situations will acquire fear early, along with the cascade of other responses that follow as a means for survival. In addition, while different types of adversity may all trigger a general fear response, we see that reactions to fear across species are varied in different situations: a creature may fight when its resources are threatened by a competitor, flee if there are escape routes, freeze to avoid detection, or feign death when the threat to survival is imminent and escape seems hopeless. This strongly suggests that there is no one response to the different kinds of abuse children may experience, whether it's emotional, physical, or sexual.

THE WOUNDS OF DENIGRATION

Children's book author Roald Dahl has captivated readers of all ages because each story pushes our imagination, turns our moral compass, and reels in our empathy. In almost every Dahl book, there are tensions between child deprivation and abuse on the one hand and child protection and resilience on the other. Whether it's Aunts Spiker and Sponge in *James and the Giant Peach* or Harry Wormwood and Miss Trunchbull in *Matilda*, all of Dahl's adults heap blistering verbal abuse upon innocent children, calling them "disgusting little blisters," "nauseating little warts," "witless weeds," and "vipers." And yet, Dahl's children rise up against the army of tyrannical adults, enacting sweet revenge in magically delicious ways. The pull of these novels is that we see the vulnerable turn the tables on their powerful oppressors. However, real life doesn't always play out as in Dahl's fiction, and even with such victories, verbal abuse is likely to have left its signature on the developing body and brain.

Millions of children all over the globe, at home, in schools and communities, are subjected to litanies of vituperative attacks that denigrate, instill fear, discriminate, and demolish self-esteem. Verbal abuse can come in many forms—belittling, mocking, denying, threatening, abandoning, scapegoating, rejecting—all designed to undermine the individual's self-worth. When delivered by a parent or caretaker, verbal abuse violates the child's expectation of serve-and-return nurturing. In a number of studies, results show that in families where parents frequently heap verbal abuse on their children, say twenty-five or more times a month, there is a significantly higher incidence of depression, anxiety, and externalizing behaviors that can show up in schools as disruptive violence. When children are verbally abused by their parents, often with the result of feeling helpless, they are more likely to vandalize school property and bully other children in order to exert some control over their lives. Sometimes, verbal abuse can make them more vulnerable to being victimized by their peers, as self-confidence is destroyed. Children who experienced more verbal abuse by the age of thirteen years showed more conduct problems and depressive symptoms at age fourteen. Children who experienced parental verbal abuse were more likely to develop bipolar disorder, and at an earlier age than those without verbal abuse.[2]

Discrimination and oppression by means of verbal abuse have consequences for a developing child just like parental verbal abuse, including intergenerational effects.[3] African Americans exposed to the intergenerational effects of structural racism are more likely to end up with more debilitating cases of depression that are longer lasting, more treatment-resistant, than non-Hispanic White Americans. In one study, the more frequently pregnant Black and Latina teen mothers experienced racist comments as reported during community hospital and health center visits, the more their infants—at six and twelve months—suffered from heightened separation anxiety and strong negative emotions such as tantrums.[4]

To dig deeper into the possibility that verbal abuse leaves a unique signature on the brain, developmental biopsychiatrist Martin Teicher and his colleagues used diffusion tensor imaging—a technique that indicates the strength of connection between brain areas by measuring the movement of water molecules. Their idea was that if verbal abuse has a specific or selective effect on the brain, then the impact of verbal abuse—in contrast to physical and sexual abuse—would show up in areas involved in language processing, particularly the arcuate fasciculus, which connects two regions of the brain critical for the acquisition and implementation of language comprehension and expression.[5] Teicher's results confirmed this prediction: children who were verbally abused, but who had no other ACEs, had weaker connectivity in the arcuate fasciculus. But interestingly, verbal abuse also affected areas of the brain outside of those associated with language. The researchers observed that connectivity in the cingulum bundle, which joins the limbic lobe to the neocortex and is thus involved in emotion regulation, was also impacted, as was the fornix, which connects the subcortical septal area with the hippocampus and plays a key role in social connectedness and bonding. The psychological and behavioral results from the damage to these three neural bridges is a reduction in language processing, auditory regulation, and emotional control, with an increase in anxiety. The anxiety is a kind of overreaction to pain—a marker of the body keeping score of verbal abuse hits.

Follow-up studies by Teicher and others have confirmed and extended these findings, including evidence that parental verbal abuse is associated with a smaller hippocampus—a critical area for memory and learning, and susceptible to selective cell death as a result of chronic stress. As Teicher notes, these results "may have public health implications, raising the possibility that parental criticism, condemnation, and ridicule can exert deleterious effects on the developing brain."[6]

When children experience verbal abuse, or their parents do, there are recognizable traumatic reactions. When children are physically abused, the sticks and stones are real and the outcomes show this.

BUCKLING TO PHYSICAL ABUSE

Shuhada, now in her fifties, recalls her childhood. She was often locked up in what she described as a "torture chamber," beaten by her mother who not only enjoyed it but forced her to repeat "I am nothing."[7] She often contemplated suicide. She regularly skipped school and honed her skills as a thief, sometimes stealing from charity tins. Her mother placed her in a home for obstinate, defiant girls and she often escaped, but with the goal of playing her guitar in talent shows. At the age of eighteen she had her first record deal. At twenty years old, she had a child, and by age twenty-one she'd achieved pop icon status. Her career went up in flames at twenty-four after she ripped up a photo of the pope on *Saturday Night Live*.

Shuhada was born Sinéad O'Connor. Shuhada is the name she adopted following her conversion to Islam. Some of the headlines of her life described above come from her 2021 autobiography, *Rememberings*. It is a life filled with physical and psychological battering that disintegrated her sense of self. It is also a life that shows some resilience and the ability to reintegrate the self. As she remarked during an interview with Amanda Hess of the *New York Times*, "Child abuse is an identity crisis and fame is an identity crisis, so I went straight from one identity crisis into another."[8]

Reading about O'Connor's childhood, and then revisiting online images of her magnetic smile and penetrating eyes during her young adult years, is a reminder that what we see on the surface may not reveal underlying ACEs. A child with a history of physical abuse may be violent or shut down, but she may also not show any externalizing behaviors at all, hibernating the pain from her past. And children with no history of physical abuse at all may manifest harmful externalizing behaviors and internalizing thoughts. The question is whether physical abuse leaves a unique signature on the bodies and brains of children and, if so, how this signature is impacted by the other Adverse Ts.

Tommy grew up with a father who was drunk more often than sober. When his father was on a bender, he would often approach Tommy, spew roaring profanities, and then punch his son, who had curled up in a ball below his towering father. Tommy started to experience this violence when he was about six years old, but it continued until he was about fourteen, though the toxicity, tenure, and turbulence decreased at around eleven, when his parents divorced and he was living with his mom. For Tommy, the smell of alcohol, an angry face, and someone standing over him were the best predictors of potential violence—as predictive as tones are for rats in a learned helplessness experiment.

Studies by developmental psychologist Seth Pollak and others show that children who have been physically abused are more accurate, faster to react, require less information, and are slower to disengage from angry faces compared with other emotional expressions. This attentional focus is not because children who have been physically abused have superior attentional skills overall. They don't. Rather, anger is specifically captivating for a physically abused child like Tommy because it is a predictor of bad things to come. As discussed in chapter 1, when young members of a species develop in highly threatening environments, it pays to develop skills to avoid such threats at an earlier age. Enhanced anger recognition is an example of a hidden talent that is specifically linked to physical abuse.[9]

The hidden talent of anger recognition becomes, over time, a cost because the child is perpetually on alert, emotionally dysregulated, perceiving danger in anything and anyone who is a reminder of the original perpetrator of violence.[10] Physically abused children are hypervigilant, emotionally revved up, and more impulsive. But they are also less adept at recognizing the cause of others' emotional states, showing a deficit in social thinking, or what is often referred to as a *theory of mind*—what others believe, intend, and desire. Mothers who were physically abused show less ability to recognize fear and sadness in others, which undermines their attachment with their own children, as they are unable to recognize their children's signals for nurturing. This is a powerful example of the intergenerational legacy of abuse.

These behavioral changes are underpinned by alterations in a child's brain and genetic expression. For children with a history of physical abuse—compared with children without this history including individuals with other ACEs such as toxic deprivation—the amygdala and hippocampus are smaller in size. In addition, the connection between these regions and the frontal lobe involved in regulating emotions, thoughts, and actions is weaker, and the child's telomeres are shorter, a sign that the child is undergoing an accelerated aging process.[11]

The result of physical abuse is that children are hypervigilant, more distracted, less able to learn, more impulsive, and more readily triggered by the sights, sounds, and smells of situations that remind them of their perpetrator. Given all the evidence on the role of adversity in animals and human children, it is also likely that children who are physically abused earlier, with higher toxicity, tenure, and turbulence, will exhibit more pathologically damaging outcomes, whether we look at their brains, bodies, immune systems, or epigenetic markers of aging. When physical abuse arises later in life, has a shorter tenure, or is less toxic and more predictable, children may leave with less intense trauma and a greater capacity to recover.

OVERWHELMED BY SEXUAL ABUSE

Neil was only eight years old when Monsignor Lawrence St. Peter of the Holy Family School anally raped him for the first time.[12] For Neil, the scars of being raped were hidden for thirty-seven years. He didn't mention it to his parents or siblings, as they were all close to St. Peter. Later in life, he didn't tell his wife or children, nor any employer. He didn't even say a word when he attended St. Peter's funeral. Neil was alone, chained to his memory of being raped as an innocent, powerless child. These assaultive memories led him to question his sexuality, wrestle with emotional turmoil, lose his bond with his parents, and even struggle to keep his marriage to Kathryn, a trauma therapist.

Neil broke his silence in 2019 when the attorney general's office of Colorado released a report indicating that at least 166 children had been raped by forty-three Catholic priests since 1950. That report included St. Peter. Neil's father learned of the report and called his son, asking him if St. Peter had ever laid a hand on him. Neil couldn't lie to his father. He also couldn't let go of the fact that he blamed his parents for allowing St. Peter to harm him. They hadn't been able to protect him.

Across the globe, we have learned of priests raping children, athletic coaches and doctors sexually abusing boys and girls under their care, adults trafficking children as sex slaves, powerful men using young boys and girls as unpaid prostitutes, and family members sexually abusing their children such as Leah and Victoria, the little girls I introduced earlier. And we have learned that organizations in power to do something about these aberrations, including the Vatican, athletic committees, the UN, and national justice departments, have at best been incompetent and at worse morally complicit by means of omission—the failure to protect children from sexual abuse when it's possible.

In some parts of the world, sexual abuse of children is even woven into the fabric of the culture. In Afghanistan, a practice called *bacha bazi*, or boy play, has been an accepted custom since the nineteenth century. Originating in Central Asia during the Ottoman Empire, it involves older men who coerce young boys to engage in sex, including slavery and prostitution. Though many countries, including the United States, consider *bacha bazi* an abhorrent human rights violation, it is not an attitude shared by many Afghani men. Between 2010 and 2016, the US military was asked to investigate approximately six thousand cases of potential human rights violations in Afghanistan with the understanding that, by law, evidence of abuses, including *bacha bazi*, would mean withdrawal of military funds. Remarkably, the investigation failed to report a single human rights violation. Follow-up investigations by the *New York Times* indicated that US military members who reported on such sexual abuses were immediately silenced and often dismissed from duty. *Bacha bazi* was alive and well, with men in positions of great power abusing vulnerable boys.[13]

The systemic cover-up of childhood sexual abuse is an urgent problem in this country as well. In 2002, the *Boston Globe*'s Spotlight team revealed hundreds of American priests who, without oversight, had raped thousands of children. And the sexual crimes by Penn State football coach Jerry Sandusky and Larry Nassar, the US doctor for the gymnastics team, have made headlines. Stories like these have brought global awareness, but as investigative journalist Jason Berry noted in a *New York Times* documentary, these crimes against children are not about one sick person but about "a sick hierarchy that's been covering up" their toxic treatment of young boys and girls.[14] In addition, there is a global epidemic of sex trafficking, with an estimated one million children annually pedaled to willing buyers.

These cover-ups allow the scars of sexual abuse to deepen. Victims often experience shame and guilt, as well as traumatic sexualization, taboo, stigma, distortion, and self-blame. For many, these changes lead to revictimization—large-scale analyses indicating that victims of child sexual abuse are twice as likely as non-victims to be revictimized. But heightened risks for being revictimized is not restricted to sexual abuse, with other forms of maltreatment such as neglect, emotional and physical abuse revealing similar patterns. Does sexual abuse, therefore, have a unique signature when it comes to a child's traumatic reactions?

I mentioned earlier in this chapter that abuse, as a type of ACE, can result in several TRACEs, expressed behaviorally as the four Fs: fight, flight, freeze, feign. Feigning, a state of going limp also known as tonic immobility, is often the last-resort response when it seems like death is imminent. Analyses of more than three thousand victims of self-reported adverse events shows that tonic immobility is a far more common response to sexual abuse than any other ACE, including other subtypes of abuse, as well as other types of violent adversities. In an investigation into Nigerian women who had been raped, one woman described her experience as follows: "I just became like a log of wood, it felt like I was paralyzed all over my body. I could not even fight for my life, though I could have." This is one way in which sexual abuse leaves a distinctive signature, an insight that provides potential inroads to recovery, and therefore hope for survivors of such adversity.[15]

Another way in which sexual abuse may leave a unique imprint is through its impact on the pubescent adolescent, a period that is naturally associated with a tsunami of hormonal and anatomical changes, as well as a wave of neuroplasticity. Several studies have revealed that children who are sexually abused experience different phases of puberty at an earlier age, an average of eight months earlier for breasts and twelve months earlier for pubic hair. This premature development may sound trivial, but it's associated with greater risk-taking and psychopathology, outcomes not observed for verbal or physical abuse.[16]

Analyses of college-age women who were sexually abused as children also reveal sensitive periods of impact on brain development—a link between **type** and **timing**.[17] When sexual abuse occurred in children who were between three and five years old, it was most closely associated with a smaller hippocampus, an area that is critical for memory and learning. The hippocampus was also affected if the sexual abuse occurred when a child was between eleven and thirteen years old, which is a period associated with puberty in most girls, and thus accompanied by extensive brain plasticity. Sexual abuse that happened between the ages of nine and ten years old was associated with a smaller corpus callosum volume, resulting in lower or less efficient communication between the two hemispheres of the brain, effectively limiting information processing. Lastly, sexual abuse occurring between the ages of fourteen and sixteen years old was associated with the smallest frontal cortex volume, an area that is central to inhibitory control, decision-making, attention, and working memory. Seemingly unaffected by sexual abuse was the size of the amygdala, a somewhat surprising result given its role in emotional processing; the lack of a relationship may be due to its early and rapid maturation, and the fact that the sample of women reporting on sexual abuse did not report experiencing it much earlier than four years old; sexual abuse may well have occurred earlier, but recollecting memories before the age of four becomes difficult at best.

In a remarkable longitudinal study spanning five decades, developmental scientists Avshalom Caspi, Terrie Moffitt, Jay Belsky, and their colleagues showed that sexual abuse in early childhood has a disproportionate impact on physical and mental health relative to all other types of adversity.[18] Out of a sample of 937 individuals followed from birth to their mid-forties, childhood sexual abuse survivors were more likely than their peers, who suffered from other types of adversity or no adversity at all, to have higher levels of internalizing problems (e.g., anxiety, depression), externalizing problems (e.g., conduct disorders, aggression), suicide attempts, inflammatory problems, sexually transmitted diseases, oral health problems, financial difficulties, and problematic social relationships. As the authors note, the cost of childhood sexual abuse is to greatly reduce both individual and societal flourishing.

It makes sense, intuitively, that the toxicity of sexual abuse shapes its legacy, and research shows this as well. In a study of 1,411 female twins, psychiatrist Kenneth Kendler and his colleagues showed that girls who were sexually abused without genital contact (such as by nonconsensual kissing or hugging) had far lower psychopathology, or none at all, compared with girls whose genitals were violated.[19] Those who were raped had the most severe psychopathology, and the most common TRACEs, including PTSD, bulimia, and substance abuse. In some cases, only one twin was subjected to sexual abuse, and consistently, it was this twin who suffered from psychopathology.

The studies I have discussed so far in this section suggest how sexual abuse becomes biologically embedded, pointing to the importance of type, timing, and toxicity. The signature of sexual abuse overlaps to some extent with that of physical and emotional abuse—it also targets the hippocampus and connections to the frontal cortex, and it has similar effects on the HPA axis, resulting in lower levels of cortisol secretion or hypocortisolism.[20] But whereas physical abuse is associated with changes in amygdala volume, and emotional abuse is associated with damage to the arcuate fasciculus connecting key language areas, sexual abuse does not appear to impact these areas.

Sexual abuse does, however, leave a unique imprint in the area of the brain called the somatosensory cortex, which holds a kind of map of our anatomy. The more nerves a particular part of our body contains for fine motor control—think of our lips, tongue, hands, genitals—the more space it gets on the map. In this way, the somatosensory cortex provides a distorted representation of the human body.

Like some other areas of the brain, it also shows remarkable plasticity for change, and not only during childhood but also adulthood. Detailed experimental studies of rodents and primates, including human primates, show that both positive and negative experiences can further distort the already distorted map. For example, if two fingers of an adult owl monkey are tied together for several weeks, the distinctive representations in the somatosensory area for each finger transform into a single representation of two synchronized fingers. If a rat pup's genital area is stimulated by an experimental device above and beyond what is typical, the somatosensory area of the genital area will increase. If a human adult loses a limb due to an accident or military combat, the area representing the missing limb is remapped to other areas—a missing thumb is linked to the jaw, a missing index finger to a cheek. As neuroscientist Vilayanur Ramachandran discovered, patients who have lost a limb and suffer phantom pain can recover by taking advantage of the plasticity in the somatosensory cortex. The plasticity is both the essence of recovery and resilience, but it is also a vulnerability if adversity has a long tenure, as it often does in childhood sexual abuse.

Among the most common reports from women who were sexually abused as children is an inability to have orgasms, a reduction in sexual pleasure, and chronic genital or pelvic pain. Brain imaging research by neuroscientist Christine Heim and colleagues shows that the area of the somatosensory cortex dedicated to the clitoris is smaller in women who were sexually abused as children than in women with no history of sexual abuse.[21] This change in the somatosensory cortex was not observed in women who were physically or emotionally abused as children.

Interestingly, Heim and her colleagues also noted that the smaller size of the clitoral area was only observed in women who were sexually abused before puberty. Women who were sexually abused after puberty, when there is relatively less plasticity in the brain, showed no difference in the clitoral area of the somatosensory cortex.

A smaller clitoral area may well be adaptive for a child living with an abusive caretaker, as in Leah's case. A reduction in libido would reduce interest in interacting with men, including sexually abusive ones. However, this change in women's bodies and brains has long-term, deleterious health consequences. What remains unclear is whether a similar signature is penned into the bodies and brains of men who were sexually abused as boys, such as Neil, who we met at the opening of this chapter, and the Afghani boys subjected to *bacha bazi*. Sadly, the odds are high, especially given the known psychopathology that ensues for men, including PTSD, anxiety, and substance abuse. However, the science of changes in brain anatomy for sexually abused boys is not yet available.

SYNERGISTIC EFFECTS OF ACES

We have learned that the different subtypes of abuse—emotional, physical, and sexual—each pen their own signature on the child's developing body and brain, with timing, tenure, and toxicity contributing important details to these signatures. We have also learned that, in general, abuse often speeds up the development of certain abilities and triggers emotional dysregulation, whereas deprivation often retards the development of systems involved in learning and decision-making, which, in turn, undermines a child's motivation. Children exposed to one type of adversity are often exposed to other types, and this includes the three subtypes of abuse. Of interest is how multiple types of adversity modify allostatic load—the burden of chronic stress—and whether a particular type of adversity has a disproportionate impact.

Recall from chapter 1 that allostatic load is a maladaptive response, one that taps—over-taps—the same physiological systems that adaptively regulate stress when it is acute. A child under chronic adversity—multiple ACEs, long tenure—will bear a heavy allostatic load, a point that was realized by the developmental psychologist Gary Evans almost two decades ago.[22] Several studies, especially by cognitive neuroscientists Katie McLaughlin and Margaret Sheridan, show that the allostatic load burden from repeated abuse in childhood shows up in terms of smaller amygdala and hippocampus volume, lowered cortisol and heart rate, lowered capacity to learn by association—especially for threatening stimuli—emotional dysregulation, rumination, chronic inflammation, and biological markers of aging. These devastating effects led the Centers for Disease Control and Prevention in the United States to declare abuse a public health risk.[23]

Though multiple ACEs exert a compounding impact on a child's developing body and brain, it's possible that some ACEs outweigh others when combined in what is known as a *synergistic effect*. A synergistic effect of a pair of ACEs arises when their combined impact on health risks is greater than the sum or product of their individual contributions. In one study by psychiatrist Frank Putnam involving several thousand women who were screened for ACEs as well as risks for complex adult psychopathology, results showed that sexual abuse on its own had a disproportionately larger impact on the risk for psychopathology than poverty, but that the synergistic effect of poverty and sexual abuse increased the risk by approximately one-third. In a follow-up study by Putnam involving a much larger sample of individuals, covering a broader range of ages during which children were exposed to different ACEs—hitting the timing and type of adversity—results showed that sexual abuse had the most significant synergistic effect of any ACE type, with bigger effects in women than men. Though synergistic effects were observed for other ACE types, especially physical abuse, emotional abuse, neglect and domestic violence, the most potent synergistic ACE pairing involved sexual abuse and physical abuse.[24]

Understanding synergistic effects can provide a guide to treatment and to policy. Knowing, for example, that sexual abuse paired with other ACEs has a disproportionate impact on psychopathology may suggest that the best treatment for a child should focus on the traumatic signatures of sexual abuse. It also offers another argument in support of looking at ACE scores in a more nuanced way. A population exposed to sexual abuse may have a lower ACE score than another population, and yet have much more risk to develop serious traumatic responses over time.

6

War: The Chaotic Mind

n 1987, I spent time in Uganda carrying out research to understand the vocal communication of chimpanzees. One day, I was observing a chimpanzee community in the Kibale Forest of Uganda, when suddenly each animal stopped silently on the path, vigilant. Then, with Navy SEAL stealth, they snuck up on an adult male intruder from another community and ripped him to pieces. This isn't hyperbole. Several males pinned the intruder down, holding his legs and arms, as others bit into his face, blinding him, and then proceeded to rip out his testicles, followed by his intestines. By the time they were done, there was little left but a skull and a few bones with some bloody flesh.

Chimpanzees are intergroup-ist, wired with a discrimination bias that means they perceive anyone from a different community as the enemy, no qualifications. Witnessing this violence as a chimpanzee within the attacking community is both stressful and exhilarating— their cortisol stress physiology rushes in while the attack is ongoing, ending with a crescendo of dopamine and endorphins to accompany the rewards of victory. For members of the losing community, it is all stress and fear. For me, watching such an attack was stressful. It was also stressful living in Uganda at that time.

To get to the forest where I was studying chimpanzees, I had to drive from Kampala, the capital of Uganda. I had to make this trip several times, as I often needed supplies in the city and was also teaching a course at Makerere University, the oldest university in Africa. On my trip, I passed numerous roadblocks manned by children holding machine guns, standing next to a pile of human skulls. Passing through these roadblocks was terrifying and disheartening. The skulls were reminders of the brutal regime of Idi Amin, who had been in power from 1971 to 1979. The armed children were reminders that, in times of war, even adolescents may be recruited, willingly or not.

Bolondemu, a young man I met in the same forest where I was observing the chimpanzees, was one of the unwilling. He was a strapping young man who spoke in a quiet voice with tenderness and sadness in his eyes. As we became better acquainted, I asked him about his family and where they lived. He told me that they had all been killed. Timidly, he recounted the events of that tragic day and what followed.

Bolondemu and his younger brother, Mukisa, were abducted as children by the Lord's Resistance Army (LRA), a Ugandan rebel group. Within days of arriving in the camp, Bolondemu was given an ultimatum: kill your brother, Mukisa, or be killed. Together with five other newly abducted children, Bolondemu cut up Mukisa with a machete and then bathed in his blood, ceremonially celebrating his first kill. Mukisa was only the first of dozens of individuals that Bolondemu would kill during his tenure with the LRA. As he recounted to me, and as verified by interviews with many other child soldiers throughout the world,[1] killing became an addiction, a need that had to be satisfied at all costs. Bolondemu had developed an appetite for killing, an adaptive response to surviving in a turbulent world of madness and chaos.

The LRA—still in operation in 2023, though in small numbers—is neither the first nor the last rogue rebel group to brainwash children, stripping them of their family and the joy of childhood. Though the number of wars on the planet is at an all-time low, it is still the case today that millions of children grow up as killers or witnesses to killing, accompanied by toxic levels of oppression and discrimination that add fuel to the fire of out-group hatred. Though we lack rigorous, up-to-date counts of child soldiers, with some experts relying on a dated 1990s estimate of three hundred thousand, the number is likely higher and growing given both the economics of warfare and the accessibility and size of arms—ideally designed for little ones.[2] Some children willingly join these rebel groups, whereas others are forced to join. For many, their exposure to family and community adversity leaves little choice but to pursue a career of violence. For many, this is not a story that ends well.

The idea of a child soldier may seem unfathomable, a phenomenon that occurs in distant countries where poverty and corruption run deep. Perhaps you've watched documentaries such as *Crisis Childhood*, which reveals Filipino children sold by their families to the militant jihadist Abu Sayyaf so that they can be used as suicide bombers or organ donors. Or perhaps you've seen fictional films such as *Beasts of No Nation*, which tells the story of a young orphan boy in Africa who is abducted by a vicious warlord and trained as a child soldier to kill, and eventually develops an appetite for it, much like Bolondemu's story. Ultimately, these stories may seem foreign to many, and yet armed children are part of a much broader landscape once we stretch the panorama to include gangs, whether they are the Latin Kings in the United States; the Hellbanianz of the United Kingdom; the Camorra of Naples,

Italy; the AUE gangs of Russia; the Bōsōzoku gangs of Japan; or the Jebitte gangs of North Korea. In the United States alone, it is estimated that one million children ages five to seventeen years are involved in gangs—a number that far exceeds even the highest estimate of child soldiers on the global battlefield.[3]

Armed and violent children are not restricted to faraway lands. They are in our backyards. Rehabilitation depends on understanding how replacing childhood with violence transforms the body and brain. As you will learn in the next section, much of the detailed scientific work on this transformation comes from research in war-torn, low- to middle-income nations. Sadly, the translation to high-income nations, including the travesties in Ukraine and the mass shootings in US schools is all too easy.

ON DEFINING "CHILD" AND "SOLDIER"

The idea of a child soldier raises two definitional problems, which are directly relevant to what "counts" as adversity and how it is biologically embedded. Problem 1: What's a child? Problem 2: What's a soldier? Problem 1, which I partially addressed in chapter 1, is intimately linked to the timing dimension of the Adverse Ts—a child according to the definition of an ACE, is anyone less than eighteen years old. Problem 2 is tied, in part, to the type dimension and the adverse experiences of a soldier.

In the context of armed forces, whether governmentally sanctioned or not, the international community generally recognizes and supports definitions of "child" and "soldier" that were inspired by a UN report from Graça Machel, a minister of education in Mozambique: a child soldier is "any person below eighteen years of age who is or who has been recruited or used by an armed force or armed group in any capacity, including but not limited to children, boys and girls, used as fighters, cooks, porters, messengers, spies or for sexual purposes. It does not only refer to a child who is taking or has taken a direct part in hostilities."[4] On the face of it, this seems reasonable enough.

But when one stops to consider cross-cultural variation in the roles children play in society, and the differences within cultures in how age cutoffs are determined for different roles, new problems emerge. In some parts of the world, children are expected to work in their early teens, if not earlier. They may be directly involved in hunting and gathering, cultivating, shepherding, and much more. In many societies, such as in North Africa and the Middle East, there is no age of consent as long as you are married, whereas in others, such as South Korea, the age of consent is as high as twenty years old.

In the United States, you can buy a gun from a licensed seller when you are twenty-one years old or an unlicensed seller at eighteen years old, yet enter the military when you are seventeen years old. You can be sentenced to life in prison or the death penalty at age eighteen. Policies around these age cutoffs have changed over the past two decades due, in part, to the scientific evidence on brain maturation. If an individual doesn't yet have the brain power to control his impulses, then he may be subject to irrational, reflexive, involuntary, and shortsighted actions that may not be his responsibility. And so, an armed child under the age of eighteen who commits a crime is not punished in the same way that an adult is. But should a twenty-year-old really receive the worst punishment the law can assign? The answer is complicated by the fact that full brain maturation, especially of the frontal lobes, which are critical for self-control, short-term memory, attention, and planning, doesn't occur until we are twenty-three to twenty-five years old. From this perspective, a culture's determination of age cutoffs for engaging in armed attacks is irrelevant. The eighteen-year-old cutoff follows the science, to some extent, but it ignores the critical changes that occur within this eighteen-year span, as well as what occurs for the five to seven years that follow.

Again, how we define "child" may seem like a tedious philosophical dive into the semantic weeds, but it's not. The rights of children depend on a scientific understanding to determine sensitive or critical periods of vulnerability. And we know, based on the evidence discussed in the last few chapters, that adverse experiences that arise early in development have a more deleterious impact on body and brain than later occurring adversities.

TRANSFORMED INTO CHILD SOLDIERS

Recruitment of child soldiers in today's world doesn't have to be targeted toward local, poor, disenfranchised, and defenseless families whose lives are threatened. With global access to the internet and the persuasive promotion of revolutionary causes pinged to anyone with a smartphone, our children are vulnerable.

The Islamic State of Iraq and Syria, or ISIS, boldly used these digital technologies to recruit young children from Australia, England, Europe, North Africa, and the Middle East to fight for their cause. In 2016, the world watched as Isa Dare, a four-year-old boy in camouflage clothing and a black headscarf, appeared in a promotional video blowing up three hostages in orange jumpsuits. Isa Dare was taken by his Muslim mom from their home in London to Syria so that he could fight for ISIS. This video was followed by another involving five children, ages ten to thirteen, believed to be from England, Egypt, Tunisia, Turkey, and Uzbekistan. After a chorus of *Allahu Akbar*—Allah is greater—they executed five hostages. In 2018, investigative journalists at the London *Sunday Times* revealed a video of a two-year-old boy shooting a hostage.[5] Additional documents revealed that ISIS had created the cubs of the caliphate, modeled after Saddam Hussein's lion cubs. These cubs, as young as three years old, were immediately indoctrinated, forced to practice by decapitating stuffed animals or carrying around actual heads from recent decapitations.[6] The sensational videos produced by ISIS grabbed international attention, raising the specter of a new generation of radicalized jihadi children vulnerable to the sway of these violent forces. Radicalization is part of the tool kit of transformation.

Interviews with child soldiers[7] showcase the transformative aspect of their experiences. Listen to the voice of a child soldier in the Democratic Republic of the Congo, reflecting back on his own transformation, influenced in part by the fact that his friends and some family members had already joined the Mai-Mai rebel group:

> *I think I joined freely. . . . In those days I was frightened.*
> *Since our home was attacked almost every night by bandits*
> *and other rebel groups as well, what did I have to lose?*
>
> —KG, age 16, recruited at age 13,
> Democratic Republic of the Congo

The transformation that many child soldiers experience as they adopt the ways of their rebel group's norms may, paradoxically, both perpetuate a cycle of violence while better equipping them for recovery when they leave the group—a finding that extends to children who join gangs and have to fight for a living on the streets.[8] As we will learn in Part III, many communities that have worked relentlessly to rehabilitate child soldiers have had success. This is striking when one considers the timing, tenure, turbulence, and toxicity of their experiences. And yet, for many, adopting the norms of their violent groups is a survival strategy and a means to gaining control. As you'll recall from chapters 3 and 5, the only way to move beyond learned helplessness is to gain control. Moreover, those who are awarded status for committing unimaginable atrocities develop an appetite for continuing, which evolves into a vicious cycle of rewarded violence, which leads to an addiction to kill—a craving to seek the pleasure of harming others that can't be turned off despite the negative consequences. The psychology of control, reward, and social rank are ingredients for success once some child soldiers end their tenure with a rebel group and begin to remake their lives.

But before we can understand how some recover, we must understand the impact of the trauma they experience. Unlike our deep dive into the Romanian orphans in chapter 3, there is no single study of child soldiers that has fully explored the impact of such adversity over time. What you will learn about next, therefore, are pieces of evidence from around the world where children have entered the armed forces of rebel groups.

To understand the emotional development of a child soldier, psychologist Maria Umiltà and her colleagues presented portraits and movies of individuals expressing different emotions—sadness, anger, fear, happiness—to child soldiers and child civilians who lived through the 1991–2002 civil war in Sierra Leone.[9] All individuals were in their early twenties and they had been exposed to the war as children for a period of about ten years. They were tested a few years after the war ended. Overall, civilians passively exposed to war were more accurate in recognizing facial expressions of emotion than child soldiers, especially when looking at the movies, where changes in emotion occur more rapidly and ephemerally. But the most striking difference emerged for one of the four emotions: sadness. Child soldiers were significantly worse than civilians in recognizing sadness, were more likely to misattribute the label of sadness to other emotions and, overall, showed a stronger tendency to use negative emotion labels—sadness and anger—when making mistakes. The most likely explanation for this pattern is that surviving as a child soldier depends on having a stiff upper lip, and being able to suppress or at least hide any feelings of sorrow and sadness. Keeping such emotions at bay, especially for children, who under normal circumstances have difficulty regulating their emotions, adds additional stress. This stress shows up in terms of a number of other internalizing problems.

Medical anthropologist and psychiatrist Brandon Kohrt and his colleagues have worked with young adult Nepalese who were children during the 1996–2006 civil war—a conflict between the Communist Party of Nepal and the Nepal government that involved the massacre of more than seventeen thousand people, including many civilians.[10] To determine whether being a child soldier has a specific impact on development, Kohrt and his colleagues compared the pathology of children who were conscripted as soldiers during this period with those who were not—civilian children—but who were nonetheless exposed to the adversities of war—long tenure, timed to several sensitive and critical periods, highly turbulent and toxic. ACEs for all of these children included fires and natural disasters, physical abuse, bombing, torture, abduction, witnessing violent death, domestic violence, and loss of a caretaker due to murder.

Nepalese child soldiers were more likely to experience bombings, torture, and abduction, and they more often witnessed violent death than civilian children. Associated with this pattern of ACEs were differences in their traumatic reactions. Child soldiers showed more significant levels of depression and PTSD, as well as greater deficits in daily functioning than civilian children. Even a comparison of child soldiers and civilians with the same number of ACEs revealed differences in their traumatic reactions, with higher levels of depression and PTSD in child soldiers, especially female child soldiers. Importantly, no single type of ACE explained the mental health challenges of child soldiers, nor did the age at which they started or the duration of time they spent as soldiers. Rather, the number of ACEs or allostatic load explained the severity of trauma among child soldiers, with some impact of toxicity—those exposed to beatings, bombings, and torture had the worst PTSD and depression.

The experience of being a child soldier matters as a type of ACE, above and beyond the traumatic experiences of war. And the detrimental changes that such children experience in their emotional well-being is accompanied by profound shifts that are seen at the level of gene expression, molecular changes that impact the body's immune system. Kohrt and his colleagues followed up their psychological assessment of the Nepalese child soldiers and civilians with blood samples that allowed them to look at a host of genes involved in regulating inflammation and viral infection. What they found is that the immune system of a child soldier is more chronically stressed than a civilian child who, nonetheless, also lives with chronic stress.

TRANSFORMED INTO CHILD GANGSTERS

The number of child soldiers pales in comparison to the number of children in gangs—often highly structured, ideologically radical groups of adolescents and adults, male and female, who inhabit the streets of cities throughout the world. Though abduction isn't part of the recruitment repertoire, children often end up in gangs in the same way that children end up as soldiers: they are either forced into it by the realization that continued poverty and threat of violence from gangs are unattractive dead ends or, because they feel lonely or marginalized, they join gangs as a means of securing social relationships, status, and an identity badge. And like the formation of armed forces with child soldiers, gangs with children are most likely to form in areas of conflict, poverty, and ethnic marginalization. Though there has been far less research on how gang-related violence is biologically embedded in children, what is known parallels the patterns for child soldiers.[11]

In one study, adolescent gang members, between twelve and sixteen years old, were more likely to have been violently attacked than non–gang members, either from physical abuse by parents or bullying from peers. In turn, adolescent gang members who have been violently victimized are more likely to have internalized mental health problems such as anxiety and depression, as well as externalized problems such as aggression, oppositional defiance, and conduct disorder. Their mental health problems are, in turn, associated with angry rumination, low empathy, guilt, and remorse—an emotional recipe for enabling further violence.[12]

Part of the indoctrination into a gang is desensitizing or normalizing the use of violence. Often this involves early exposure to using weapons, with the threat of being beaten or shunned if a child refuses. When violence is normalized in this way, it creates a sense of moral disengagement. For example, compared with children who are never in gangs, gang members are more likely to assign the responsibility of the harm they have done to others. And they often blame their victims. Gang members are also more likely to sanitize their violent actions by dehumanizing their victims—a transformation that turns others into dispensable objects or eradicable vermin and parasites.[13] Gangs didn't invent these strategies. They are ancient ingredients in an ancient recipe for destroying the competition without moral injury, including genocidal purification by Nazis of Jews, Gypsies, and people with disabilities; Hutu attacks on Tutsis, Serbian attacks on Muslims and Croatians; and, as I write, Russian attacks on Ukrainians.[14]

Recall that in our discussion of child soldiers, I raised the idea that some may develop an appetite for killing others, and that the rewarding nature and status of such proactive violence may, paradoxically, buffer their traumatic reactions and make them more likely to have success later in life. In contrast, reactive violence—a response to threat—is often associated with emotional dysregulation and anger and commonly leads to PTSD or DTD. Like some child soldiers, not all gang members will kill someone else, but they may well be involved in nonlethal violence. Some of this violence will be reactive and some will be proactive. As psychologists Anselm Crombach and Thomas Elbert note: "An insecure and violent environment not only provokes reactive aggression but also seems to foster a trait for appetitive aggression. Becoming a perpetrator instead of a victim, winning fights and thereby regaining a feeling of control in insecure and dangerous living conditions such as in the streets, could be the prerequisite for the activation of this trait. Feelings of power, control, and effectiveness in violent situations lead to the enjoyment of violence and a craving for more."[15]

Insights into the nature of appetitive violence comes from a study by Crombach and Elbert of street children in Burundi. These children, all boys ages eleven to twenty-four years old, were living in a highly turbulent environment, with significant uncertainty and insecurity around food and violence, including being beaten in school, at home, and on the streets. Though they were not strictly part of a gang, these children were exposed to and perpetrated violence, and some used guns. Though all children of all ages had a significant number of ACEs, those who engaged in appetitive violence had significantly less severe PTSD symptoms than those who engaged in reactive violence. This prophylactic effect was, however, dose-dependent in much the same way that the negative consequences of ACEs depend on numbers: for children with one to eight appetitive violent attacks, those with more attacks had less severe PTSD symptoms. As we will discuss in greater detail in Part III, the counterintuitive protection that appetitive violence provides children is not a public service announcement to promote such brutality. Rather, it provides further evidence of why it is important to understand individual differences in how the Adverse Ts shape the ways in which adversity gets under the skin.

Given the parallels between child soldiers and child gangsters, it is surprising that gang involvement has barely touched policy. Article 38 of the UN Convention on the Rights of the Child dictates that children—under the age of fifteen—should be protected from being recruited into armed forces, whereas Article 39 dictates that states have a responsibility to rehabilitate children who were victimized by being recruited into armed forces or otherwise exploited. As psychologist James Garbarino argues, these articles must be expanded from a focus on child soldiers to any child involved in violent groups, which would include gangs.[16] As I argued earlier in this chapter, to fully protect a child's rights, the age cutoff for the definition of a "child" should minimally be eighteen years, and if we want to look at it through the lens of brain maturation, and especially the circuitry that contributes to greater responsibility and control over one's actions, it should be twenty-three to twenty-five years.

When children perpetrate violence during childhood, whether as a member of a rogue terrorist organization or a street gang, it leaves a different imprint on their brain and body than when they are exposed to violence. Exposure to violence can arise within a family when children see verbal and physical aggression between parents, but it can also arise during war and community violence. Though children may not be directly involved in such battles, they often feel the impact on their own development, as well as the costs it imposes on their family. We will look at this phenomenon in the next section.

LIVING THROUGH BATTLE

In one sense, it was a special Friday night because it was Eid al-Fitr, the end of Ramadan—a celebration of the month when the Muslim holy book, the Qu'ran, was first revealed to the Prophet Muhammad. In another sense, it was a special night for the al-Hadidi children, Suhayb, Yahya, Abderrahman, and Osama, because they were going to celebrate Eid with their cousins in the Shati refugee camp, just outside of Gaza City. They even convinced their father to spend the night. The next day, the celebration was promptly ended by a bomb, killing all of the al-Hadidi family except Omar, the five-month-old baby who was pulled out of the rubble, lying next to his dead mother.[17] For Omar, loss arrived early in life and the road ahead would present many additional adversities, including displacement to different homes; the lack of an attentive mother; physical, emotional, cognitive, and social deprivation; and exposure to war, poverty, oppression, and discrimination. Omar was on a path of chronic stress, with a heavy burden and a horrifically high allostatic load.

In 2019, 1.6 billion children were living in war zones, with the densest concentration in Africa and the Middle East.[18] Though war has always resulted in casualties—lethal, economic, health, social—the nature of war has changed in ways that more directly impact children. In many areas of conflict, armed groups take over or destroy schools and hospitals, with direct costs to education and healthcare. Not only are children less likely to gain an education and the healthcare they need, but when schools are taken out as safe havens, children are more likely to be exploited. In the mid-1990s, thanks to the internet and the broader reach of humanitarian efforts such as Doctors Without Borders, there was a new global awareness of children living in conflict zones. Now the scientific evidence for the imprint of war on children's bodies and brains has begun to emerge.

Baby Omar, like Nadine, who we met in chapter 6, knows little else but war. For children growing up in Gaza, sirens, explosions, rubble, death, abuse, screaming, uncertainty, and loss are all too familiar. For children born into and growing up with war, the Adverse Ts are many typed, timed early, and associated with several sensitive and critical periods, highly toxic and turbulent, long in tenure. Though Palestinian children like Omar and Nadine are far more often exposed to the casualties of war than are their opponents, the Israelis, our understanding of how such adversities get under the skin comes from far-reaching studies of Israeli children by developmental neurobiologist Ruth Feldman.[19] These studies parallel, in many ways, those on Romanian orphans discussed in chapter 4 in that the same children were followed for many years, using different assessment tools to understand what is affected, when, and how badly.

Instead of starting this story with a child's developmental path forward after war, which we will get to, I want to reach further back and begin with the mother's journey under chronic stress, from conception to delivery and beyond. You will recall from chapter 1 that Dutch mothers who conceived during the winter famine of World War II were more likely to give birth to babies who became mothers with physical and mental health problems than mothers who conceived outside of this period of famine. This suggests an intergenerational impact of stress.[20] Feldman and her team built on these results by exploring how an Israeli mother's empathy is impacted by the chronic stressors of war. They assessed the pathology and empathy of mothers and their children, as well as the synchrony of their attachment styles, contrasting those exposed to war with those who were not. All of the mothers showed activation in the sensorimotor area of the brain in response to images of people experiencing pain to different parts of the body; recall from chapter 5 that this is the brain region that provides a map of our body. All mothers also showed activation in the visceromotor cortex, an area that is involved in cognitive control over the body's internal environment and gives rise to the uniquely human features of our empathy. Critically, war-exposed mothers showed significantly lower activation in the visceromotor cortex, lower empathy, and more asynchronous attachment styles. Mothers who have lived through war can't put themselves in their child's shoes, can't see when they are in pain and thus fail to respond with comfort and nurturing if their child is crying, screaming, or shutting down. Though exposure to war in and of itself did not negatively impact the prosocial skills of children—that is, their kindness, sympathy, and empathy—a disruption in synchrony did. Children with more asynchronous serve-and-return relationships had weaker prosocial skills.

Feldman and her team assessed emotion recognition and executive functioning in war-exposed Israeli children at average ages of three, seven, and nine years old and compared them to children of the same age without war exposure. War-exposed children made more errors in recognizing emotional expressions of happiness, sadness, and anger, and showed weaker ability to inhibit actions—an essential element of executive functioning. Children with compromised executive functioning were more likely to have compromised parental care, suggesting that inadequate attachment may be related to delays in the development of inhibitory control. But there was one more intriguing finding: war-exposed children with stronger parasympathetic systems were less likely to show deficits in executive functioning than war-exposed children with weaker parasympathetic systems. As I explained in chapters 1 and 2, the vagus nerve plays a critical role in the parasympathetic system and, in particular, in regulating and maintaining the body at rest—keeping it relaxed and exerting low energy. Children who innately have calmer dispositions are less impacted by the adversity of war. This is the voice of biology's resilience.

Some children exposed to war react to the extreme violence and loss by dissociating, a form of psychological distancing or separation that hibernates memories and anesthetizes pain. Feldman's research shows that war-exposed children who avoid their adverse experiences have higher levels of the stress hormone cortisol and more compromised abilities to recognize facial expressions of emotion than either war-exposed children who acknowledge the pain of such adversity or children who haven't been exposed to war. These avoidant children are more likely to show the traumatic symptoms of PTSD, or perhaps more accurately developmental trauma disorder (DTD), the related but distinct form of childhood psychopathology that manifests as dysregulation, self-hate, weak attachment to caregivers, distrust of others, and dissociation from reality. This mixture of traumatic reactions complicates treatment, as many different and often supportive systems are broken; we will pick up this conversation again in Part III.

What we have learned thus far is that children who have been exposed to war, especially those who have weak parasympathetic systems, high cortisol levels, and who do not experience consistent comfort and care from their mother—as well as those who show avoidance in facing their trauma—have the most significant deficits in executive functioning and emotional development. These deficits in executive functioning parallel other studies of chronic stress in early childhood and adolescence.

We must, however, avoid drawing a causal connection between the experience of war and a child's response to it, as some children are more vulnerable to adversity and others have the capacity to be more resilient. Analysis of the developing brains of children exposed to war offers some clues about why some children have a layer of protective armor.

Feldman used brain imaging to assess patterns of activation in the default mode network (DMN), an arrangement of different brain regions that are active when we are at rest, daydreaming, walking down memory lane, thinking about our experiences, choices, and emotions. This network's activity is unique to each individual—it has a "brain print." Healthy individuals have brain prints characterized by brain regions that work together, like synchronized swimmers. Unhealthy individuals have brain prints with brain regions that work more on their own, like freestyle swimmers doing their own thing. Children and adolescents with synchronous brain prints have more accurate and richly textured memories of the past and are better able to cope with their experiences of war. Children and adolescents with asynchronous brain prints have avoidant, dissociative responses to their experiences with war and are more likely to have anxiety disorders in adulthood. Essentially, synchrony of the brain regions within the DMN provide protection against the adversity of war, whereas asynchrony enhances vulnerability.

We have grown accustomed to hearing about the devastating impact of war on children living in the Middle East, on the African continent, in many parts of South and Central America, and in Asia, while savoring the peace enjoyed by children in Europe, Australia, and North America. And yet, the eruption of war between Russia and Ukraine in 2022 is a sad reminder that even peace can rapidly turn to war. As reported by the *New York Times* and UNICEF, there are 5.7 million children in Ukraine, many suffering from traumatic reactions to war, a third forced to leave their homes, more than half having lost their schools, and many orphaned or separated from their parents—devastation not seen since World War II.[21] These statistics show that war deals children a handful of ACEs and, for many, a hand of TRACEs.

We have reached the end of an arduous journey through the lethal landscape of ACEs. Though I have often discussed the scientific evidence in a detached, dispassionate voice, I have kept the voices of children—my daughter Sofia, my Ugandan friend Bolondemu, my students Sean, Ellie, Leah, Aliya, Victoria, Ethan, Kevin, and Tommy—who have suffered from adversity alive in my heart and mind. Their voices, and for many their ability to survive and surmount, is a testament to their strength and the strength of their enveloping communities. Some are more resilient; some carry more risk. By understanding how such individual differences arise, we can enable the vulnerable to join their resilient brothers and sisters.

part three

HOPE: ROADS TO RESILIENCE AND RECOVERY

*The world breaks everyone and afterward
many are strong at the broken places.*
—ERNEST HEMINGWAY[1]

Immunity: The Ingredients of Change

ike all clever viruses, COVID-19 caught our species off guard. From our individual immune systems to our global medical, political, and economic systems, we just were not ready. These failures allowed COVID-19 to kill millions of people, decimating economies, destroying families, orphaning children, crushing mental health, and shaking up our trust in health policy. But only our immune system responded with lightning speed to its initial poor showing, as it was engineered to do.[1]

Our immune system has two distinct parts, one innate and one acquired. The innate system has been fine-tuned through evolution, dating back five hundred million years ago to the jawed fish, and it is designed to protect us against foreign invaders that can harm our bodies. The acquired system develops to fend off threats as we experience the world, starting in utero and continuing until we die. Our body was not ready for the first variant of COVID-19, but thanks to its memory, anchored in B cells, it was ready for future variants. B cells not only remember bacteria and viruses, but they rapidly mount a series of responses. Some are designed to attack the detailed architecture of the invader, and others counter future variants. For every human living on the planet today, our evolutionarily ancient immune system provides hope that we can surmount the rapidly evolving coronavirus. Though our grudge-holding B cells may not provide us with complete protection against future variants of COVID-19, they may give scientists time to further perfect the mRNA vaccines that add a layer of protection.

Like our immune system, our systems of resilience also include an innate and acquired component. To understand what causes variation in our responses to adversity, let's first look at the variation itself, returning to a study by Rasmus Birn and colleagues that I described in chapter 2. This study explored the relationship between early life adversity and subsequent engagement in risky behaviors. The results showed that children with greater early life stressors tended to exhibit higher levels of risk-taking behaviors. But there was considerable variation swarming around this correlation, with one cluster showing no risky behavior at all despite the fact that some of the individuals had high levels of childhood adversity. This pattern of variation is observed in other research, including a large-scale genome-wide association study of 1.5 million individuals that suggests variation in risk-taking is mediated by differences in neurochemistry and activation in the reward areas of the brain.[2]

In a study by a team of developmental scientists including Seth Pollak, whose work on adversity and facial emotion recognition I discussed in chapter 4, results showed that children exposed to higher levels of adversity had weaker connectivity in brain areas associated with reward processing.[3] This reduced connectivity was, in turn, associated with a reduced capacity to use negative feedback in learning. Deficits in reward learning—a common signature of deprivation that was clearly documented in the Romanian orphanage study—can

undermine educational success. But like Birn's findings on risky behaviors, there was also significant variation around the relationship
between connectivity, adversity, and reward learning. One group of
individuals had weak connectivity within the reward circuitry, but
some had low toxic adversity, whereas others had high toxic adversity.
A second group of individuals had strong connectivity within the reward circuitry, but some had low toxic adversity and others had high
toxic adversity. In other words, neither the signature of connectivity
within the reward area nor the toxicity of adversity are sufficient to
predict who will have traumatic outcomes and who will have resilient
ones. We must take a deeper dive into the nature of vulnerability and
resilience.

HOW BIOLOGY SCULPTS FUTURE OPPORTUNITIES

Caenorhabditis elegans is a one-millimeter-long transparent nematode
worm whose identity is partially defined by being male or hermaphrodite; there are no pure females. Pure males have to reproduce with a
hermaphrodite. Hermaphrodites can either reproduce with a pure
male or self-fertilize. That's it for the relationship between sex and
identity. Experiences with the environment layer in another component of this worm's makeup. Since *Caenorhabditis elegans* is a slithering
land dweller without bones, a heart, or a circulation system, the temperature of the soil has an adverse impact—excessive heat is a major
stressor to adaptive functioning. But it could also be a major stressor to
future generations who were not directly exposed to the heat. Experiments show that if a mother worm experiences acute heat while she is
carrying fertilized eggs, these offspring will start their lives with their
mother's memory of stress from the heat, but the grand-offspring will

not. If a mother worm is exposed to chronic heat, however, both her offspring and grand-offspring maintain this memory of stress. These are epigenetic changes that are not permanent alterations of the DNA, but rather, they are alternations of genetic expression.[4]

Let me be clear: We are not worms. But there are several reasons why this little creature provides an interesting case study in thinking about the nature of resilience. For starters, C. elegans has approximately the same number of genes as we do, and we share similar molecular machinery that control our developmental programs. And we now know that our identity, including our strengths and weaknesses, are also shaped by our histories, including the genetic and environmental lotteries that generate current and future opportunities.

But for humans, it is not just environmental stressors that shape how the generations after us thrive. Where we depart from our distant relatives is that we can reflect upon our identity, our sense of self, our propensities, desires, and goals. Our sense of self can be fragmented into pieces by exposure to chronic adversity, including adversity brought on by how our parents treat us.

Research shows that mothers who were maltreated as children are more likely to be depressed as mothers. As a result, they are more likely to maltreat their own children, and are more likely to show poor serve-and-return interactions with their children. The children are more emotionally dysregulated, have more compromised executive functioning, weaker social attachments, and are more likely to be perpetrators of violence.[5] The paternal side plays a role as well. Grandsons of grandfathers who smoked had higher body mass index (BMI), and grandsons with grandfathers who were undernourished had higher mortality risk, suggestive of a compromised immune system.[6] A child enters the world with predispositions that have been determined by their parents.

When we ask about the development of a child's identity or attemp to answer Bruce Perry and Oprah Winfrey's question—"What happened to you?"—we must not only look at a child's direct experience with adversity, but her indirect experience as relayed by her parents' generation, and her parents' parents' generation. We must understand how each child's biology, passed down from previous generations, interacts with experience to shape the possible identities that they could acquire.[7]

I met thirteen-year-old Badrick as he was being restrained by four teachers, all substantial in size. He was in a rage. Every muscle in his body was tense, his eyes bloodshot, spit and venomous language pouring out of his mouth:

"You fucking cocksuckers. I'm going to kill you when I get out of here. I have knives at home. You White pieces of shit. Don't ever turn your back on me or I'll slit your throats. And I'll find your houses and kill your family. Wait until I get out of here."

This was neither the first or last of Badrick's many restraints and vituperative responses within the school, one focused on children with emotional disabilities.

Badrick grew up on the streets of Kingston, Jamaica, poor. His parents were rarely around to supervise him, as both worked. When they were around, it was often unpleasant, with his mom yelling and screaming in response to her husband's beatings. Badrick was frequently absent from school in Kingston. He was street savvy, knew how to fight, and had racked up an impressive record—just like his father. His father's response to any problem he had at school was to beat him. Badrick didn't trust anyone and was quick to pull the trigger at the slightest provocation. He was impulsive. So was his father. He was part of an intergenerational relay team, grabbing the baton of violent norms and running with it.

The sciences of genetics and behavior provide some insights into how such inheritance might work, setting the stage for understanding the constraints and opportunities for children like Badrick to recover.

Studies of mice suggest that the monoamine oxidase A (MAOA) gene may play a role in our violent tendencies. MAOA is responsible for creating an enzyme that breaks down neurotransmitters that play a role in mood-motivation-reward, fight-flight reactions, and impulse control–emotion regulation. These are states of the body and brain that, we have learned, can be impacted by adversity. Mice that lack the MAOA enzyme, either due to a natural mutation or an experimental knockout, are more aggressive toward intruders than mice with the enzyme.[8] Because the MAOA gene is on the X chromosome, and since males have one X and one Y chromosome, a mutation is more likely to be associated with problems for males than females, who have two Xs and can compensate. This kind of experimental evidence suggests that the MAOA enzyme, by means of its regulation of neurotransmitters, plays a role in the expression of aggression—individual mice with the enzyme are less aggressive than those without it. Just because it plays a role doesn't mean that MAOA is the only player, the key player, or the engine of aggression. Rather, it points to one biological ingredient that may shape the propensity for aggression.

Like mice, we also have the MAOA gene, and it also plays a role in regulating the same enzyme that breaks down essential neurotrans-mitters. In 1993, a report was released about a large Dutch family who all lacked the MAOA enzyme.[9] The men in the family were all extremely violent, impulsive, and showed signs of intellectual impairment. This wasn't ordinary violence. One of the men used a pitchfork to attack a caretaker in an institution for the mentally ill and also raped his sister; one tried to use his car to run over his boss; one used a knife to force his sisters to take off all of their clothes. At least part of their propensity for violence, as well as poor self-regulation, appeared to be associated with an MAOA mutation—a finding that parallels the results reported for mice.

An important addendum to the studies of MAOA mutations in mice and humans is research exploring the interaction between two variants of MAOA—MAOA-L and MAOA-H—and different environmental experiences. The MAOA-L variant is associated with lower levels of the neurotransmitters serotonin and norepinephrine in development than MAOA-H, as well as more impulsive violence. Consistent with this pattern is an association between more violent cultures and a higher frequency of the MAOA-L variant, a relationship first observed among the fierce Maori of New Zealand.[10]

These studies captivated molecular biologists, neuroscientists, psychologists, anthropologists, and journalists. The MAOA gene became a hot research topic and journalists concluded that scientists had discovered the *warrior gene* and that some of us are *born to rage*.[11] Lawyers also jumped on the idea of using genetic evidence to defend their clients and some still use this strategy twenty-five years later, much like the insanity defense. The reasoning is that a person who can't understand or control their actions isn't responsible for them—they are psychotic or delusional, and thus, not culpable. A person with a faulty MAOA gene is a zombie, essentially incapable of overcoming his or her wiring. Though none of the MAOA cases returned a verdict of "not guilty," in several instances the conviction was reduced.[12] If we accept this argument, it could be the basis to eliminate the death penalty—at least in the United States and fifty-four other countries where it still is an option.

But we need to be careful here since association is not the same as causation. We know, for example, that the MAOA gene also plays a role in our capacity for self-control.[13] It may be, therefore, that those with the MAOA-L variant are more impulsive, and when triggered by a threatening situation, are less able to control their aggressive tendencies than those with the MAOA-H variant. Badrick and his father may well have had the MAOA-L variant or the MAOA mutation, but they were also impulsive, having grown up in environments where violence was more normative.

The upshot of this research is to emphasize the importance of biology in understanding violence, recognizing that genes, not a gene, play a role in sculpting our identities, guided by our environmental experiences. We can use this information to understand risk, resilience, and the likelihood for recovery.

THE DANCE OF NATURE AND NURTURE

There are three different ways in which genes and environments interact: *genetically altering, environmentally triggering,* and *environmentally regulating.*[14] Under *genetically altering* conditions, a person has a cognitive, emotional, or behavioral genetic disposition that, in turn, leads them to create, modify, or become drawn to a particular environment. For example, people with genes that bias them toward heightened impulsivity might seek out more risky situations that give them immediate gratification. Or, as discussed in chapter 1, a child with the heritable callous-unemotional trait—such as Sean—may be more likely to have outbursts or morally inappropriate social interactions because he does not have the emotional feedback to preempt such behavior.[15]

Under *environmentally triggering* conditions, the significance of a particular genetic variant is only seen in certain environments. Thus, the environment brings about or triggers the expression of the gene. For example, a variant of the DRD4 gene, involved in the regulation of the neurotransmitter dopamine, is associated with greater than average fat intake in children living in low SES environments, but not in high SES environments.[16] Living in a worse-off environment triggers the expression of this particular genetic variant, resulting in health problems for the developing child.

Under the *environmentally regulating* condition, certain experiences control both when and how genes are expressed—essentially, an epigenetic effect. As we've discussed before, DNA methylation is an example of such an effect, and several studies show that these can have a deleterious impact on the autonomic nervous system, resulting in health risks.

All three of these gene-environment interactions impact where a child lands on the vulnerable-resilient landscape and, as we will soon learn, guide how we develop approaches to recovery.[17]

To address the possible interaction between genes and the developmental experience, behavioral geneticists Avshalom Caspi and Terrie Moffitt looked at the relationships between the variants of MAOA, parental maltreatment, and antisocial, aggressive behavior in five hundred sixteen-year-old boys.[18] One cluster of boys had little to no antisocial behavior, but they had a mix of MAOA-L and MAOA-H variants, and they were all living with parents who treated them well. This shows that having a particular MAOA variant isn't necessarily associated with or predictive of antisocial behavior, nor is it associated with parental maltreatment. Another cluster of boys had extremely high antisocial behavior, the MAOA-L variant, and severely abusive parents. Directly below them on the data plot were boys with much lower antisocial behavior, the MAOA-H variant, and parents who severely mistreated them. These two clusters suggest that if you are born into an environment with severely abusive parents, and by luck of the draw you get the MAOA-L variant, you are much more likely to engage in antisocial behavior than if your luck hands you the MAOA-H variant.

Caspi and Moffitt's results raise two tentative conclusions about the relationship between the genetic and environmental lotteries. One: If, by chance, a child wins the supportive-parent ticket and either the MAOA-L or MAOA-H ticket, he will have good odds of developing socially appropriate behaviors as a teenager. Here, the interaction between genetic and environmental lotteries doesn't result in detectable changes in outcomes. Two: If, by chance, a child has an abusive parent, the odds are good that he will develop more significant antisocial behaviors as a teenager if he has the MAOA-L variant than the MAOA-H variant. A child with the MAOA-L gene and abusive parents is more at risk of developing pathological behaviors, whereas a child with MAOA-H is more resilient. The environment triggers the impact of MAOA on a child's identity. This adds more nuance to the example of the violent Dutch family I mentioned earlier in this chapter. We know the men had an MAOA mutation, but don't know what kind of environment these men were raised in as boys and how that may have triggered gene expression.

Caspi and Moffitt's study was followed up by several other studies exploring the relationship between MAOA variants, gender of the child, **type** and **timing** of childhood adversity, and antisocial behavioral outcomes or pathology.[19] Consistently, males with the MAOA-L variant were more significantly impacted by childhood adversity than females with MAOA-L. Males with the MAOA-L variant were more significantly impacted by violent adversity (e.g., physical or sexual abuse, assault, severe physical punishment) than by other types of adversity (e.g., low SES, peer interactions, smoking by mother during pregnancy), irrespective of whether the adversity occurred during early childhood or adolescence. Here, the type dimension matters, but timing does not. In addition, MAOA-L boys who were mistreated exhibited more intense antisocial behaviors than mistreated MAOA-H boys. This suggests that MAOA-L boys are more likely to start off on the vulnerable side of the landscape, whereas MAOA-H boys are more likely to start off on the resilient side. Again, MAOA is one among a myriad of biological ingredients associated with the development of aggressive tendencies, but this points to the fact that some children may be predisposed to negative outcomes. And one reason they may be more predisposed to negative outcomes is because they can't control their impulses—they have poor self-control.

SELF-CONTROL AND
THE AFTERSHOCKS OF ACES

There's a children's game called King of the Hill that starts with a race. The first one to the top of the hill becomes the self-anointed king. To displace the king, you literally knock them off. Depending on the rules, you can knock them off with a touch, but often it involves more aggressive shoves and takedowns. I played this game growing up, but most schools have now banned it, as emotions can run hot and many children don't have the ability to tamp down those impulses. For young children, the brain's emotional circuitry is king and it takes years—up to twenty-three to twenty-five years from birth—for the inhibitory circuitry of the frontal lobes to take over the rulership. The emotional circuitry is always vying for control of decision-making, but maturity brings greater self-control—a skill that is critical to individual and societal welfare. In the same way that some are born to be kings, both through royal and biological inheritance, so, too, are some born with greater inhibitory talents, starting in their biology and cultivated by their environment.

Profound insights into how this developmental process works come from a longitudinal study spanning several decades by Moffitt and Caspi.[20] Moffitt and Caspi joined Phil Silva, a primary schoolteacher in Dunedin, New Zealand, who first started studying a population of approximately one thousand children in the 1970s. These children were followed for forty years, with the first battery of physical and mental health assessments carried out when the children hit their third birthday. For each individual, additional information was collected on their family, including SES, education, and health. Like the original ACEs study, Moffitt and Caspi's work also allowed them to examine the relationship between a child's experiences and later life outcomes. But unlike the original ACEs study that focused on adults' recollection of childhood adversity and assessed physical and mental health problems in adulthood, Moffitt and Caspi's research followed children over time, recording adversity and other experiences as they occurred, with continuous assessments of physical, mental, and social well-being measured at the level of genes, brain functioning, and psychological capacity.

Moffitt and Caspi's headline result:

A CHILD'S PROPENSITY FOR SELF-CONTROL AT AGE THREE PREDICTS HER HEALTH, WEALTH, EDUCATIONAL, AND CRIMINAL OUTCOMES AT AGE THIRTY-TWO

Three-year-olds who had weaker self-control were more likely to grow up to be thirty-two-year-olds with worse health, less savings, lower educational attainment, higher criminal records, higher incidence of teen pregnancies, higher rates of substance abuse, and a higher frequency of hospitalizations for mental and physical health problems than three-year-olds with stronger self-control. The benefits of strong self-control were above and beyond IQ and family background—two factors that, in hundreds of studies, explain considerable variation in life outcomes. Adolescents with strong self-control, as evidenced by lower incidences of substance abuse, school dropout, and teen pregnancies, had some of the biggest payoffs in adulthood in terms of wealth, mental and physical health. Among siblings, those with stronger self-control had better outcomes in adulthood, suggesting that the propensity for self-control on its own is more important than family experiences.

The predisposition for self-control is essentially linked, throughout life, to outcomes that matter for human flourishing. Individuals starting off life with poor self-control are more likely to end up on a pathological path, whereas those who begin with strong self-control are more likely to end up on a resilient path. Though an individual's propensity for self-control is relatively stable over the course of development, changes arise, with decreases linked to weaker outcomes and increases linked to stronger outcomes. This suggests that there is plasticity in our capacity for self-control, opening the door to interventions. But first we need to consider other dimensions of self-control, including some hidden costs.

Again, childhood adversity is often associated with inflammation, a biomarker that the body's immune system has been taxed and isn't working properly. Inflammation can also be associated with psychiatric disorders such as autism, depression, and schizophrenia. Moffitt, Caspi, and their team revisited the Dunedin population, but this time, the individuals were thirty-eight years old. Using blood plasma samples, they extracted two biomarkers of inflammation. Because of the longitudinal data, they were also able to look at different dimensions of risk during development including poor health, poverty, high number of ACEs, low IQ, and weak self-control. Each of these risk factors on their own, but also when combined into an overall risk factor, were strongly associated with higher levels of inflammation. These risk factors were important even when BMI and smoking—two dimensions known to be linked to poor health—were statistically extracted from the analysis. These results add another biological layer to our understanding of vulnerability and resilience: individuals with poor self-control are more likely to end up with higher body inflammation, whereas those with strong self-control are more likely to have lower inflammation, indicative of a stronger immune system. This raises the intriguing possibility that anti-inflammatories, including psychedelics, might be a helpful therapy, which we will discuss more in chapter 9.

But the hard work it takes to keep things under control is taxing for a child, especially when it's something he must do all of the time. And it may not always be an overall win. For Jamaican-born Badrick, the simple act of riding the bus to school for a good forty-five minutes each day was challenging—he had to keep his cool, avoid being triggered by annoying kids, and then keep his composure for the rest of the school day and then again while riding the bus back home. For Bolondemu, once he was liberated from the Lord's Resistance Army by Ugandan forces, he had to squelch the appetite he had acquired for killing, navigate the social world under new norms, and make an effort to find work. Badrick increasingly gained self-control over the years I was with him in the school, while Bolondemu had clearly managed to regulate his emotions, maintain focus on his work, and successfully develop and maintain social relationships, including having a family with a wife and two children.

A study by psychologist Gregory Miller and colleagues shows that for young adults living in poverty, as was the case for Badrick and Bolondemu, constant exertion of self-control pays off on the surface while creating hidden costs.[21] Using DNA methylation as an epigenetic marker of aging, results showed that low SES individuals with strong self-control had lower rates of aggression, depression, and substance abuse, but were biologically older. By maintaining self-control, poor adolescents are more successful than those without self-control but pay for it with wear and tear on their body and brain. And sometimes, especially when the environment is unpredictable and resources for survival are fleeting, exerting self-control may be less adaptive than impulsively going for it and grabbing what's on offer when one can.

Having propensities to think, feel, and act in particular ways are like nudges, guiding us down certain paths in life. Whether we are focused on the genetic, immunological, neural, hormonal, or psychological level, these nudges do not determine the end point. Inherent in all of these biological systems is plasticity, the capacity to change. Plasticity is opportunity. But the extent of plasticity is limited and dependent on the Adverse Ts of experiences—type, timing, tenure, turbulence, and toxicity.

THE PLASTICITY POTENTIAL OF PUBERTY

It has long been understood that early childhood is a peak time of brain growth and malleability, but new research shows that puberty may offer an incredible window for change that we are just now beginning to grasp. An exquisite experimental study in mice of social rewards, oxytocin, and the psychedelic MDMA—more commonly known as ecstasy—helps us understand what opens and closes plasticity during particular periods of time. Neuroscientist Romain Nardou and his colleagues raised small groups of young mice in an enclosure with one kind of bedding material and then, after twenty-four hours, put each mouse on its own in an enclosure with a different kind of bedding.[22] What the mice were learning, therefore, was that there was one kind of bedding for socializing and another kind of bedding when alone. Socializing is rewarding for young mice, whereas solitary confinement is frightening. After experiencing these two environments, the mice were then allowed to wander between them. These young mice consistently spent more time in the enclosure associated with the social bedding than the solitary bedding. Like people who hang out at a local bar or coffee shop to meet others, mice hang out in bedding, where they are likely to meet other mice. Hanging out is socially rewarding. But interestingly, Nardou only observed this effect with young pubescent mice, not with mice who were younger or older.

Puberty in mice is a critical period associated with considerable plasticity in the nucleus accumbens, a reward area in the brain involved in the regulation of the hormone oxytocin, or the "feel good" hormone. But once puberty occurs, plasticity of the nucleus accum-

bens and the flow of oxytocin stops and so the socially rewarding nature of being with others becomes less powerful. Nardou wondered,
Might it be possible to open that window again?

To find out, he served mature mice one dose of the psychedelic
MDMA and then presented them with the social and solitary bedding
enclosures. Remarkably, these mature mice acted like pubescent juve-
niles, preferring to hang out on the social rather than solitary bedding,
reaping the social rewards, driven by a rejuvenated nucleus accumbens and its active oxytocin receptors.

Though our own neural and hormonal changes during puberty are
not identical to those observed in rats, they are close enough to shape
understanding of the plasticity potential. In the studies of Romanian
orphans that we learned about in chapter 4, experience of highly toxic
deprivation covered the opening and closing of the sensitive period of
the HPA axis activity for stress regulation. As a result, these children
developed an HPA system that was less reactive than noninstitutional-
ized children, including a blunted cortisol response, critical for regulating stress. Since the window for HPA axis activity had closed, the
orphans were looking at a future with reduced potential for change.
But what if, as suggested by the research on mice, puberty could be
another critical period of flexibility—a second-chance opportunity to
recalibrate the HPA?

Developmental psychologist Megan Gunnar explored this possibility by looking at HPA activity in children who started life in an orphanage and were then placed with a nurturing foster care family.[23] To test
for changes in HPA activity, Gunnar assessed foster-reared and biologically reared children with the commonly used Trier Social Stress Test
during different stages of development, including before, during, and
after puberty. The Trier required children to answer math problems in
front of an unfamiliar group of adult judges. Stress was measured by

extracting cortisol from their saliva, a simple, noninvasive, and accurate measure. Unlike children who remained in an orphanage and showed a flattened or blunted cortisol response to stress, the foster care children going through puberty showed a reactive cortisol response, much like their biologically reared counterparts. Importantly, this more typical, reactive cortisol profile was not seen in the foster care children before or after puberty. As Gunnar argued, puberty is a period that enables the HPA system to recalibrate, undoing in some sense the damage caused by earlier deprivation. This is the plasticity potential of puberty.

The HPA's recalibration appears to be dependent on both the quality of foster care and the relative severity of deprivation.[24] In a parallel study carried out with children who started off in the Romanian orphanage and were then placed in Romanian foster care, there was no evidence of recalibration. The Romanian foster care parents appeared less nurturing and supportive than the foster care parents in Gunnar's study. The toxicity of the deprivation experienced by the Romanian children was also greater than in the Gunnar study. Both the quality of care and the toxicity of the deprivation greatly impact the effectiveness of foster care interventions, which we'll look at more in chapter 8.

ADAPTIVE BRAIN CHANGES

In this book, we have learned that there are different sensitive and critical periods associated with different developmental systems. These periods are associated with tremendous plasticity—opportunities for change. Plasticity is typically considered a positive process of development, especially if the environmental experiences a child has during this time are what is expected or required for a particular skill or knowledge. But if a child is in a harsh or insufficient environment for the developmental leap to take place, then plasticity becomes a curse. A harsh experience can cause damage to a developmental program, whereas insufficient experience can stultify it. As I alluded to earlier, however, adverse experiences can sometimes enhance plasticity overall and also, depending on the nature of the adversity, accelerate development.[25]

In chapter 5, I mentioned the observation that children who experience abuse learn to recognize fear and respond to threats at an earlier age than children who are not exposed to abuse. Children who are exposed to physical and sexual abuse, domestic violence, absence of a father, and frequent displacement from the home begin puberty earlier. These changes, over the long haul, may well damage the developing child's body and brain. But they also reveal that developmental programs are designed to be flexible and change in response to unpredictable fluctuations in the environment. Essentially, along with the damaging aftershocks of adversity in childhood, there can actually be adaptive outcomes that may benefit the child in both the short and long term.[26]

This brings us back to the start of this chapter and the idea of individual differences, including its causes and consequences. What, in particular, allowed Bolondemu to show resilience and recovery in spite of his adversity, whereas Aliya, the Sudanese refugee girl we met in chapter 3, showed numerous traumatic reactions, years after the adversity ended? Recent studies on individual differences in the brain, generated from our biology and sculpted by experience, provide the start of an explanation for why some individuals are vulnerable to traumatic responses and others are resilient.

Child psychiatrist Nuria Mackes and her colleagues looked at the relationship between brain volume and the timing and tenure of deprivation within the Romanian orphanage.[27] Despite significant differences in tenure—the children were in the orphanage anywhere from three to forty months during sensitive and critical periods of development—there was no apparent impact on brain volume for some children. This suggests that some individuals are wired for resilience, immune to the negative impact of deprivation, including differences in timing and tenure.

To dig deeper into the wiring for resilience, Martin Teicher looked at the brains of adults who had experienced comparable childhood maltreatment, and compared the scans of those who had developed mental health problems and those who didn't.[28] Maltreated individuals—compared with non-maltreated individuals—had a sparser set of connections among many of the key neural players involved in emotional processing, memory, attention, and cognitive control. In addition, individuals who were maltreated, irrespective of whether they showed mental health problems in adulthood or not, had the same damaged areas: reduction in the size of the hippocampus and frontal lobes, greater activity in the amygdala, weaker activity of anterior cingulate for cognitive and emotional control. Those who had suffered childhood maltreatment but who did not develop mental health problems, showed even sparser connections to the damaged areas. In other words, the damaged brain areas have less of a voice, a silencing that seems to allow the rest of the brain to avoid corrupt chatter. For those with developing mental health problems, things get worse if the adverse experiences continue during the ages of fifteen to twenty-four years, a period when the executive functions of the brain are maturing. Most psychiatric disorders emerge during adolescence and are mediated by emotional dysregulation, which may start with individual differences in brain wiring.[29]

HIDDEN TALENTS

Jacques hadn't eaten in days, so he snuck into a chicken coop, grabbed a couple of hens, and started to head out, before he was stopped by a snarling German shepherd. With little time to think, he put the hens down, grabbed a rock, and smashed the shepherd in the nose, killing him instantaneously. Jacques was only ten years old at the time. He was alone, his parents far away, a strategy of separation deemed critical to avoid being caught by the Nazis. For the entirety of the war, his parents placed him in homes with trusted others for a few months at a time before reuniting for a few days, and then repeating the cycle. Sometimes he was with families who were part of the resistance, sometimes it was in a church run by Jesuits. At a young age, Jacques confronted several different types of adversity, for five years, with high toxicity and turbulence: war, community violence, poverty, home displacement, and neglect (physical, social, cognitive, and emotional). Throughout, Jacques managed to adapt, flexibly and cleverly changing to meet the ever-shifting landscape of a country at war. The rural peasants beat him up because he was a Parisian elite, but he fought back. When he had to costume up as a Christian to fit in with the Jesuits, he did so. When he had to hide his Judaism to fit in at a school that was often checked by the Nazis, he did that, too—anything to avoid a strip search that would reveal a signature trademark of Jews, circumcision.

Jacques and his parents made it through World War II, but few of his relatives did. In his late teens, he left France, got a PhD in physics from Harvard, got married, had two children, worked as a research scientist at Bell Laboratories for more than thirty-five years, retired to France at fifty-five to become an alpinist, while further refining his hunger for fine food, wine, literature, and opera. Jacques is ninety years old today. Jacques is my father, a man with superpowers, not only resilient but equipped with hidden talents.

As I mentioned in chapter 1, *hidden talents* are relatively advanced skills or abilities that emerge in response to adversity.[30] They represent a form of plasticity that is sensitive to the Adverse Ts. Children who grew up in poverty for the first ten years of their life, with highly unpredictable and uncontrollable family situations, showed stronger abilities to shift their attention in a task that was associated with declining and uncertain economic conditions than children growing up in the absence of poverty and with predictable family situations. Children exposed to divorce, separation, and non-biological caretakers had stronger memories of early childhood experiences than children living with married parents. Children ages four to nine years old, who experienced sexual and/or physical abuse, showed stronger attention and memory for highly emotional, negative, and stressful events than children without such abuse. Formerly incarcerated youth, with prior histories of several ACEs, living in unpredictable and uncontrollable environments, with high toxicity, long tenures, and cutting across multiple sensitive and critical periods, showed enhanced abilities to read cues of danger and determine the integrity and honesty of others—reading minds. These examples suggest that adversity can result in enhanced skills in some contexts, and that we are equipped with developmental programs that are plastic and able to change in response to novel, even unexpected, experiences when they are forced to. They hold out hope that from adversity can come strength.

Community: The Caring Cultures

was a really short thirteen-year-old, a few inches shy of five feet. Being vertically challenged is never a good thing for a young boy, but perhaps especially in junior high school. Over the course of two years and change, I was the constant target of bullying by three much larger boys—Ronnie, Lionel, and Chris. Yes, I remember their names and every detail of what happened to me about fifty years ago. All three, either as a team or individually, would push me, knuckle punch me, call me midget, and shove me into a locker—one specific locker. This was particularly stressful and embarrassing, as they shoved me into the locker right before our math class. You see, I had a crush on the math teacher, Miss Kabida. She would hear banging in the locker outside her class, come out, open the locker door, and then ask, "Marc, what are you doing in here?" Why she assumed I was willingly going into the locker was beyond me. Each bully also developed their own unique tactics. Lionel's was the most petrifying. He was huge. In the summer, he would find me in the community pool and push my head underwater.

Often, I felt as if I would drown. I had nightmares of drowning. I felt helpless, like the rats discussed in chapter 3 who couldn't escape shock.

One day I told my mom that I couldn't go to school. I don't think I had missed a single day since preschool, except perhaps for a sick day or two. This declaration was clearly out of the ordinary. My mom asked if I was sick. I said no. My mom asked if there was something going on at school. I burst out crying. It took a while for me to stop. I finally mustered the courage to tell her. She suggested that we speak with the principal about what was happening. I vehemently rejected this option, as it would be far too embarrassing and cowardly. When my father came home, I told him as well. He told me about his experiences in France during World War II, some of which I alluded to in the last chapter.

My father's parents took him out of school in Paris in 1939 and fled to the countryside to avoid being caught by the Nazis. At the time, France was highly centralized, with all intellectual, cultural, and educational happenings in Paris. The rural areas were, as my father described, mostly uneducated farmers, what he called "peasants." When my father went to school, he was immediately tagged as a snobbish Parisian, and promptly beaten up, relentlessly and repeatedly. One day he fought back. He didn't win, but he gained respect. As he finished telling me his story, he looked at me with intensity and affection and said, "Marc, you have to fight back."

I heard my father's wisdom, but felt petrified, my confidence frozen. I told my father that I couldn't fight back, as there were three bullies, not one, and each towered over me. They were inseparable, a team, all black belts in bullying. My father then proposed that he take me out of school each day for lunch, as this was the time that I was most vulnerable. I would go to school but skip out for an hour each day. The principal agreed. So did I.

The support from my parents buoyed me. They were my life raft to resilience. I soon felt the courage to strike back, accepting the moral of my father's story. I knew that I couldn't take on Team Bully at once. I had to get one of them alone. I waited for the ringleader, Ronnie, to be by himself. With his back to me, I tapped him on the shoulder and swung as hard as I could, hitting him solidly in the gut. It was like a fly bouncing off a window. Nothing. Nada. I teared up, realizing that Ronnie would clobber me. But he didn't. He looked at me and said, "Why did you do that?" With the little air that I had left in my chest, I managed to tell him that I was tired of being beaten up by Team Bully, tired of being shoved into the lockers, just plain tired. Ronnie looked at me and said, "Okay, we'll stop."

Families and communities can be the cause of adversity, the fabric of cultural dysfunction. But they can also be the source of healing and hope. Bullying was my one ACE, one with a long tenure, timed to early adolescence. My parents were my source of healing and hope—my road to recovery. For children in orphanages, adoption by a certain age provides healing and hope. For children abducted by rogue militias, liberation and return to their villages can provide healing and hope. For children living in unpredictable, uncontrollable, and unsafe home environments, safe schools with kind, predictable teachers can provide healing and hope.

FOSTERING THE DEPRIVED CHILD

Mikey,[1] a rhesus monkey infant I observed on the island of Cayo Santiago, Puerto Rico, was born with two legs that never worked. As an infant, this didn't matter much because he was carried by his mother. But as he approached his first birthday, his weight had increased to the point where it became harder for his rather frail mother to carry him. When his mother and sisters moved away from him, he would cry. Sometimes, his sisters would come back, pick him up, and carry him to the next event. Less frequently, his mother would pick him up. This seemed rather cruel, but rhesus monkey mothers—like all mothers—have evolved an instinct to assess the odds that an infant will survive. Mikey's prospects were poor. Fortunately, he had his older sisters, little allomothers—caretakers—helping out and honing their own skills as future moms.

One day, Mikey attempted to walk on his arms. At first, he just flopped over. But he was persistent. One of his sisters, Jackie—the most dedicated allomother—would sit by and wait, watch, and sometimes give him physical support. Soon, Mikey was walking on his arms. Then he was running on his arms, keeping up with his group as they moved to feed, rest, or play. It was hard not to cheer for this powerhouse of courage.

Mikey's mother interacted with him but didn't carry or feed him. Jackie and his other sisters played with him. He seemed to be developing all of the species-typical social behaviors, including the submissive screams, retracted ears, and grimaces that are common when subordinates submit to dominants.

One day, I searched and searched the island but couldn't find Mikey. I asked Edgar, one of the research staff on the island. Edgar told me that Mikey was found dead, most likely due to injuries from more dominant animals. His sister Jackie was seen walking around the island, occasionally crying, searching for her brother, who she would never see again.

You will recall that in chapter 4 I discussed the deprivation experiments on infant rhesus monkeys carried out by the psychologist Harry Harlow. These experiments showed the irreparable psychological damage caused by separating infants from their mothers. In the absence of species-typical maternal care, including the essential serve-and-return interactions between mothers and their offspring, infants fail to develop species-typical behaviors. This failure to develop fits with the idea of a critical period as the damage appears permanent.

In the mid-1970s, Harlow's research efforts pushed in a direction that not only added an important wrinkle to the earlier findings, but added hope for his deprived monkeys and for the millions of deprived children all over the world.[2] Led by one of his students, comparative psychologist Melinda Novak, they showed that infant rhesus monkeys who had been deprived for either six or twelve months, and who exhibited severely dysfunctional behavior toward themselves and others, could acquire species-typical social behaviors if introduced to a *therapist* monkey—a younger female peer whose primary social interests were friendly, like Jackie, who supported her brother, Mikey. By removing the potential competitive element of a same-age or older peer, Novak allowed maternally deprived infants to interact with nonthreatening infants who simply wanted to groom, play, and huddle. This therapeutic approach helped infants reared in isolation reduce their anxiety to a new environment, halt atypical interfering behaviors, and engage in positive social behaviors—and these appropriate, species-typical behaviors continued into young adulthood at age three years. For rhesus monkeys, even one year of complete maternal deprivation can be reversed with access to a good therapist—an unthreatening, patient, friendly allomother.[3]

In her book, *The Orphans of Davenport*, psychologist Marilyn Brookwood describes a case study from the 1930s that suggests the power of allomothers for human orphans. She tells the story of Wendell Hoffman, who was born in an Iowa hospital and taken from his mother, Viola, after she failed an IQ test given by hospital staff. As was typical at the time, and horrific by today's norms, Viola was deemed intellectually unfit to raise a child or have future children. After she gave birth to Wendell, she was sterilized, and Wendell was sent to an orphanage.

Eventually Wendell, along with several other children from the same orphanage, were moved to a state-run institution for individuals with mental impairments. Though the physical conditions of the orphanage were lacking, these children received care from a group of women who were loving, caring, attentive, and nurturing, though they had the mental capacity of nine-year-olds. Soon, Wendell and the other children began to thrive, play, laugh, and learn, and their IQ scores increased, especially in contrast to those children who had been left behind in the orphanage without dedicated allomothers. This resoundingly positive result, hailing the transformative power of allomothers to rescue children from the deprivation of an orphanage, remained dormant for several decades. It was awakened in the 1990s by the Bucharest Early Intervention Project that I described in chapter 4.

In the BEIP, some children were moved from their orphanage and placed in foster care with allomothers, or more accurately, alloparents. Since this was a randomized control intervention—effectively, the researchers flipped a coin to decide who was staying in the orphanage and who was leaving, and at what age—any positive effect of foster care would most likely represent a critical *causal* ingredient. If the intervention resulted in positive outcomes, the goal was to re-create policy changes in Romania to eliminate the orphanages and increase the availability and support for foster care.

Developmental scientists Charles Nelson, Nathan Fox, and Charles Zeanah not only developed the foster care intervention, but they had their eye on the long game in terms of evidence. Their thinking was that because there are different sensitive and critical periods (timing) for different abilities—emotional awareness, recognition, and regulation; understanding of one's own and others' beliefs and intentions; comprehension and production of the sounds of one's native language, along with its words and grammar; and the executive functions of working memory, attention, self-control, and planning—they would need to observe and assess foster care children until they reached their late teens, if possible. The other Adverse Ts were a factor to consider in their results: some children left the orphanage at six months, whereas others left at thirty months (tenure), some children had unpredictable and uncontrollable changes in the number of different foster care parents (turbulence), and some children experienced other adversities after placement in foster care (type), including some that were highly toxic.

The results of the BEIP study offered hope for allomothers as essential guides on the road to recovery. Placing infants with nurturing alloparents enabled them to shift from a delayed pathology or chronic pathology path—the paths I described in chapter 2—to a delayed resilient or resilient path. But, as we will see, not all body and brain systems responded in the same way or at the same time, and herein lies the significance of considering the Adverse Ts.

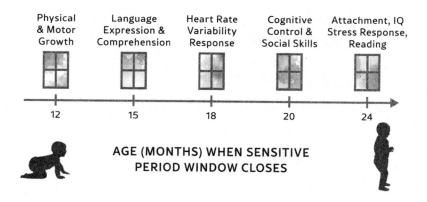

Physical & Motor Growth	Language Expression & Comprehension	Heart Rate Variability Response	Cognitive Control & Social Skills	Attachment, IQ Stress Response, Reading
12	15	18	20	24

AGE (MONTHS) WHEN SENSITIVE
PERIOD WINDOW CLOSES

The illustration above shows important and defined developmental periods for child development. One of the earliest sensitive periods ends at twelve months after birth and is linked to measures of physical growth. Children placed into foster care before twelve months caught up in weight and height to the level of children raised from birth by their biological parents, especially children with foster care parents who were sensitive, respectful, and nurturing. But children placed into foster care after twelve months, especially those with low birth weights, failed to catch up, and showed the most significant delays with respect to head size and one broad measure of intelligence—IQ. Given that many orphaned children have low birth weights and given that twelve months is a sensitive period for weight and height growth, it is all the more important that children living with toxic deprivation enter into foster care at the earliest age possible, and critically, before the twelve-month window closes.

Children who remained in the orphanage after the twelve-month window closed also showed more repetitive, stereotyped behaviors, which indicate problems with motor and sensory systems that may also have been associated with their delayed physical growth. These included such behaviors as pacing and rocking in place, as commonly seen in captive animals who are under-stimulated, living in impoverished environments. For animals, these actions arise from poor connectivity between cortical structures and the basal ganglia, a brain region that is essential for motor control. Stereotyped behaviors like rocking, hand flapping and, in extreme cases, head banging, are also seen in many autistic children, and it is well established that autism is associated with problems of sensory integration and regulation. Romanian orphans who were placed in foster care before twelve months either lost the stereotyped behaviors they had developed or never developed them at all.

When a child is fifteen months, the window for language acquisition is thought to close, which is a far more complicated system than height, weight, and stereotyped actions. As I've discussed in previous chapters, language acquisition relies on generative systems dedicated to processing unique sounds or signs, concepts, and rules so that we can create meaningful thoughts and expressions that others will understand. This process is buoyed by our more general systems such as working memory, attention, and motor control. When we listen to others speaking, we must attend, maintain the information in working memory, consider how we will respond, or if we will respond. When we speak, we also have to cue up in working memory our thoughts and intentions, evaluate the attention of our audience, their understanding of a topic, and then articulate what we have in mind.

To determine the impact of deprivation on language acquisition, and the possibility of recovery following placement into foster care, the BEIP team gathered evidence from caretakers about the children's comprehension and expression while they were in the orphanage. They then assessed the children who were moved to foster care. These two groups were compared with children who were raised from birth by their biological parents. Children in all three groups showed earlier comprehension of language than production, a pattern that fits with all studies of language acquisition. For children placed into foster care before fifteen months, patterns of language acquisition matched those who were never in orphanages. Even children who were placed in foster care between sixteen and twenty-four months ultimately caught up to their age-matched, biologically raised peers when tested at thirty and forty-two months, and developed not only richer vocabularies but also the ability to use more complex grammatical structures. And those children who remained within the orphanage for two years or more showed significant deficits in both language comprehension and expression. So while the window for language acquisition appears to close down at fifteen months, it is not fully closed—at least for the elements of language observed—until twenty-four months.

Again, the sensitive period for language acquisition is more complicated to interpret than that for weight, height, and stereotyped actions because it doesn't occur in isolation—it is linked with other developmental systems like memory, attention, and associative learning. To show that there is a specific language delay, rather than a delay in the systems that support language, it is necessary to run a comprehensive battery of tests. For example, in a study by neuropsychologist Alfonso Caramazza, results from a comprehensive series of tests showed that a patient who couldn't produce nouns had no problem producing other linguistic elements such as verbs and adjectives, and also had no problem with the systems that support language such as memory, attention, and perception.[4] Not only has this type of comprehensive testing yet to be carried out for children raised in orphanages, but we know that such children suffer from extreme deficits in the development of attention, working memory, cognitive control, and associative learning—even when they are placed with alloparents early in life. It is likely, therefore, that what appears as a language delay is more accurately explained as a delay in the executive functions, systems that support language.

The next developmental window in our timeline is associated with the autonomic system and, in particular, stress processing and regulation. As we've established, deprivation, like many other types of adversity, is stressful. As a result of this chronic stress, and as we discussed in chapter 4, children in orphanages have blunted heart rates and cortisol responses relative to children raised by their biological parents. Children who start life in an orphanage but are adopted into foster care before eighteen months recover normal heart rate patterns, and if they are adopted before twenty-four months, they return to normal cortisol responses. Intriguingly, as we learned in chapter 7, there is some evidence that the cortisol stress response of deprived children can recalibrate during puberty, but this was not the case for the Romanian orphans, apparently because of the high toxicity and tenure of their deprivation.

The last two windows explored by the BEIP team involved developmental programs for cognitive control—the ability to flexibly process, regulate, and respond to information—and social skills. Children who were placed into foster care by twenty months showed developmentally appropriate abilities for cognitive control and social skills when assessed at eight years, including the willingness to engage with peers, communicate in conversations, and express secure attachment to their primary caretaker, and flexibly adjust to changing goals. Children who were placed into foster care no later than their second birthday showed normal IQ levels at four and a half years, normal levels of brain electrical activity when assessed at eight years, normal levels of attachment to caretakers, and grade-level appropriate reading skills. Importantly, the positive impact of foster care on brain activity, attachment, and social competence was lessened if there were disruptions in foster care placement, including moving between families—an example of how heightened unpredictability and uncontrollability—turbulence—disrupts development.

Overall, leaving the impoverished conditions of an orphanage before the age of two years, and entering the loving home of foster care parents, greatly improved the ability of children to flourish. This was our experience with our daughter Sofia, whom we brought home at age twenty-two months, though it was not the kind of outcome Julie had when she adopted her six-year-old son, Ethan.

Some developmental programs were stubbornly resistant to change even with a positive foster care experience, suggesting that they rely on an extremely early critical period for success. For example, children who were placed into foster care before twenty-four months continued to show deficits in executive functioning, including attention, working memory, inhibitory control, cognitive flexibility, and associative learning. This shows that the developmental programs that create executive functioning may take hold during fetal development and the first year of life.

On the flip side, children made important gains in some domains no matter when they were placed in foster care. Children who left an orphanage across a wide range of ages showed significantly fewer psychiatric disorders and improved emotion recognition compared with children who stayed in an orphanage for the first twelve years of life. This shows that foster care, at any time before twelve years, may reduce the risks of psychiatric disorders.

In chapter 4, I described the experiments carried out by cognitive neuroscientist Margaret Sheridan and the BEIP team in which children played two computerized games, one involving the ability to link actions with rewards and the other with the ability to link numerical patterns to actions. Though children placed into foster care before the age of two years showed significantly greater skills on these two associative learning tasks than children who remained in the orphanage, their skills were weaker than age-matched peers raised by their biological parents, and this was especially noticeable on the numerical pattern task. In addition, children placed into foster care before the age of two years, and then assessed at eight and twelve years old, failed to recover developmentally typical skills in visual and spatial working memory and learning, flexibility in switching between rules, and planning—abilities that support virtually all educational goals, as well as many of the language and social skills we discussed earlier. It is thus highly likely that what appear to be deficits in language and social thinking are, in fact, due to deficiencies in the supporting players that help us communicate and develop relationships.

The fact that foster care fails to rescue the executive system from the impact of early deprivation should not be taken as evidence that we've hit a dead end in altering the brain's plasticity. As we will see over the course of this chapter and the next, other interventions are possible and hold out promise. But what the BEIP team's results show is the devastating impact of early toxic deprivation on a fundamental capacity of human brain function, one that enables us to grow healthy relationships, learn in school, plan for the future, and create a meaningful life.

Children in orphanages with toxic deprivation are stuck in a Beckettian *Waiting for Godot* scenario, waiting for the warmth, tenderness, protection, and tutelage of a mother or father, waiting to be guided and nurtured in their endeavor to lead meaningful lives, waiting for experiences that our DNA has programmed us to expect. Many never receive the basic human needs for flourishing. Others are saved by the allomothers they desperately need. For Sofia, my wonderful daughter, flourishing defines her—she is strong, creative, sensitive, and beautiful. For some, the rescue is too late—or its quality insufficient—as the damage from early deprivation has left its mark, irreparably harming a child's ability to attend, learn, remember, recall, and emotionally regulate.

The good news is that austere orphanages such as those in Romania have closed down across the globe; and in places where orphanages remain, such as those I am working with in Kenya, there have been significant efforts to increase the quality of care, including cognitive, emotional, social, and physical nurturing. And in some countries, including many low-income nations, orphanages may well provide better care than foster parents.

So far we've discussed how allomothering can positively impact a child who has gone through tragic deprivation. But for children exposed to the adversities of war, including those who have carried arms and killed, there are different tools to use to set them on a path to healing.

HEALING THE ARMED CHILD

As we saw in chapter 6, child soldiers show a disproportionately higher rate of mental health disorders like PTSD when compared with non-conscripted children exposed to war. Analyses by political scientists Roos Haer and Tobias Böhmelt reveal that conflicts involving child soldiers last longer and are more likely to reoccur than if there are no minors involved.[5] This suggests that child soldiers, once engaged, may be more resistant to change their beliefs and violent inclinations. A child abducted into an armed group, or who has joined one willingly, will have experienced a deeply rooted transformation in his perception of the world. He may also have committed acts—touched dead bodies, killed others—or been subjected to violence or sexual abuse that are outside the norm of the culture he grew up in. And he might be physically displaced from his village, ending up in one that is socially, morally, religiously, and legally very different.

Interventions designed to help child soldiers recover must first pave the reintegration road, whether it is to their community of origin or a new home. Reintegration is a reciprocal process between the soldier on one side and the community on the other. For the soldier, reintegration may require coping with mental health, violent tendencies, substance abuse, a change in beliefs, the lack of education, and the minimal opportunities for obtaining a job and developing resources. In the absence of economic opportunities, ex-soldiers may resort to theft and violence, or substance abuse to cope with the misery of a bleak future. For community members, engaging in reintegration may require coping with their own mental health issues, their beliefs about the cause of war and its direct or indirect impact on their own well-being. Communities may also experience moral outrage that ex-soldiers are receiving resources that they could well use and surely deserve.

Research by medical anthropologist Brandon Kohrt, whose work on Nepalese child soldiers appeared in chapter 6, provides an illustration of the challenges of reintegration. Consider Raj, a boy from a lower caste who was taken into a Maoist armed force at the age of fourteen years. In his own village, he had become a shamanistic healer.[6] But when he became part of a Maoist armed militia group, he was coerced to beat shamans for their spiritual and unscientific beliefs. These experiences were corrosive for both Raj and his family, as his mother describes: "He couldn't follow the rules of the shaman god, so he started. He dreamed only about war. He has nightmares. He worries all the time. He is very sad because he had to quit his studies."

Raj expressed similar concerns, while noting his eagerness to engage in the ritualized healing that is necessary for his own and his family's well-being: "We do not have the money to follow what my deity told us to do. I still have not done the puja [ceremony] that the deity told me to do. I think my parents and my brother also have become sick because of this. We are hoping to do the puja soon."

In Raj's case, there was harmony between his own and his village's perspective on ritual and reintegration. For Maya, a girl who joined the Maoist armed forces, there was dissonance, as a return to the norms of her village meant a return to patriarchy and violence against women. Her village's attitude toward girls who were part of the Maoist armed forces is captured by a teenage girl who didn't join: "Everyone treats girls badly who leave the village. As soon as she leaves, everyone assumes she took off with some boy and is now impure. I want to escape all the hardship of life here. . . . Instead of suffering here, it would be better to deal with the Maoists."

For Maya, leaving the Maoists and agreeing to spiritual cleansing meant going back to a society that discriminates against women, prevents them from working to earn money, and turns a blind eye to domestic violence. From Maya's perspective, the best therapy for her trauma was to build up wealth and independence through work: "The NGO helped me open a grocery shop. I have a business. . . . Now I feel my status improving and I feel that I can do something. . . . I would like to show that even an insulted outcast girl can do work like this."

With these tensions and cultural issues in mind, Kohrt collaborated with the government of Nepal and UNICEF to design a two-pronged intervention aimed at ameliorating the physical and mental health of child soldiers through the lens of their community, while simultaneously healing and building the resilience of the community. The first prong focused on stigma. Because child soldiers often feel stigmatized by their communities and may also feel shame or embarrassment associated with receiving specialized treatment, Kohrt's team disseminated pamphlets to child soldiers as well as other children and families within a village, raising awareness about mental health, including risk and protective factors. The second prong, carried out by trained Nepalese psychosocial workers, was an intervention focused on promoting inclusion and acceptance of child soldiers who are often discriminated against.

Kohrt's intervention revealed several short- and long-term benefits to child soldiers, with important differences emerging on the basis of educational, socioeconomic, and moral perspectives across villages. Child soldiers who returned to lower-caste villages had stronger mental health recovery and well-being than those returning to higher-caste villages, suggesting that the stigma may have been less in lower-caste villages, and the support relatively higher. Six years after the war ended, child soldiers were more likely to be married with children than non-conscripted individuals, revealing the impact of both therapeutic and educational resources on relationship and reproductive health.

An important feature of Kohrt's research, as well as other international researchers', is the discovery that therapeutic treatment must be sensitive to the local cultural norms and economic conditions of the community and carried out by community members who are not only trusted but have been equipped through training with skills to help victims of childhood abuse and violence. Clinical psychologist Thomas Elbert, whose work on child soldiers and appetitive violence we discussed in chapter 6, has implemented a therapeutic approach called Forensic Offender Rehabilitation through Narrative Exposure Therapy (FORNET) for ex–child soldiers in Uganda and the Democratic Republic of the Congo, as well as street children in Burundi.[7] FORNET is delivered over the course of several weeks by locally trained community members, focusing on ex–child soldiers who, as a result of exposure to war and perpetration of violence, have PTSD and often have continued to engage in violent behavior. The therapeutic process starts with individuals reconstructing key events in their life—their *lifeline*— including exposure to stressful adversity, perpetration of violence, and positive experiences. Reflecting on positive childhood experiences is an important element in many therapeutic approaches, as it helps children see that there is lightness and joy within the moments of dark from the past, while helping the therapist identify what a child enjoys. Next, they are taught ways in which they might regulate their emotions, recognize anger, and find friends who can support them through hard times. Lastly, the therapist helps them discuss recent situations in which they were violent, as well as those in which they avoided violence. This last step is often carried out in groups to enable ex–child soldiers to work with each other and grow in the absence of a therapist.

Results from a randomized control trial in the Democratic Republic of the Congo showed that FORNET decreased appetitive violence and PTSD symptoms in ex–child soldiers when they were assessed at three to five months, as well as six to nine months later. This pattern held for individuals who were recruited before eighteen years, as well as older adult recruits, suggesting that at least the child vs. adult distinction doesn't matter with respect to recovery in this situation. A somewhat surprising result was that FORNET also led to a decrease in substance abuse among ex–child soldiers even though this was not a target of treatment. Given the common observation that veterans of war turn to substance abuse to help relieve the pain of their experiences, this side-effect of FORNET is significant.

HEALING CHILDREN OF WAR

In 1994, the Rwandan Hutu tribe committed genocide against the Tutsi tribe, killing approximately eight hundred thousand people within one hundred days. Thousands of children were recruited as soldiers, but a much larger number were exposed to this civil war, including the adversities of violence, death, parent loss, destruction of home, discrimination, and oppression. Carine, a Tutsi teenager, lived through this carnage.[8] In her first confrontation, she was sliced across the face with a large knife on her way to a pit of dead bodies, the decimation from a recent school attack by the Hutu. Though she had no desire to join the inhabitants of this pit, her next two confrontations brought her close to the edge. She was gang-raped multiple times, bitten, and beaten. She made it to a hospital, but it was overrun by Hutu rebels before the doctors were able to fully heal her wounds. As Carine noted, "I couldn't run away. I couldn't go because everything was broken. . . . Whoever wanted to have sex with me could. If the perpetrators wanted to urinate, they could come and do it on me."

The civil unrest ended after one hundred days and Carine received the medical treatment she needed. She returned home to her village but, remarkably, given the severity of her injuries, she was pregnant. Despite the taboo of rape in her village—and most other Rwandan villages—Carine refused to abandon her son, accepting that she might have to harbor the stigma forever, push her trauma into hibernation, and withhold her son's birth story.

For many, perhaps especially people living in Western, high-income nations, Carine's childhood exposure to war may seem utterly unfamiliar and unrelatable. And yet, as I write these words, the war in Ukraine—a Western, high-income nation—rages on. There are no child soldiers in Ukraine, but of the seven million children, most have already been exposed to the war, with more than a thousand killed or badly injured, and many young girls have been raped.[9] Healing these war children will take a village.

An essential hub for a child's recovery from the adversity of war starts with her parents, if they are alive and willing to engage in psychological, emotional, and physical rehabilitation. Recall from our earlier discussions that children expect serve-and-return interactions from their parents. When mothers are able to return their child's serve in a timely and appropriate manner, they help buffer the stress response, either by reducing the magnitude of their child's reaction or enabling quicker recovery. As developmental neuroscientist Ruth Feldman has shown in her longitudinal studies of Israeli children growing up in the war zones around the Gaza Strip, the health impact of chronic stress is reduced when mothers are in sync with their child's needs, specifically when a mother can empathize with her child.[10] In this sense, healthy mothers have healthier children because they empathize with their needs and buffer them from stressful experiences. The problem is, of course, that in many of these war zones, mothers are either unhealthy or dead. In these cases, villages can come to life, helping struggling mothers recover or providing a network of allomothers.

Public health scientist Theresa Betancourt led a group of epidemiologists, economists, and social workers in an effort to implement a home visit intervention to villages throughout Rwanda.[11] The goal of the intervention, called Sugira Muryango, or "Family Strengthening," was to enhance caretakers' understanding of early child development from six to thirty-six months old, the importance of serve-and-return care, and the skills required to reduce family violence through conflict resolution and emotion regulation.

Observations of more than a thousand families showed that those receiving Sugira Muryango compared with those who didn't were more likely to engage in serve-and-return interactions with their children including stimulating them cognitively and emotionally; more likely to provide them with a diversity of nutritionally rich foods; more likely to be sensitive to their physical needs when they were sick; more likely to create a healthy home environment; less likely to experience mental health challenges such as anxiety and depression; and less likely to engage in violent behavior, either with each other or with their child. In other words, children living in villages who had experienced the Sugira Muryango approach had fewer ACEs, including deprivation (physical, social, cognitive, and emotional), abuse (physical), poverty, and domestic violence, during a suite of sensitive and critical periods. And the lasting adversity they'd expect to go through as a result of war was of shorter duration and lower toxicity. They had fewer TRACEs.

Another promising approach to healing children of war is work carried out by the Global Trauma Project,[12] focused on survivors of the civil war in Sudan, as well as other regions of Africa. Like the work in Nepal and Rwanda I described above, the work in the Sudan starts with empowering and training community members to understand the impact of adversity—including war, community violence, abuse, and poverty—on an individual's body and brain, including children. It's an approach they call Trauma-Informed Community Empowerment. Strikingly, following engagement with their community-led therapy, there is a 64 percent decrease in PTSD symptoms, a 26 percent decrease in emotional dysregulation, and a 15 percent decrease in heart stress response. These positive changes not only remain stable a year after the therapeutic intervention but are associated with decreases in violence and dissociative disorders, as well as an increase in motivation to work. Initiatives such as the Global Trauma Project provide evidence that villages can function, at a large scale, to heal the suffering of children exposed to war.

HEALING THE OPPRESSED
AND DISCRIMINATED CHILD

Tania always wore black—all of her clothes, dyed hair, mascara, and choker. For most of the school day, she either sat at her desk, head down, or was in a time-out room, yelling or being restrained.

Tania was born to Brazilian parents. The students in her mostly all-White school made fun of her skin color with comments such as "You trying to be Black!" and "Why is it always so dark around here when you're around?" Tania was born Tristao, the Brazilian version of Tristan. She changed her name around the seventh grade when she was twelve, right after puberty. The kids at her school continued to call her "Tristan" or "Tranny Tris," and often punched her in the chest, saying, "No boobs, Tristan!" When she started wearing earrings and mascara, she was beaten up. When she tried to enter the girls' bathroom she was shunned. Repeatedly, the boys shoved her into their bathroom and hit her. Her school seemed both blind to Tania's situation and unable to help her. Eventually, Tania's parents pushed to have her moved to an alternative school, one that was sympathetic to her transformation and that cultivated an atmosphere of inclusion and equity, celebrating diversity rather than discrimination and oppression—another ACE within the domain of cultural dysfunction.

As I discussed in Part I, discrimination and oppression are forms of adversity that, whether experienced directly or indirectly as part of an intergenerational relay, wear down the body and brain. Discriminatory comments, in the form of verbal abuse, put-downs, social exclusion, and nonverbal gestures—often referred to as *microaggressions*—result in physiological changes that are signatures of stress, including increased blood pressure, increased heart rate, decreased heart rate variability, and increased epigenetic changes associated with accelerated biological aging. These changes cannot only be detected in the moment, when the microaggression occurs, but over longer periods of time, including changes in key language areas that we covered in chapter 5.[13]

Unlike many other forms of adversity that we have discussed, the health tab of discrimination and oppression is often more subtle or difficult to detect because they often entail microaggressions, as opposed to the full-bore macroaggressions of outright violence that one may more often consider. Victims of microaggressions may or may not be consciously aware of their impact. Though microaggressions can be deployed by any group that oppresses another, we have become far more aware of their impact on victims of racism. Studies show how microaggressions adversely transform the stress response, which impacts learning, and can lead to delinquency and risk-taking, often resulting in lost opportunities for employment, and even epigenetic aging that increases the odds of early death.[14] But as with war and community violence, communities can enable children to recover from racial injuries and build resilience to it. And as with the heightened impact of adversity on younger children, so, too, is it the case that interventions that start early have the best chance to help kids build resilience and recover.

Biases toward our own tribe and against other tribes start early in life, with evidence that infants under one year prefer to look at, approach, and listen to individuals from their own race, as opposed to other races. This own-race bias can, however, be influenced by the early rearing environment, with evidence that infants growing up in racially diverse neighborhoods show less of an own-race bias.[15] These early developing biases can mature and become ingrained, especially in cultures where discrimination is palpable. In schools throughout the United States, explicit awareness of racial inequities in academic achievement—grades, standardized testing, dropout rates—as well as in suspensions and other disciplinary actions, has led to initiatives to both reduce racial biases among students and teachers, as well as to build resilience among children of color and other minority groups that have been discriminated against.

Social psychologist Greg Walton and his colleagues set out to assess whether a short, forty- to seventy-minute online intervention for American middle school students (ages twelve to fourteen years old) could reduce the significant disparity in suspension rates among racial-minoritized students, especially Black and Hispanic children.[16] It is clear that all children are harmed by suspensions, increasing their negative feelings about school, dropout rates, vulnerability to substance abuse and crime, and decreasing their friendships and sense of belonging. But children of color bear the brunt of this harm. The intervention focused on the double-edged sword of racial biases in school: teachers who perceive misbehavior as a fixed character trait of racially stigmatized groups, while racially stigmatized students expect unfair treatment by teachers. Walton's intervention, called an *empathy mindset*, attempted to develop working relationships between teachers and students, premised on respect and understanding, with the goal of learning and growth. Teachers read scientific articles and wrote reflective essays on how helping all children learn and grow is an ideal, that all children have this potential, and that positive relationships must be maintained even in the face of misbehavior. From this perspective, there are no fixed character traits or personality, but rather, the potential for growth. With an empathy mindset, teachers put themselves in their students' shoes, trying to understand their struggles and how they might help. It is a powerful counter to racial bias or any other form of discrimination.

Walton launched the empathy mindset intervention in twenty middle schools, located across seventeen cities, and involving a racially diverse group of close to six thousand students. Teachers were randomly assigned to either the empathy mindset training or a control group with no training. Strikingly, especially given the brevity of the intervention, suspension rates among Black and Hispanic students dropped by 45 percent if they were paired with teachers trained on the empathy mindset. Students with prior records of suspension also showed lower suspension rates in the following year, including students of color. Students with disabilities—another group that is often discriminated against—also showed a reduction in suspensions if they had teachers who went through the empathy mindset intervention. This intervention also had staying power and a direct impact on the students' own sense of well-being and belonging, as those who moved from seventh to eighth grade had lower suspensions despite the fact that they were with new teachers who didn't take part in the empathy intervention. And for children, schools may provide the ideal context for reducing the adverse impact of discrimination, as well as other forms of adversity, especially given that they may be exposed to such adversities within schools.[17]

SAFE SCHOOLS, RECOVERING CHILDREN

Sasha missed the first two months of school. She refused to get on the school bus and even refused to be chauffeured by her parents to the front door. Her parents eventually convinced her to accept the ride, but when they pulled up to the school, she put the brakes on, refusing to leave the car.

One day, Sasha's attitude toward school changed. Greeted by two smiling teachers, both wearing T-shirts with Pokémon characters—Sasha's passion—she opened the car door, walked into school, and into a play area with a table, three chairs, and a Pokémon board game. The teachers asked if she wanted to play, noting that they were aware of her fierce skills in the game. Sasha smiled and nodded her head. The teachers asked her to explain the rules and to keep track of the scores. Sasha then asked, "Is this school?" Carrie, one of the teachers, answered, "Absolutely. You just explained the instructions to Pokémon, which shows you are a good listener and explainer, and you have been keeping track of the score, which is math. In this school, we do a lot of different things so that students like you can both show us what you already know and so that you can learn new things." Sasha smiled again and her body followed, relaxed, calm, happy.

Sasha lived in an environment that made her feel unsafe. Her home was a run-down apartment in a high-crime neighborhood. Gunshots, sirens, homeless people, and drug deals were common experiences. She lived with her four siblings, mother, and stepfather—her father having passed away two years earlier, killed by a gang. Though her stepfather was kind, she didn't trust him. For Sasha, school would be her safe space, a place where she could learn to trust others, feel calm, and build confidence to cope with what might always be a turbulent home environment.

Sasha's school was part of a global movement to bring trauma-informed practices to educators and the children they teach.[18] A trauma-informed school is anchored in the 4 Rs:

- Realizing that exposure to childhood adversity is common
- Recognizing the different signatures of traumatic reactions to adversity
- Responding to children with trauma by understanding what happened to them and providing them with the skills to build resilience and recovery
- Resisting re-traumatization by building protective systems and awareness within and outside the school

In the same way that I noted in chapter 1 that much of the medical community was unaware of the magnitude of ACEs in the population prior to and even after Vincent Felitti and his colleagues reported their initial results, many schools across the globe are unaware of the magnitude of adversity that children experience, or if they are aware, they don't understand what it does to the developing body and brain and what can be done to help them. And as many experts have noted, even when a school is trauma-informed in the sense of Realizing and Recognizing, there is far less evidence to support the impact of Responding and Resisting, including schools throughout the United States and Europe. A powerful exception comes from the Horn of Africa.

In East Africa, including Kenya, Tanzania, and Uganda, reports suggest that abuse of children is high, with 56 percent having been physically abused, 36 percent emotionally abused, and 9 percent sexually abused.[19] The irony, given the focus of this section on schools, is that teachers contribute to the physical and emotional abuse of children, despite the fact that corporal punishment is legally forbidden in all contexts in Kenya, and legally forbidden in schools in Uganda; Tanzania remains legally uncommitted, with no official ban in schools. It is with this backdrop that the efforts of Raising Voices, a Ugandan nongovernmental organization, stand out.[20]

The Ministry of Education and Sports in Uganda made corporal punishment in schools illegal in 2016. However, research in schools by Raising Voices showed that 90 percent of children eleven to fourteen years old reported physical violence, 88 percent reported being caned—hit by a stick—and 8 percent reported being burned, choked, or cut. To address this violence, Raising Voices developed the Good School Toolkit (GST), an evidence-based approach to changing school culture that directly engages with stakeholders—teachers, students, education officials, parents, and community members. The GST is implemented over a period of about eighteen months and involves trainings and activities around the conditions for healthy learning and development, the importance of teacher-student relationships, positive student engagement, positive discipline instead of violence, and the cultivation of safe, nurturing, learning environments that can be celebrated and passed on to future generations. All of these trainings are accompanied by data collection systems that establish the starting point or baseline for all stakeholders and then continue to track changes in actual violence, perceived safety and well-being, and direct engagement in school activities. To assess the direct impact of these interventions, Raising Voices compared schools who received GST with schools who didn't, but were on a wait list.

Schools using Raising Voices' GST approach showed a 42 percent decrease in violence by staff toward students. Compared to control schools, where 41 percent of students reported being caned, only 23 percent of GST students reported caning. Though the GST approach didn't completely eliminate violence by teachers toward students, the severity and frequency of injuries was greatly reduced, including a significant decrease for students with disabilities, who are often—globally—disproportionately targeted. Students who were involved in GST schools were more engaged in creating rules for positive discipline, including the creation of student courts where peers evaluate and decide on consequences for misbehavior. In GST schools, there were also significant decreases in violence among peers and an increase in a sense of belonging to the school and safety, including increases in the perception of connectedness to teachers and other students. As an interesting side effect, parents whose children were in GST schools reported lower acceptance of physical and emotional abuse at home as a form of discipline, suggesting that interventions that directly include parents can have benefits outside of school.

Raising Voices' success in creating trauma-informed schools is due, in large part, to their emphasis on strong evidence, together with a focus on culture change, one that includes the direct involvement of students, teachers, school administrators, parents, and the local community. Culture change, especially when it entails historically entrenched beliefs about the consequences of misbehavior, can't be grounded in accusatory finger-wagging. Rather, culture change comes from providing alternative approaches such as forging respectful relationships, compassionate understanding of childhood adversity, and the use of positive discipline to promote change.

Though Raising Voices has been singularly focused on violence against children, similar trauma-informed approaches have been effectively implemented in schools and their communities to address other forms of childhood adversity, including children growing up in regions of intense conflict, displacement as refugees, poverty, neglect, and discrimination.[21] Where these approaches have fallen short is in seeing that different types of adversity, linked to the four other Adverse Ts, leave distinctive signatures on the child's developing body and brain, signatures that cry out for more customized interventions. One exception to this shortfall are interventions focused on self-control, most carried out in the United States and Europe. As I discussed in chapter 6, many different types of adversity, occurring early in development, can undermine the self-control system, leading to greater emotional dysregulation, greater focus on the present, a singular interest in immediate gratification, lower curiosity, and higher criminal convictions. These psychological transformations often manifest in a child's behavior in school, but there are methods to reverse them, which we will discuss in the next section.

CREATING HABITS OF MIND

Charlie had a hard time sitting still and an even harder time keeping his focus on the lesson. Whenever he wanted to say something, he just blurted it out, unable to raise his hand or wait for a turn. When his teacher asked him to wait, he blew a fuse, often resulting in a full-on tantrum with screaming, projectile insults, and property destruction. The source of Charlie's emotional dysregulation and inability to focus was a past and present that tormented him—a long tenure of emotional and physical neglect, home displacement, and parents with mental illness—made his environment highly turbulent. But Charlie was also brilliant, a hidden talent that was often covered up or accompanied by his emotional dysregulation and lack of attention. One class in particular illustrated Charlie's teeter-totter between talent and torment.

In the middle of a fourth-grade class on human nature, I asked the students to come up with an example of our uniqueness and to raise their hand when they had an answer. At the time, it wasn't clear to me that Charlie was listening, as he was looking around the room, out the window, and out the door. All of a sudden and before anyone raised a hand, Charlie literally leapt out of his chair and answered, "Sentience." My jaw dropped. Not quite sure of his answer, I asked him to clarify. "Did you say 'sentience' or 'sentence'?" Charlie rolled his eyes, flipped his desk over, and then exploded. "What the heck, Marc, why would I say 'sentence'? That's not even an answer?" Walking over to Charlie, trying to calm him down, I said, "My bad. You know I'm old and often don't hear well!" Charlie smiled, his body calming down. I then asked the class if anyone else knew what *sentience* meant. Crickets. I asked Charlie to explain. He stood up, started pacing, looked around the room, and then explained, "Well, okay, so sentience is the feeling of having an experience, of knowing what it's like to experience something. Like, I can know what it's like to be afraid, but you can't really know what my feelings are like. And I certainly can't know what it's like to be another animal." I then asked Charlie where he learned about sentience. Staring out the window, Charlie answered, "YouTube, of course, and those guys who I think are philosophers or scientists, Dennett, Block, Pinker, and Chalmers." My jaw dropped farther as Charlie pounced: "What's the matter, Marc, haven't you listened to those guys?"

For Charlie, like many other school-age children who are emotionally dysregulated, impulsive, and inattentive, the difficulty starts with poor self-control. As discussed in chapter 6, weaker self-control in early childhood is predictive of poor success in adulthood, including measures of wealth, health, education, and crime. For decades, it was believed that self-control could be strengthened like a muscle. Unfortunately, there has been little evidence to support this perspective, and striking evidence that those who appear to be in control actually have developed work-around strategies to avoid using self-control, including creating habits of mind.[22]

One particularly effective habit of mind is called *mental contrasting with implementation intentions*, or less formally *WOOP*, for *Wish-Outcome-Obstacle-Plan*, developed by social psychologists Peter Gollwitzer and Gabriele Oettingen.[23] Mental contrasting involves thinking of a desirable future goal or wish, along with potential obstacles. Implementation intentions are IF-THEN plans, designed to achieve the wish or future outcome. The IF sets up the situation, whereas the THEN determines the desirable response. For example, Charlie had two wishes—to be less fidgety and distracted, and less volatile when upset. Charlie identified potential obstacles, including his difficulty sitting still and his frustration with peers. We then helped Charlie turn these wishes and obstacles into two IF-THEN plans: IF I'm fidgeting, THEN ask to go on a walk with staff; and IF I'm frustrated with a peer,

THEN close my eyes and start deep breathing. Once the plans are created, they must be repeated like a daily mantra so that they become habits of the mind. Perceiving the IF situation literally triggers, like a reflex, the THEN action—for Charlie, fidgeting triggered a request to go for a walk, and frustration triggered deep breathing. Evidence from schools shows that IF-THEN plans work for children who are challenged by emotional dysregulation and attention deficits.

Developmental psychologist Angela Duckworth and her colleagues designed a study to close the academic achievement gap often associated with children experiencing the adversities of low SES environments—neglect, poverty—by using the WOOP approach. Each student practiced mental contrasting to establish positive thoughts about the future and possible hurdles that might get in the way of achieving them. Next, they created IF-THEN plans to establish when and where to leap over these hurdles. The entire WOOP training only required three hours, and no special resources, making it highly effective and scalable. Results showed that children who went through this training ended up with better grades, higher attendance, and lower behavioral conduct problems than control children who only thought about their positive wishes.

To help children with attention deficits and emotional dysregulation, psychologist Caterina Gawrilow and her colleagues carried out a series of WOOP experiments with children ages eight to fourteen years old.[24] In one experiment, children with attention deficit hyperactivity disorder (ADHD) played a computerized game where they had to tap a key in response to pictures of animals or transportation vehicles, but hold back the tap when a sound preceded these same images: this is a classic Go/No Go psychology experiment that requires both attention and self-control. Before playing the game, one group of children rehearsed the goal statement, "I will not press a key for pictures that have a sound." The other group rehearsed an IF-THEN plan of "IF I hear a tone, THEN I will not press a key." Results showed that individuals who formed IF-THEN plans performed better than children who formed goals, and those with more severe ADHD benefited more from the IF-THEN plan than those with less severe ADHD.

In a second experiment by Gawrilow and colleagues, children with ADHD either worked for two weeks on their learning styles (e.g., how well they learn in visual or auditory modalities)[25] or worked on learning styles while also creating WOOPs for particularly meaningful, challenging, and attainable goals. Students who used WOOP were rated by their parents as more competent with school activities and as more self-regulated, especially for those with more severe ADHD.

WOOPing effectively helps with self-regulation, especially when children have time to practice their IF-THEN plans, modifying them over time, supported by teachers and counselors in school, as well as parents and therapists outside of school.

Before my class on human uniqueness ended, I saw Charlie close his eyes and whisper to himself, "If I'm frustrated, then breathe."

TECHNIQUES FOR
CALMING IN RESPONSE TO STRESS

Frank was a teenager in a class of mine a few years ago. He had been physically and emotionally abused by his father, lived in a rough part of town, and had a hefty criminal record involving assault and robbery. The class I'd designed was called *Think It*, and it was focused on critical thinking and, in particular, helping students like Frank who are often impulsive and impatient to slow down and reflect. We were discussing the nature of right and wrong, and I introduced the idea of a moral dilemma by presenting a pair of classic runaway trolley problems: one in which a bystander can flip a switch to turn the trolley away from five hikers and onto one hiker, and a second case in which the bystander can push one innocent hiker in front of the trolley, thereby saving the five other hikers. As I was about to ask the students for their judgments of these cases, Frank flipped his desk and stormed out. I froze, not knowing what to do. One of the students in the class piped up, "Dude, that wasn't a good choice. Frank's best friend just died on a train track."

I felt horrible. I walked out of the classroom to speak with Frank, who was sitting with his school counselor in a quietly lit room, on the couch, doing meditative breath work to calm down. I apologized for my poor choice of examples and his terrible loss. He shrugged. I told him that when he was ready, I would be pleased to have him back, but to take all the time he needed to feel okay.

I tried to process Frank's experience and my unintentional re-traumatizing him. I had just accidentally violated the Resisting component of trauma-informed care. I tried to think about the fact that children who live in communities with violence and loss—two types of ACEs—not only live with chronic stress, but the acute stress of daily adversity derails performance in school. Experiencing community violence disrupts sleep, worsens encoding, retrieval, and updating of information, and significantly reduces attention and self-control.[26] Not only would this put Frank in a difficult position to return to my class, but to be in class more generally. I knew that other students who knew about Frank's friend would also be affected, and that they were experiencing comparable kinds of adversity as well.

Halfway through the class, Frank walked back in, sat down, and stared at me. He seemed poised to speak and so I asked him, "Frank, something you want to share?" With little hesitation, he erupted, "Yeah, I have something to share. What's moral about my best friend getting whacked by a train? What's moral about him being homeless? What's moral about him not having any support from his parents? That's all morally fucked-up." We all froze, mesmerized by Frank's comment. In the calmest way I could, I replied, "You're right Frank. There's nothing fair or right or just about what happened to your friend. It is morally fucked-up." I wanted Frank to experience my empathy mindset, despite the inappropriateness of my using the F-bomb.

It's important for educators to be aware of how stress, that may be carried into the school from home or triggered by experiences in school, can alter the ability of children to learn. To appreciate how acute stress plays into a child's learning in school, consider the figure opposite, illustrating how different stages of learning and memory unfold in relation to the timing of stressful events. In the best of all possible worlds, a child is exposed to new material—the alphabet, order of operations in math, social norms in school—and encodes it into memory, sleeps on it for consolidation into long-term memory, retrieves it at a later date when it is needed, and then updates the memory as new, relevant material is provided.

In the real, messy world, stressful experiences intrude on this process. A stressful event that occurs well before new material is introduced, such as Frank's experience of losing a friend to a train accident, would interfere with encoding, such as the lesson on moral reasoning I introduced. However, and somewhat counterintuitively, sometimes stress actually helps learning. If a stressful event occurs right before encoding—let's say a child is triggered by a male substitute teacher who looks like his abusive father right before he teaches a lesson—the encoding of new information might be strengthened because it binds to a strong emotion. Similarly, a stressful experience that occurs prior to consolidation could also enhance what learning takes hold. However, if the stress occurs before retrieval and updating—like, before a child takes a test—it will derail these memory systems. Educators must therefore be vigilant to the experiences of children prior to, during, and after school, while also equipping children with the tools to cope with stress.

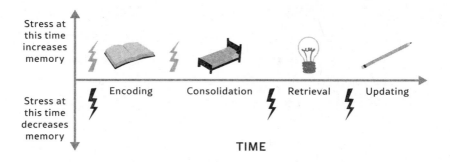

Over the past decade or so, schools around the world have integrated techniques for calming the body and brain, borrowing directly from different meditative practices that focus on increasing body awareness. Meditative practices are ideally suited for coping with emotional dysregulation and attention because they are designed to lower heart rate and heart rate variability, help us gain sensitivity to our patterns of breathing, increase our ability to focus attention on different parts of our body as well as different thoughts, and fine-tune our attention and our ability to understand our body's signals. In studies of adults, it is well known that meditative practices that focus on staying present in the here and now significantly reduce inflammatory biomarkers of earlier adversity, a form of erasure that we will dig into in the next chapter.[27] For children ages five to eighteen years, meta-analyses of multiple schools and thousands of children reveal that breathing awareness (noticing how heavy or fast it is), body scans (closing one's eyes and traveling across the body, stopping at key landmarks such as feet, lap, stomach, chest, shoulders, etc.), meditation, and mindful movement improve social-emotional well-being and academic performance, reduce stress, lower conduct problems, improve grades and attendance, and decrease mental health symptoms.[28] And the beauty of these approaches is that they require few resources, relatively short training, and can be used during any phase of learning and memory. For example, a child who experienced a highly stressful event, such as the loss of a friend, a couple of days before listening to a new math lesson, could be coached to use breathing to calm down along with focused attention on the here and now, including the task at hand. Or if a child like Charlie, who we met in the last section, arrived in school without breakfast or after a poor night's sleep due to being in a new home, he could be taken to a calming room, given the chance to close his eyes, gain awareness of his body and breathing, and given a meal to stop his hunger—all before being asked to take a test, where retrieval is key. These coping strategies are lifelong partners on the road to recovery.

The *Think It* class with Frank came to an end. Before he graduated, I had the chance to talk with him, but it was just after he had returned from being convicted for robbery. He was wearing an ankle bracelet, monitored by the local police. I wanted to talk with him about his postgraduation plans, so I asked, "If you could have any job, any career, what would it be?" Frank looked at me and responded, "Oh, I don't know, perhaps something at Walmart, stacking boxes in the warehouse." I was shocked, and I tried to model some ideas for him, but it was clear that it wasn't registering. Frank didn't want to play the what-if game about his future. Or perhaps, Frank couldn't play the what-if game. Frank's history of abuse, poverty, and family dysfunction had either obliterated his ability to imagine or shoved it into hibernation. Equally unsurprising was Frank's apathetic attitude about cognitive behavioral therapy and exposure therapy, approaches that rely on imagination.[29] Frank often dissociated to avoid the unbearable pain of the past and its reach into the present, and at that point, he seemed unable to reimagine a new life for himself.

I ran into Frank when he became a teller in a bank, several years after he had graduated. He was wearing a dress shirt and tie. Seeing me in line, he got up and came out to greet me with a hefty handshake and hug. We talked for a bit about what he had been doing since graduating from high school. Frank explained that he had finished a college degree at the local community college, focusing on business. Before I left he sent me off with a comment that I will never forget: "You remember all that calming stuff you guys taught me in school? That helped a lot, but even more important was that it allowed me to imagine a bigger what-if. Thanks, man."

EMPOWERING TRAUMA-SENSITIVE TEACHERS

As I mentioned earlier on in this section, for many children living with adversity, the Adverse T of turbulence brings with it uncertainty about food, shelter, caretaking, and abuse—uncertainty that takes away control and adds significant stress. When schools work well for such children, they provide predictability on all fronts, especially the social front. For many students, perhaps especially those with emotional disabilities that arise due to ACEs, predictable relationships with teachers and other school staff are essential.[30] It is for this reason that programs like Teach for America that place teachers for a couple of years in a school before moving them on, or nonprofit organizations that take short-term volunteers are, unfortunately, unhelpful because they add to the child's uncertainty. Just when a child develops a relationship with a trusted staff member, they leave. Or if they know that staff rotate in and out of a program, then they never attach in the first place. Teacher turnover is natural, but when the rotation cycle is too rapid—say a few weeks or even months—it eliminates the role of stability and predictability that schools can provide. For this reason, there needs to be significant public and private investment in schools to support teachers in their work while also contributing to wellness programs for teachers given the difficulty that working in a trauma-informed school presents.

When COVID-19 consumed the globe, and children were forced to stay at home, many government-run family services reported a substantial decrease in cases of abuse and neglect. This wasn't due to a decrease in cases, but rather, a decrease in vigilance from teachers who know their students and know when something is off. At the same time, hospitals reported an increase in mental health crises, especially for adolescents.[31] Without the social fabric of a school, teenagers were not only deprived of a biological need that is satisfied by their friends and teachers, but were often living their adversities day in and day out without any break.

In many parts of the world, including the United States, educators working in schools with children who have experienced adversities are underpaid, overworked, highly stressed, and underappreciated. COVID-19 pushed many educators over the edge, with little recognition of how taxing it is to their empathy and compassion, day after day. If we are going to empower schools to help our most vulnerable, governments will have to do better to provide them the needed resources, support, and appreciation that they deserve. Part of this support must include improved training around how adversity gets under a child's skin, including the Adverse Ts, especially since many trauma-informed programs have failed to make an impact because of insufficiently precise interventions.[32] It must also include empowering teachers to use these insights to strengthen resilience and provide the tools to recover from adversity.

Teachers provide eyes on children, acting as witnesses to signs of adversity on the home front, including signs of abuse, neglect, and family dysfunction. Schools offer food and shelter for children living in poverty. Teachers can build trust and confidence in their students by giving them stable, predictable relationships. Schools furnish students with skills to manage emotions, calm stress, strengthen memory, and believe in growth. Sometimes, schools—in consultation with parents or other caretakers—recruit outside therapies because a child's response to adversity is so severe that standard treatments fail. These supplementary treatments may include promising new technologies that can actually erase the traumas from their past. In the next chapter, we meet these supplements.

Neuroengineering: The Transformation of Maladaptive Thoughts

ionna was aggressively erasing her drawing. She wasn't happy with the color or style of the little girl's hair. She wasn't happy with the shape of the mother's eyes or where she was looking. She wasn't happy with the size of the bear. She wasn't happy most of the time. If only Fionna could have used her eraser to magically wipe away the past eleven years of her life.

Fionna had been repeatedly raped by her father. Her mother was bipolar, often drunk or stoned. Fionna's mother was the only caretaker at home, as her father left when she was nine. Many of Fionna's ACEs occurred during critical stages of language development—the acquisition of social thinking, emotional awareness, and the core executive functions. Some of these experiences, such as her history of sexual abuse and living in a dysfunctional home environment, were long in tenure and highly toxic and turbulent.

Fionna was often checked out of the real world, inhabiting a dissociative state in which her body felt separated from her brain, a feeling of unrecognizable identity, clinically a dissociative identity disorder.[1] The bear in the picture was imaginary, her friend, her confidant, her defender. She often rolled her eyes up and then spoke to her bear friend, indirectly letting us in on her pain and sadness. When she wasn't engaged in imaginary play, she was either limp and tuned out or hyper, unable to sit still, body twitching, eyes darting, breath heaving. Few of the standard school approaches, including the WOOPing and breathing techniques I noted in the last chapter, enticed Fionna to engage or calm down. She needed a different approach.

We learned in chapter 5 that women who were sexually abused as children, especially before puberty, have smaller somatosensory areas associated with the clitoris. The body and brain manage the ledger. Similarly, research shows we can think of our bodies as a kind of heat map for our emotions: brilliant reds, oranges, and yellows show activity in highly triggered areas and cool blues represent areas that are deactivated. Studies by psychologist Lauri Nummenmaa indicate that the heat maps for different emotions are consistent across cultures, suggesting a universal code.[2] Though studies of these maps come from healthy individuals, they show that when we are angry, our bodies are hot from the waist up, and especially hot in our jaws and mouth as well as our hands—we have a fighting stance. There are also some hot spots in our feet. Fear, a common response to abuse, is hot right up the middle of our bodies, with less heat in the hands than for aggression, and again, some activity in our feet, presumably so that we can be ready for escape. On the other side of the heat map scale is depression, where the body is effectively shut down, revealed by the cool blues throughout. Things heat up again in the center of the body, from the waist up, when we experience anxiety and shame, the latter being a core emotional response to sexual abuse. Interestingly, for shame, the forearms, hands, waist, and legs are all cool blues to black, revealing that they are shut down, turned off, which is characteristic of the tonic immobility associated with sexual abuse that we discussed in chapter 5.

In a somewhat different approach to mapping how the body keeps its own ledger, clinical psychologist Aline Zoldbrod asked childhood sexual abuse survivors to indicate where on their bodies they could be touched (green), perhaps could be touched depending on the situation (yellow), and definitely could not be touched (red).[3] Both men and women colored the genital areas red, some from their waist down to their knees, and many used red around their lips or the entire head. As Zoldbrod remarked, body maps such as these can be used to explore how different therapeutic approaches might transform the body's pathological responses to sexual abuse, effectively erasing the reds and yellows where appropriate and replacing them with green.

Fionna had good reasons to want to erase everything. Like many children who have suffered from sexual abuse, as well as other types of adversity, she wanted to dissolve the past. Unfortunately, her attempts to erase her history were as incomplete as her attempts to get rid of parts of her drawings. Fionna was dissociated, her sense of self fragmented—broken shards of memory, perception, emotion, and body awareness.[4]

Fionna, like many children who express TRACEs such as dissociation and emotional dysregulation, was in therapy and on medication. Therapeutically, she was engaged in a combination of cognitive behavioral therapy, which typically focuses on how to recognize and modify problematic patterns of thinking and behaving, and dialectical behavioral therapy, where the focus is on emotional regulation and navigating interpersonal relationships. In terms of medication, Fionna was taking Abilify and Concerta to try and tamp down her aggression and tantrums, and help her attention and focus. But for Fionna, like many other children, perhaps especially those with developmental trauma disorder, therapy and medication wasn't sufficient. As clinicians Joseph

Spinazzola and Bessel van der Kolk wrote in 2020: "Children with developmental trauma rarely have a satisfactory response to currently available evidence-based psychotherapeutic and pharmacological treatments."[5] The good news is that there are treatments that provide more satisfactory responses. Some involve biofeedback—nudging the signals of body and brain toward a healthier state of functioning. Other treatments involve directly altering brain activity—zapping underdeveloped or damaged circuitry to bring it up to speed. And yet other interventions involve directly changing the neurochemistry of the brain—using psychedelics with therapeutic support to open the mind to alternative ways of thinking and being. Many of these approaches are new, with tantalizing results that await more robust confirmation. Some are only effective in specific populations. Some are restricted, thus far, to adults. Several of these techniques are radical and controversial, but all point to more hopeful roads to recovery.

NUDGING THROUGH BIOFEEDBACK

When our youngest daughter, Sofia, was in her early teens, we often provided her with two options when it came to certain household chores or other responsibilities, such as going to bed at a reasonable time or turning off her iPhone at dinner. Giving her two options provided her with a sense of agency, the ability to freely choose. But we always designed our options so that one was far more attractive than the other. For example, Sofia could either finish her homework or clean the toilet and shower. She could either turn off her iPhone at dinner or clear the table and do the dishes after we finished eating. Sofia always had a choice, but we designed the choice space with a bias in our favor— biased toward what we believed were the healthier and more positive choices with respect to core values. In the words of behavioral economists Richard Thaler and Cass Sunstein, we were *nudging* Sofia to make the right choice.[6]

Biofeedback is a form of nudging in which the individual's body and brain are guided toward an alternative way of responding—of making healthier choices. Though different forms of biofeedback have been in existence for more than seventy-five years, it has enjoyed a renaissance within the past decade or so due to extraordinary technical advances in imaging autonomic and central nervous systems along with deeper understanding of how the brain and body are altered by adversity and mental health problems.

In the earlier chapters, I discussed the important work of Stephen Porges and his polyvagal theory. A key component of this theory is the idea that in highly social mammals, including us, the vagal nerve evolved as a critical component of the parasympathetic nervous system, and it is active when we are in a relaxed social state, taking care of others as well as ourselves. The vagus is directly involved in regulating heart rate. Like anything with a beat or rhythm, the heartbeat falls within certain frequency ranges. High-frequency beats are associated with parasympathetic activity, and thus represent control by the vagus nerve. Differences in duration between heartbeats is called heart rate variability. The measure we are interested in, because it maps onto different emotional states, is high-frequency heart rate variability, or HFHRV. When we are stressed, HFHRV is low. When we are calm and socially engaged, HFHRV is high. More social mammals, such as wolves, dogs, and nonhuman primates, have higher HFHRV than asocial mammals such as cats. Domesticated animals have higher HFHRV than their wild types—think dogs versus wolves. People who are depressed or angry—and thus clearly not in a social mood—have lower HFHRV. Autistic people, who often have a different perspective toward social interactions than non-autistic people, including less empathy and awareness of others' beliefs and desires, have lower HFHRV.

Altogether, this points to the fundamental role of the vagus nerve in social engagement, in part by means of its role in regulating heart rate variability.[7] And it suggests that if we can nudge up the HFHRV of victims of adverse experiences who are emotionally dysregulated and socially isolated, then we may be able to create a path to healing.

Decades ago, psychologists and clinical scientists used electrocardiograms linked to a monitor to show people what their personalized HFHRV looked like. Today, there are apps for that, including ones for your smartphone or watch.[8] By matching your breathing to a visual of high HFHRV, you can nudge your vagus to change its regulation of your heart so that you experience greater calm, lower stress, and more stable social engagement.

Social neuroscientist Tania Singer, who has long been interested in understanding how empathy, compassion, and other-oriented processes work at the level of the body and brain, set out with her colleagues to determine if they could manipulate the vagus to nudge heightened HFHRV, and then maintain this state even after the nudging stopped.[9] In this way, she was looking at the creation of habits of the mind, helping people reach greater calm and social well-being.

All of Singer's subjects, who were healthy adults, watched as an animated ball on a screen, linked to a direct readout of HFHRV, bobbed up and down. Singer only told subjects to keep the ball up high as much as possible, but not how to do this—if they kept the ball up, their HFHRV was high. To prepare, subjects spent three months in some kind of training. One group learned a meditative training involving body scans and controlled breathing. Another group experienced a meditative training focusing on social and emotional competences such as compassion, gratitude, and kindness, which sometimes involved interacting with another person. The third group spent their training meditating about their own self-awareness and identity as well as others' perspectives, again while sometimes interacting with another person. The last group did not do anything special for three months—they were the control group. All three meditative groups focused on body awareness. The second two meditative groups focused on social interactions. In their work, all three meditative groups were, unconsciously, nudging their vagus nerve. The idea was that this practice would help them nudge the ball to bop higher in the screen exercise, and as a result have a higher HFHRV reading.

It worked. All three of Singer's meditative groups showed higher HFHRV than the control group. There was no difference between the three meditative groups—each kind of training powered up the regulatory action of the vagus. After three and six months, all three groups maintained their high HFHRV. Nine months later, however, the benefits disappeared. Vagus nudging with biofeedback thus has some staying power, but there are limits, at least with present techniques.

Singer observed another intriguing result, related to the fact that the vagus nerve is chock-full of oxytocin receptors.[10] We encountered oxytocin in chapter 6, where I reviewed Romain Nardou's experiments showing that mice treated with the psychedelic MDMA reopened the critical period for social engagement by means of increasing the flow of oxytocin from the nucleus accumbens, a key reward area of the brain. We also discussed oxytocin in chapter 6 in research by Ruth Feldman, showing that mothers with a particular variant of an oxytocin gene had children who were more resilient to the travesties of war. In Singer's work with biofeedback and meditation, results suggested that individuals with a genetic variant associated with lower oxytocin initially had lower vagal control over heart rate variability, or lower HFHRV. But through biofeedback training, these individuals compensated for their initial deficit, a nudge that ramped up HFHRV to the level of those with the higher oxytocin variant. Given that early childhood adversity is associated with lower levels of circulating oxytocin,[11] introducing heart rate biofeedback is a hopeful nudge.

Considering the potential staying power of a biofeedback nudge to increase HFHRV, it is necessary to consider how other approaches might both take advantage of this window of opportunity and stretch it. Singer's experiment involved adults, but the same approach with children might result in longer staying power, depending on timing and the nature of adversities encountered. In addition, taking advantage of a six-month period when an individual is under greater emotional control, more social, and more calm might enable them—with the help of schools, communities, and therapy—to cement greater habits of control and become resilient to future stressors, thus enabling them to stay on the road to recovery.

A more direct approach to engineering change is a specific form of biofeedback called neurofeedback. Instead of nudging heart rate variability, neurofeedback involves observing and working to nudge brain activity, which the patient sees from EEGs with high temporal resolution, fMRIs with high spatial resolution, or a combination of both. Neurofeedback has proved particularly effective with stubbornly resistant stress disorders that often result from exposure to violence and abuse. And like biofeedback of cardiac activity, there are also commercially available devices to record and modify brain activity, an indication that such methods might soon be expanded on a large scale, helping low- and middle-income nations ramp up their efforts to treat mental health.[12]

Neurofeedback can work to target specific areas of the brain that have been impacted by adversity. As we learned in chapters 5 and 6, exposure to physical abuse, domestic violence, war, or community violence often results in a hyperactive amygdala and poor regulation from the frontal lobes. The level of hyperactivity of the amygdala is, in turn, associated with the severity of PTSD following exposure to adversity and, in many cases, can result in a kind of emotion blindness known as *alexithymia* in which the individual has difficulty identifying and expressing different types of feelings. This includes an inability to understand the relationship between facial expressions and emotions, having a hypersensitivity to physical sensations linked to emotions, a limited ability to explain what causes feelings, rigid imagination and perspective taking, and an aloofness to social relationships.[13] From these observations, it follows that if we can help children calm their amygdala as a protection against future adversity or reduce its activity following adversity, we can greatly diminish their suffering.

To determine if neurofeedback might help individuals effectively calm their amygdala, neuroscientist Jackob Keynan and his colleagues designed a study focused on young adults following a highly stressful military training program.[14] To provide neurofeedback, they used the readout from an EEG centered on the amygdala, otherwise known as amygdala electrical fingerprinting feedback. One group received feedback targeting the amygdala, another group received traditional neurofeedback that did not target a specific brain region, and the control group didn't receive any feedback at all. Over the course of six sessions, subjects in all three groups increased their emotions by watching a fairly intense hospital emergency scene with people protesting at the counter. Within each session, the two neurofeedback groups alternated between an *attend* and a *regulate* period. During attend periods, subjects were told that their own brain activity had no impact on the people protesting, so they were simply passive observers. During regulate periods, subjects were told that because their own brain activity was linked to the protesters, any calming mental strategy they developed would cause the protesters to sit down and stop protesting.

At the end of these neurofeedback sessions, both groups also received a session in which they were told to look at a cross on the monitor and try to use the same calming strategies that were effective during the hospital scene, without the help of the feedback. In the last part of the study, Keynan presented all three groups with two tasks, one involving memory retrieval and one involving emotional self-control, and they gave the subjects an alexithymia assessment.

Although both neurofeedback groups showed better emotional regulation, recognition, and processing than the controls, the individuals using amygdala neurofeedback showed significantly lower alexithymia and greater emotional self-control. Surprisingly, even though the frontal lobes were not targeted for neurofeedback in the amygdala group, these individuals showed stronger connections between the frontal lobes and the amygdala than the other groups. It is this neural bridge, in particular, that is essential for calming down a hyperactive amygdala. By nudging the fingerprint of activity from their amygdala, these individuals developed greater emotional control, greater emotional awareness, and greater resilience to future stressors.

Keynan and his colleagues then followed up this study with one using the same amygdala fingerprinting feedback, but this time with individuals suffering from clinically diagnosed PTSD.[15] In addition to watching the hospital emergency room scenario, the amygdala fingerprint group also watched a scenario that was directly related to their specific adverse experience. Being exposed to a visual of the adversity was designed to raise their emotion in a highly specific way, and thus provide them an opportunity to quell this response. Amygdala fingerprinting feedback resulted in the most significant decrease in symptoms of PTSD, and was also associated with significant calming of the amygdala.

The effectiveness of neurofeedback in treating adults who suffer from mental health problems cannot be debated. Insurance policies in many parts of the United States cover neurofeedback, especially targeting pain and attention disorder deficits. For children, the research on neurofeedback has focused mostly on ADHD.[16] Though there are many developmental pathways leading to ADHD, including a strong genetic component, there is a significant association with childhood abuse and neglect. There is also evidence that ADHD and conduct problems can occur hand in hand, and that this particular suite of externalizing behaviors is more often associated with abuse and neglect.[17] Several studies show that neurofeedback can reduce inattention and impulsivity in children with ADHD, sometimes more effectively than traditional medications such as Ritalin. It is thus imperative to add neurofeedback into the tool kits of parents and teachers to help reduce behaviors that may open a child up to increased victimization.

The research on neurofeedback and mental health issues in children is still developing. Joseph Spinazzola, Bessel van der Kolk, and their colleagues provided the first use of neurofeedback to treat children who were six to thirteen years old and suffering from developmental trauma disorder or complex trauma.[18] In addition to diagnoses of PTSD, these children also had other *DSM* diagnoses including attention disorder deficits, depression, anxiety, oppositional defiance, and conduct disorders. After two weekly sessions of neurofeedback over the course of twelve weeks, the children showed a significant decrease in PTSD symptoms as well as behavioral and emotional dysfunction. However, follow-up observations one month later revealed that these positive effects had dissipated. Just as there is a restricted window of opportunity for nudging heart rate variability, neurofeedback also has a limited time horizon, at least with the methods used in this study. Layering in more advanced neurofeedback methods, such as amygdala fingerprinting described earlier, may well help prolong its positive effects.

Biofeedback is a benign, relatively noninvasive approach to nudging our bodies and brain toward a healthier state and to boosting our resilience against future adversities. It has proven highly effective in situations where more traditional approaches, including different styles of therapy and medication, are ineffective.[19] Increasingly, there are off-the-shelf commercial devices that provide a low-cost way for a wider diversity of individuals to access the benefits of neurofeedback. Though some of these devices are limited in their effectiveness, including how long positive gains last, they hold out greater hope for children like Fionna. Fionna benefited from repeated neurofeedback, together with medication and cognitive behavioral therapy out of school, and dedicated teachers and counselors in school. Fionna's bear friend gradually faded from her drawings and conversations. A few years later, she graduated from high school, with several friends and a boyfriend, and started a nursing program.

ERASURE THROUGH BRAIN STIMULATION

In 2009, I had one of the most memorable public conversations of my life. I was onstage in Sydney, Australia, with His Holiness, the Dalai Lama. We were discussing the science of morality. After our public conversation ended, we went to lunch. I mentioned the gorgeous work that cognitive neuroscientist Liane Young—my graduate student at the time—had carried out with a technique called repetitive transcranial magnetic stimulation, or rTMS.[20] This technique uses a magnetic coil, shaped in a figure eight, to deliver rapid, repetitive, magnetic pulses to different parts of the brain, causing the targeted areas to go offline temporarily—in effect, a reversible lesion. Young used rTMS to turn off a part of the brain involved in representing our beliefs and intentions. When this area is turned off, and individuals think about moral dilemmas, they ignore what someone believes or intends, focusing strictly on the outcome. For example, if Bill intentionally sticks his foot out and trips John, or John accidentally trips over Bill's foot, from John's perspective there is no moral difference in why Bill's foot is placed where it is. The only thing that matters is that he fell and injured his face.

His Holiness thought about Young's brain stimulation results for a moment and then quietly replied: "I wonder if we could use this technique to change the Chinese perspective. Wouldn't that be nice—zapping for global change."

There is a long history of scientists who have tried to manipulate the electrical and chemical activity of the brain, both with good and evil intentions. The good intentions come from a desire to help people suffering from mental health issues. The idea is that if we can alter the electrical and chemical signals of a brain that is malfunctioning to reset them back to their default mode, then we can help people surmount their illness.

The media has, all too often, been less than helpful to the medical community by focusing on the visually horrific aspects of these treatments. In the movie *A Beautiful Mind*, brilliant game theorist John Nash undergoes insulin shock therapy for schizophrenia. It's terrifying to observe: Nash is strapped down in a hospital bed with bite sticks inserted into his mouth, while his body violently contorts. In *One Flew Over the Cuckoo's Nest*, McMurphy undergoes electroconvulsive shock therapy as punishment for his recalcitrant behavior. It's equally upsetting to watch, as McMurphy writhes in his bed, immobilized by his medical team. Such imagery has not only discouraged many patients to seek treatment, but it has painted a picture of rogue practitioners with Frankensteinian ambitions. Insulin shock therapy was designed with humane goals, but ultimately abandoned because of its side effects and inability to sustain positive change. The origins of electroconvulsive shock therapy were also well-intentioned, but it was halted for some time both because of its misuse and the lack of evidence supporting its efficaciousness. There are substantive ethical and policy issues here, ones that I will return to later in this chapter. But thanks to our growing understanding of brain function, especially how memories are formed, activated, and reorganized over time, both chemical and electrical treatments of mental health have gained increasing scientific support, guided by more rigorous ethical guidelines.

Many of the children I have worked with and discussed in earlier chapters illustrate the intrusiveness of memories associated with adverse experiences. Fionna and Leah often thought about their sexually abusive caretakers, and when they'd see men who looked like their perpetrators it would trigger the imagery and emotion they had attached to their abuse. Bolondemu and Badrick often thought about fighting and killing, and those thoughts and feelings were reactivated when they felt cornered or challenged. Tommy and Kevin often thought about being beaten by their fathers, and those memories would be reactivated by male teachers. Aliya often thought about her lack of food and caretakers in Sudan, which she'd remember when she saw a bounty of food in the cafeteria or witnessed loving parents who picked up their children from the bus. Adverse childhood experiences are embedded in memory networks that can be readily awakened, sometimes into conscious awareness, paralyzing some and revving up others. New technologies aim to erase or fade these memories.

Over several decades, scientists have developed noninvasive tools to suppress or enhance brain activity using both magnetic and electric currents called transcranial magnetic stimulation (TMS) and transcranial direct current stimulation (TDCS). Before stimulating an area of the brain, they use neuroimaging to map out anatomical landmarks. Establishing these landmarks is essential in guiding stimulation to the appropriate area. So what are the appropriate areas? In thinking about the traumatic responses to childhood adversity that I have discussed in this book, it seems clear that the circuitry driving emotions, self-control, and memory are prime targets. We also learned that a common traumatic reaction—especially in cases of abuse, domestic and community violence, and war—is the intrusiveness of memories, traces of the past that are disorganized, confusing, and debilitating. Several studies now show that brain stimulation, especially magnetic,[21] can minimize these relived experiences and reduce emotional dysregulation.

To understand whether the frequent replays of a horrific experience could be tamped down, cognitive neuroscientist Giuseppe di Pellegrino and his colleagues used a fear-conditioning approach—just like the ones used in mice—with healthy adults, who watched different images on a computer monitor.[22] Some images went by without anything happening, whereas others were associated with a shock. Evidence that subjects had learned the association between image and shock—and anticipatory fear of the shock in particular—came from measuring skin conductance, a measure of anticipatory sweating. Next, some subjects came back to di Pellegrino's lab a day later, and without warning, had their fear triggered by seeing the images again, then waited in silence for ten minutes. Afterward, they received fifteen minutes of repeated TMS (rTMS) to an area of the frontal lobes called the dorsolateral prefrontal cortex, which is known to be involved in emotion regulation, including modulation of the fear and threat response. The next day, they were presented with the same set of images as on day one—some were associated with a shock and some were neutral. If rTMS worked, the subjects would not have the anticipatory fear associated with shock images.

The results were incredible: rTMS to the dorsolateral prefrontal cortex decreased the anticipatory sweat response. As a result, the images previously associated with shock did not upset the participants at all. rTMS is an eraser when it comes to acquired fear memories, at least for healthy adults.

The intrusive memories that barge into our lives, whether they emanate from experiences of chronic or acute adversity, in childhood or adulthood, are often associated with powerful visual imagery. Bolondemu's experience of killing his brother with a machete and then bathing in his blood; Kevin's experience of competing for dinner with his sister, Joani, in the dog cage; Leah's experience of being repeatedly raped by her uncle; Tommy, balled up in a corner as his drunken father beat him, night after night; Nadine, surrounded by bombed-out buildings, dead bodies, frightened siblings—all gifts of war. Might rTMS erase the imagery of adversity, without erasing other details—what happened, who it happened to, when it happened?

Cognitive neuroscientist Noa Herz and her colleagues carried out an experiment to determine if rTMS could erase visual imagery.[23] Healthy adults lay down in a brain imaging scanner while Herz localized the tip of the calcarine fissure—an area of the visual cortex known to be involved in imagery. Then each subject watched a film with highly distressing content, including animal cruelty, self-injury, surgery, a car accident, an animal attacking a human, a person being stabbed, and a tooth extraction. Before and after watching the film they filled in a mood survey and responded to a visual memory recognition test using images from the film. For the next few days they also filled out a diary, recording any intrusive memories. On day two, subjects watched images from the film, and ten minutes later, some individuals received rTMS to the visual cortex and some received rTMS to a control area, outside the visual area. On day five, they received the visual memory recognition test again.

Herz's results reveal the power of visual imagery in intrusive memories of adversity and the power of rTMS to erase them. Individuals with a stronger connection between the visual cortex and the amygdala, the connection between imagery and emotion, showed more intense responses to the disturbing film images. As Herz notes, this may provide a biomarker of who is more vulnerable to experiencing pathological responses to adversity and who is more resilient. Individuals who received rTMS to the visual cortex experienced less emotionally intense intrusions than individuals who received rTMS to the control region, but the location of the magnetic coil had no impact on the ability to remember scenes from the disturbing film. Stimulating the visual cortex erased the disturbing emotional connection to the adverse experiences, but kept the who, what, when, and where of the memory intact.

Di Pellegrino's and Herz's rTMS results are joined by others targeting different parts of the circuitry underlying the trauma of adverse experiences, including the amygdala and hippocampus, as well as different populations, including adults with major depression disorder and PTSD, using different methods of stimulation.[24] Stimulating the amygdala can reduce the emotional intensity of previously threatening images or memories, thereby resulting in reduced symptoms of PTSD. Stimulating the hippocampus shows that this area of the brain is critically involved in not only memory retrieval but creative imagining. Recall from our earlier discussions the point made by many psychotherapists, including Bessel van der Kolk, that adverse experiences resulting in PTSD or developmental trauma can undermine imagining an alternative world. TMS to the hippocampus holds out hope of helping individuals who suffer from adversity to envision an alternative, more promising future.

Research using TMS with children is still in its infancy, especially children who have suffered from adverse experiences.[25] One reason for this is that it took time for scientists to confirm the safety of this method with less developed brains. A second reason is that imaging studies of infants have only just begun to localize functional brain regions, a critical first step in using TMS to nudge the brain to a different state.[26] With safety ensured and functional brain localizers in place, stimulating the brain to change in response to adversity can be added to the space of hopeful treatments for vulnerable children.

NEW HORIZONS FOR MEDICATION

When we are stressed by an experience, including the memory of the experience, adrenaline and other hormones are released from receptors located in the heart and muscles, causing our blood pressure to rise, our hearts to race, and our bodies to sweat. Medication can dull this impact, and the effects of beta-blockers are particularly promising. Beta-blockers block the impact of adrenaline, enabling blood pressure to drop and heart rate to slow down, effectively silencing the sympathetic nervous system to give voice to the parasympathetic nervous system. Beta-blockers have long been used in human and animal medicine to help individuals with high blood pressure or heart rhythm disorders. But they are also effective for people who are anxious or stressed, helping them to reach greater calm. Experimental studies of mice suggest that the drug propranolol, a beta-blocker, can interfere with both acquiring a fear response that is normally experienced when a tone is first paired with a foot shock—consolidation—and when the tone recurs to predict an impending foot shock—reconsolidation.[27] The idea is that propranolol may reduce the physiology of fear while the memory is in an alterable state. When reconsolidation occurs, the memory that is tucked back in has a weaker body signal—people experience a muted heartbeat, relaxed muscles, as well as a blurrier mental image and sensation of fear. In this way, propranolol may work like a molecular eraser.

Psychiatrist Alain Brunet was the first to explore the possibility that propranolol might help us erase the painful part of our memories, the part that creates pathology following adversity.[28] In the first experiment, people who were uninformed about the group they had been assigned to either swallowed propranolol, a placebo, or nothing at all, either before or after they looked at upsetting images associated with a story. To make sure that the story and its imagery evoked changes in body and brain, Brunet recorded heart rate, skin sweatiness, and facial muscles associated with different emotions.

As expected, the emotionally upsetting parts of the story caused changes in sweatiness and facial muscles in all subjects. This shows that the images and story were effective modulators of emotion for all participants. Also, as expected, those who took propranolol—whether it was given before consolidation or after—had a lower heart rate than those who took the placebo or nothing at all. This shows that propranolol is working as decades of medical research proves. But the critical effect of propranolol on memory depended upon timing. Swallowing propranolol right after learning and recall didn't impact memory consolidation or reconsolidation—it was like swallowing the placebo. But swallowing propranolol before learning and recall was associated with significantly weaker memory consolidation and reconsolidation. These promising results with healthy adults suggest that taking propranolol right after a traumatic experience or after significant recall of the experience may help sufferers of PTSD weaken future reconsolidation of their painfully traumatic memories—weakening their relived experiences of the past.

Brunet and his colleagues then turned to adults with chronic PTSD, randomly assigning them to either the propranolol or placebo treatment. Over the course of six visits, separated by one week, individuals first swallowed propranolol or the placebo, and then an hour later, wrote about their specific adverse experience, including what they considered traumatic and what they felt in their body—their own personal ledger of the score. Once they finished writing they read their narrative out loud to a therapist, with instructions to read as if they were experiencing the traumatic event. Over the course of the six weeks, each individual self-evaluated their own PTSD symptoms using a validated survey, and a trained clinician evaluated their PTSD symptoms.

Overall, propranolol was associated with a significantly lower self- and clinician-evaluated PTSD score than the placebo. This effect was not observed within the first two sessions, only from session three on, suggesting that the process of awakening and reconsolidating the memory of the adverse experience had to go through a few cycles before lowering the emotional intensity of the memory. For a smaller number of individuals who were seen six months after the propranolol treatment, but with no intervening treatment, PTSD symptoms remained lower than the placebo group. This suggests that propranolol may have an enduring therapeutic impact—the memory of the adverse experience isn't erased, but the emotional intensity associated with it is diminished. People are able to relive the trauma as an emotionally detached observer.

Brunet and his colleagues next turned their attention to Syrian refugees between seven and fourteen years old who were living through the horrors of war, including the adverse experiences of bombs, executions, and forced displacement from their homes. Like the study with adults who suffered from PTSD, the children first wrote about their adverse experiences, including what was traumatic to them and how their body responded. Unlike Brunet's laboratory studies of adults, however, this study was carried out in Syria, under less controlled field conditions, thereby limiting the intervention to only propranolol, with no placebo or control group. Also, many, if not most of the children were likely to have had complex PTSD or developmental trauma disorder—pathology that propranolol wasn't directly designed to address. All children received propranolol on five consecutive days, prior to reading their narrative about the adverse experiences of war, out loud, to a therapist.

One month after the propranolol treatment, the Syrian children showed a 37 percent decrease in PTSD symptoms, and by three months, the symptoms had dropped by 64 percent. These same children also showed a significant decrease in symptoms of depression and anxiety one month after propranolol treatment; symptoms of depression continued to lessen three months later, whereas anxiety increased—a change that was consistent with the turbulence of their living conditions, including uncertainty around food and shelter, as well as continued bombing.

Brunet's results, along with others, suggest that propranolol may provide relief from the intrusive and often debilitating memories that typify PTSD, including the reduction of fear and anxiety. Though we have much to learn about how propranolol works, including its effectiveness in relation to the Adverse Ts, it provides a promising solution for those who suffer from traumatic responses to adversity, one that can potentially be scaled up for use in remote parts of the world.[29]

Where some see hope with these new technologies, others see harm. Some worry that altering memory by using propranolol or rTMS will change a person's identity, destroying the continuous narrative that underwrites our individual lives. But our memories are constantly subjected to editorial revisions as part of their natural life cycle. Your memories of a vacation with family may shift as time passes, and may be different from what another loved one on that trip with you remembers. So revision, in and of itself, isn't necessarily harmful. When a child suffers from PTSD or DTD as a result of adverse experiences, the dissociative symptoms that commonly follow happen because a person's memories have been scrambled. Chemical and electrical interventions are in some cases like glue, putting the narrative pieces back together, and in other cases like an eraser, taking out unwanted storylines.

Some worry that propranolol or rTMS could be misused to erase knowledge of immoral, illegal, or criminal activity without seeking consent. This is a serious concern and is why regulatory policies are necessary. Before transcranial magnetic stimulation could be used for therapeutic treatment, it had to jump through a number of ethical, legal, medical, and scientific hoops, including experiments that were carried out by multiple investigators, in different, independent labs, using government funds to remove any bias that might come from commercial gains. When the Food and Drug Administration signed off on TMS for treatment, it only approved one device (i.e., the Neuronetics NeuroStar TMS), and only for individuals who were medication-resistant for depression. Neither propranolol nor transcranial direct current stimulation have yet jumped high enough to pass these gold star criteria, but the landscape is changing fast.

MIND EXPANSION THROUGH PSYCHEDELICS

I had just returned from following chimpanzees in the Kibale Forest when one of our Ugandan collaborators, John, rushed up to me, breathless, smiling, and anxious to tell me about his own observations. He had been following a big adult male who, while resting at the bottom of a Balanites tree, ate several ripe fruits. The Balanites fruit is about the size of a grapefruit and when they sit around on the ground for a while, ripen into alcohol. I don't know the actual conversion of Balanites to alcohol, but a good guess would be that our male chimp slugged down a good shot of whiskey. After finishing, he slowly lumbered up the tree to a large horizontal branch. Preparing for his siesta, he slowly put his elbow down and missed the branch completely, falling about ten feet to the ground below. Lying on his back, he looked up at the sky, unfazed by the fall, but clearly soused. Barely controlling his laughter, John remarked, "They're just like us—they drink, they fall down, no problem."

Chimpanzees and gorillas may well have been the first consumers of alcohol, though their original interest was unlikely to have been on attaining a buzz or some alternate state of reality. As the first apes to climb out of the trees and spend a significant amount of time on the ground, chimpanzees and gorillas were immediately exposed to low-hanging fruit, literally. But these fruits were high in fermented yeast and ethanol, requiring a novel digestive engine. Corresponding with their descent out of the trees, these apes evolved a unique version of alcohol dehydrogenase, an enzymatic engine that is forty times more efficient at metabolizing alcohol than the earlier monkey edition.[30] This opened the foraging landscape to nutritious edibles, but with a hidden punch, one that our species inherited and then revved up through the invention of technology. Armed with efficient means of extraction, *Homo bacchanaliensis* was poised to inhabit alternative realities, sometimes to hide pain.

People living in the Bossou region of Guinea, West Africa, place metal taps into palm trees, and then attach a bucket so that it can collect the fermented, alcohol-rich sap. Opportunistic chimpanzees have invented tools to tipple from the buckets—palm leaves inserted into fermented sap and then downed like a shot. For many, inebriation follows, an unsurprising response given that the alcohol content of the fermented sap is anywhere between 3 and 7 percent. Because this is pure liquid consumption, with no fruit intermediate, it is more likely that chimpanzees are attracted to it for its hidden psychological punch—an alternate reality. From the chimpanzees' perspective, the Guineans have offered free rounds.[31]

Chimpanzees, and many other animals, also ingest plants as a means of self-medication. Here, the primary function is to counteract the impact of parasites or cope with digestive problems. In parallel with chimpanzees co-opting human ingenuity to scale up alcohol extraction from palm trees, we have co-opted animal ingenuity for self-medication.[32] Indigenous populations have—and still do—take advantage of animal discoveries to treat their own ills, specifically those of the body. But here is where the similarity ends. We uniquely tapped into the plant world to self-medicate for purposes of mental health, enabling us to go where no mind has gone before. And as for alcohol, we have revved up our access to mind-altering ingredients by inventing technologies for mass production, including the synthesis of novel variants. These ingredients are psychedelics, the users are psychonauts, and the universes of exploration are hidden dimensions of the ego and the mystical.

Psychedelics—derived from the ancient Greek words *psykhē*, meaning "soul," and *dēloun*, meaning "to make visible or reveal"—take the human mind into alternate realities, opening doors to fragments of our past, present, and future that can be frightening, exhilarating, and liberating. Frightening because psychedelics shine a spotlight on toxic memories and distasteful aspects of our character that have been in hibernation. Exhilarating because psychedelics inspire hyperconnectivity between brain areas that have rarely communicated, while reducing the pathological inflammatory responses that come from chronic adversity and stress. Liberating because psychedelics can empower individuals to move beyond the suffocation of adversity and into a deserved life that is healthy, joyous, and meaningful.

Some of you may be approaching this section with caution, aware of the tumultuous, moral panic history of psychedelics, which were touted as revolutionary agents of positive change in the 1960s and then soon after slammed and banned as agents of evil transformation.[33] Others may be approaching this section with enthusiasm, bolstered by recent headlines in the popular press, along with the eloquent and passionate defense of psychedelics in Michael Pollan's books *How to Change Your Mind* and *This Is Your Mind on Plants*. Both caution and enthusiasm are warranted. On the positive side, scientific evidence for the transformative impact of psychedelics on body and brain are growing; US and European governments have approved the use of some psychedelics for some medical conditions; some people with treatment-resistant PTSD and depression have taken psychedelics and emerged from years living under dark clouds. But, on the other hand, we still don't have the full picture when it comes to the research and there are significant commercial interests in marketing psychedelics, for both recreational and medical use, leading to conflicts of interest between scientists, doctors, insurance companies, and stock-ready corporations.

DMT is one of the psychedelics now getting a lot of attention. In 2019, while archaeologist Melanie Miller was digging in a cave in Bolivia, one inhabited by our species at least four thousand years ago, she uncovered a pouch made of three fox snouts.[34] Unsure of the pouch's function, she returned to her lab, put the pouch through mass spectrometry, and awaited its chemical analysis. The results were mind-blowing. Not only did Miller's analyses reveal that the pouch had been used to carry plant material, but it contained five psychoactive plants including harmaline and dimethyltryptamine (DMT). When brewed, the vines from the caapi plant release harmaline, whereas the leaves of the chacruna shrub release DMT, combining together to create the Amazonian brew ayahuasca—which means "vine of the soul" in the Quechua language. For millennia, ayahuasca has been used by natives of the Amazon to create vivid hallucinations and out-of-body experiences, including the ability to transform into an animal to reach the supernatural. Within the last five years, ayahuasca—and DMT on its own—have been used in scientific experiments to determine how they impact the body and brain, and how they might be used for therapeutic purposes.

DMT is naturally found in more than fifty plant species but, when ingested on its own, has no psychoactive properties because it is rapidly broken down by the monoamine oxidase (MAO) enzymes before reaching the blood-brain barrier. In chapter 7, I discussed the role of MAO in breaking down the neurotransmitter serotonin and the association between particular variants of the gene expressing MAO and both violence and self-control. Not deterred by this barrier, and perhaps motivated by it, several human cultures have developed snuffboxes and smoking methods to get DMT into the brain. Other cultures marry DMT with harmaline to create the ayahuasca brew, as harmaline blocks the effects of the MAO enzyme. All cultures that have used ayahuasca report, whether in ethnologies, brain imaging studies, or clinical investigations, that like many other psychedelics, ayahuasca opens the mind to novel ways of reexperiencing prior adversity, enables greater awareness of our beating heart, and reduces self-destructive rumination.

For many people, the experience of taking ayahuasca can be one of their most meaningful life experiences. When Amber reached her thirtieth birthday, she finally allowed herself to confront the painful memories of being sexually abused as a child. In some ways, this confrontation was liberating. For the next seven years, she tried various forms of therapy, meditation, and yoga. But none of these approaches helped her loosen the grip of sexual abuse. Amber still felt broken. A podcast gave her the inspiration and courage to travel to Costa Rica for an ayahuasca retreat. Though little happened on the first night, the floodgates opened on the second:

> *I realized in that moment the medicine had shown me who I had become, which was someone who felt they weren't worthy of love. . . . I pulled my heart out of my chest. . . . I asked the spirits to heal my heart. . . . It was the most beautiful experience of my life.*[35]

Amber's feeling of transformation is vivid and moving. But like many who have gone on ayahuasca retreats, we must be cautious in our interpretation of the transformation due to the potential biases, including the placebo effect—wanting to be better and believing that the treatment is working can make you think that you feel better, without the treatment playing any role at all. Fortunately, serious scientific studies have addressed these problems head-on.

At about the same time that Miller discovered the fox pouch with ayahuasca ingredients, a group of Brazilian researchers ran a double-blind, randomized control trial to test the impact of ayahuasca on patients with treatment-resistant depression—individuals, numbering close to one million globally, who suffer from chronic depression despite repeated attempts at erasure with standard medication and therapy.[36] The study was double-blind because both the investigators and the patients were kept in the dark with respect to who received ayahuasca and who received the placebo. The placebo was designed to look and taste like the ayahuasca brew—brownish, bitter, and sour—and to cause a similar, short-term, upset stomach, but without the psychoactive properties. As in all studies of psychedelics that use some form of psychotherapy, patients were first prepped by a trained therapist or guide who educated them about the rationale for the study and the procedure. Next, patients consumed the ayahuasca or placebo while sitting in a comfortable reclining chair, in a living room–type atmosphere, with calm lighting. During their experience with ayahuasca or the placebo, there were two trained guides available in case patients were in distress. To avoid any bias, these guides only spoke to the patients if asked questions, and in no case did they provide advice or comments about the patients' experience. During the final phase, initiated after the psychedelic experience had ended, patients discussed their experience and completed a clinically validated assessment of depression symptoms.

One dose of ayahuasca, when compared to the placebo, was sufficient to decrease symptoms of depression on day one, with further improvements on days two and seven. Even remission rates of depression were higher on day seven, with 36 percent for ayahuasca and 7 percent for the placebo. Though several patients felt some psychological distress and some nausea during the ayahuasca experience, these were short-lived. All patients felt safe, with no side effects to the body or brain. The sense of safety and lack of side effects is particularly important given the intensity of the ayahuasca experience.

The Brazilian team's experimental findings with ayahuasca, together with others using different doses and settings, provide encouragement for people suffering from depression. Though we do not yet know in detail how ayahuasca transforms body and brain, what we do know suggests that it tamps down the activity of the default mode network (DMN)—an area critical to our sense of self, our autobiographies, and hyperactive in people with depression—while increasing the connections between other areas of the brain, including areas involved in visual imagery and memory.[37] As we've learned from earlier chapters, these are brain areas that are commonly damaged by childhood adversities.

Perhaps our deepest understanding of the transformative power of naturally occurring psychedelics comes from mushrooms of the genus *Psilocybe*, with more than three hundred species popping up in wooded areas all over the world. The magic of these mushrooms is derived from psilocybin, which, when ingested, is converted by the body into the psychoactive ingredient psilocin. When psilocin binds to receptors in the cortex, the brain becomes very plastic, enabling people to open their minds to alternative ways of thinking and being.

Consumption of mushrooms for hallucinogenic experiences dates back to Mesoamerican cultures, some 3,500 years ago. Like ayahuasca, magic mushrooms have enjoyed promotion from both the under- and aboveground cultures, and coverage by Gwyneth Paltrow's Goop Lab team, *Newsweek*, *Rolling Stone* magazine, and the *New York Times*.[38] Scientific studies of the healing potential of psilocybin have also grown within the last ten years, peaking between 2020 and 2022 with an FDA designation as a breakthrough therapy for treatment-resistant depression.

In 2022, a team of neuroscientists and neuropharmacologists led by Richard Daws published the results of a remarkable study in the journal *Nature Medicine*.[39] The study involved two experimental interventions. The first was an open-label design, meaning everyone knew in advance what the medical intervention would be. Patients with treatment-resistant depression ingested two doses of psilocybin, each dose separated by seven days. Because patients knew, in advance, that they would take psilocybin, results must be treated somewhat cautiously due to the possibility that biased expectations may create false positives—a placebo effect. The second intervention, involving patients suffering from major depressive disorder, was a double-blind, randomized control trial—the gold standard in clinical research. One group received psilocybin and the other group received an active placebo control called escitalopram, an SSRI commonly used to treat depression and anxiety, but neither the patients nor the psychotherapists knew who was in each group. In both studies, researchers used functional magnetic resonance imaging to assess patterns of brain activation and, especially, potential changes in connectivity between different neural circuits before and after treatment.

Of particular interest to Daws and his team was the possibility that psilocybin, through its impact on serotonin receptors, would tamp down the hyperactive and dominant DMN that is a signature of depression, and rev up connectivity between previously subordinate networks. Such changes, if observed, would be consistent with the commonly reported sense of ego dissolution—a melting away of negative self-absorption and microscopic rumination—that is the signature of magic mushrooms and other psychedelics.

Patients in both studies experienced significantly fewer symptoms of depression within one to two weeks of ingesting psilocybin, a remarkably rapid change that persisted without additional psilocybin for up to six months in the open-label study and up to six weeks in the double-blind study. Though patients on escitalopram also experienced a decrease in symptoms of depression, the magnitude was far lower than for psilocybin. The improvement in depressive symptoms on psilocybin, but not escitalopram, was also associated with a silencing of the DMN's dominant voice and an amplification of otherwise subordinate networks and their connections, including the salience and executive networks. This seems to show that our neural universe before psilocybin is ruled by a dictator, but after psilocybin the power of that dictator is diminished, resulting in a more democratic voice.

Unlike the psychedelics ayahuasca and psilocybin that come from nature's pharmacy, MDMA—3,4-methylenedioxymethamphetamine—more commonly known as ecstasy or molly, comes from the laboratory's pharmacy. Unlike ayahuasca's and psilocybin's recreational use in retreats and spiritual experiences, MDMA has been part of the rave party scene. Part of MDMA's appeal to partygoers is its ability to loosen inhibitions and open social desires and attractions. As I discussed in chapter 7, neuroscientist Romain Nardou used MDMA to reopen a critical period for sociality in mice. Adult mice on MDMA become less shy and transform into youthful socialites, a process orchestrated by increases in serotonin and oxytocin. If partygoers and mice can experience greater sociality, more openness, and weaker inhibition, might this psychedelic work its magic on long-term sufferers of PTSD who are often shut down, afraid, stressed, and consumed by intrusive memories?

Rick Doblin, director of the Multidisciplinary Association for Psychedelic Studies (MAPS), and longtime activist for the scientific understanding and therapeutic use of psychedelics, set up a randomized, double-blind, placebo-controlled, phase 3 clinical trial using psychotherapy-assisted MDMA. The target: close to one hundred patients suffering from, on average, fourteen years of severe PTSD.[40] For individuals with severe PTSD, between 40 and 60 percent do not respond to the FDA-approved SSRIs sertraline and paroxetine, even when accompanied by therapy. For individuals with severe PTSD, many also suffer from childhood traumatic experiences, depression, dissociation, substance abuse, and suicidal ideation. As with other studies using psychedelics, Doblin's was randomized in the sense that patients were randomly assigned to the MDMA or placebo groups. It was double-blind in the sense that neither the patients nor the therapists were aware of who received MDMA and who received the placebo. It was considered phase 3 clinical because of prior clinical trials evaluated by the FDA, including the designation of MDMA as a breakthrough therapy. All patients first received therapy and a PTSD assessment, then three eight-hour sessions of psychotherapy-assisted MDMA or placebo over the course of eighteen weeks, as well as a post-treatment assessment.

Compared with the placebo, three doses of MDMA with therapy resulted in a significant drop in PTSD symptoms. This drop occurred irrespective of other comorbid mental health challenges, such as depression, anxiety, suicidal ideation, and dissociation, and irrespective of when the PTSD started (timing), its cause (type), and the individual's experience with SSRIs. By the end of the study, 67 percent of patients no longer met the *DSM-5* criteria for PTSD. Critically, especially given the FDA's evaluative oversight, there were no significant side effects. This means that three doses of therapy-assisted MDMA meets the gold standards for safe treatment of severe or complex PTSD.

The research on psychedelics is encouraging, but many unknowns remain. We have no idea how such psychedelics would or could work with children or adolescents. Also, current evidence suggests that the positive impact of psychedelics is at best up to six months. And the current sample of patients in these studies is both small and lacking in diversity, especially in terms of race, SES, nationality, age, and underlying causes of PTSD, depression, childhood trauma, and anxiety.[41] But there is renewed hope for long-term sufferers of severe PTSD. It is clear that psychedelics have the potential to not only turn off the derailing thoughts and emotions associated with traumatic experiences, but also reduce the inflammatory responses of the body's response to stress. Therapy-assisted psychedelic treatment is a cost-effective, scalable approach, one that can reach developing nations with few resources, including countries consumed by war and poverty.

The Way Forward: A Deserved Life

I will never forget Albert's smile, a sign of hope, a way forward for our most vulnerable.

Albert was left at the entrance to an orphanage in Kenya when he was about five years old. He was mute, depressed, filthy, emaciated, and barely able to walk. Without a way to recount his autobiography, and with no family, he had no name, no birth date, no history. By the time I met him, several months after he had arrived, he was clean, well-dressed, healthy, and had just started talking. When Albert smiled it was in response to my handing him his first cuddly stuffed animal, a hand puppet lion. Albert put it next to his face and said, "Simba," the Swahili word for lion. He carried Simba all day, into bed, and for weeks to come. Simba came to represent stability, predictability, comfort, and attachment—essential elements of a deserved life.

Albert's journey from birth to early childhood, like the journey of millions of other children all over the world, wasn't expected by the biology that he inherited from his ancestors, nor their ancestors, nor the generations of ancestors that preceded them back to the origins of our species. Young children don't expect to be abandoned, forced to fend for themselves for food, shelter, love, protection, and comfort. The extreme deprivation that Albert experienced early in life may have left him with permanent wounds, including challenges associating actions with consequences, be they positive or negative. Other wounds are beginning to heal thanks to his own grit together with caring allomothers from the children's home, teachers in the local school, doctors at the hospital, and a pastor from the nearby church. Albert's gritty nature and loving nurture have paved the way for recovery, back onto the path of a deserved life.

Albert's journey is a reminder of the reality of childhood adversity, the signatures of traumatic responses, the importance of individual resilience, and the critical role of caring cultures in enabling children to grow despite the stressors of their past. His journey is also a reminder that helping children build resilience and overcome trauma depends on understanding how adversity gets under their skin, recognizing the developmental signatures that emerge in response to different types of adversity, their timing, tenure, turbulence, and toxicity—the dimensions of the Adverse Ts.

What we have learned is that ACEs are not the province of any particular nation, gender, race, religion, level of wealth, or educational bona fides. ACEs are omnipresent. But the risks of experiencing ACEs increases for some children in some situations, such as children with disabilities and those with parents who have ACEs. We have also learned that an accumulation of ACEs before the age of eighteen years greatly increases the risks of physical and mental health problems, and that the earlier in life they occur, the more devastating their potential impact—damaging human health, culture, economics, education, and human thriving. Given this understanding, it should be clear to all nations that childhood adversity and traumatic injuries are the number one public health crisis, one that deserves the energy and expertise of an international army of doctors, scientists, social workers, therapists, educators, and policymakers. I believe there are at least six important pathways to help us move forward and create hope for future children.

The first pathway builds on the positive impact that the ACE score has had on policy in different countries, specifically, alerting public health workers to the potential risks to the child's developing body and brain.[1] Given the attention received, it is now time to inform policymakers as well as other professionals working with children about both the limits of the ACE score and the advances that have been made in deepening our understanding of the Adverse Ts, as well as individual differences that may result in traumatic or resilient responses to adversity. Though the nitty-gritty details of Albert's brief history on earth was unknown, his life out on the streets was associated with physical, emotional, social, and cognitive neglect, as well as poverty, loss of parents, home displacement, disease and, most likely, exposure to community violence. These different types of adversity hit Albert during critical periods of development, with a long and toxic tenure, entirely unpredictable and uncontrollable, impacting basic elements of language functioning, social processing, attachment, and physical growth. Albert's treatment involved talking and reading to him to reengage a dormant and muted language system, comforting him with caring and trustworthy peers and adults to build his social relationships and attachment, providing him with coping strategies and memory aids in school, and providing him with a stable home and predictable food to aid his growth, while reducing his insecurity and anxiety. This kind of treatment, underpinned by an understanding of the Adverse Ts and an appreciation of the different signatures of traumatic and resilient responses, is more likely to recruit the international army of professionals that can help children such as Albert, but also Leah, Tommy, Kevin, Aliya, Victoria, Bolondemu, Badrick, Serena, Sasha, Charlie, and Frank, each with different Adverse T profiles, each with different traumatic and resilient signatures.

The second pathway is to close the gap between scientific understanding and practice, working collaboratively with all professionals who are involved in child welfare.[2] As I discussed in the first two parts of the book, scientists have accumulated a wealth of knowledge concerning how childhood adversity transforms the developing body and brain. This knowledge must be fully integrated into coursework or trainings for developing and practicing professionals in medicine, education, counseling, social work, law, and policy. For example, though some legal cases have introduced adverse childhood experiences as potentially mitigating evidence for crimes including murder and substance abuse, there is an opportunity to educate lawyers and judges about how such experiences can undermine an individual's social thinking, moral sensibilities, language, and ability to link actions with consequences. Equipping legal experts with such knowledge ought to shift understanding of responsibility for a crime and liability for punishment. Closing the gap between scientific understanding and practice will require the creation and dissemination of a trauma-informed curriculum that enables doctors, teachers, counselors, therapists, police officers, lawyers, and judges to not only recognize the signatures of different traumatic experiences and how best to respond—as I've developed in this book—but to build in mechanisms for screening, prevention, and treatment. This kind of curriculum should be not only mandated but also certified so that professionals in different organizations can coordinate care around a shared understanding of adversity, trauma, resilience, and recovery.

A third pathway is through the coordination of organizations and professionals concerned with childhood adversity and trauma, helping all see the importance and relevance of collaborators and developing a common language and set of procedures. The National Child Traumatic Stress Network, a US-based organization I mentioned in the first chapter, provides extraordinary resources and training to government organizations, schools, and parents, focused on children who have been abused and neglected. The Raising Voices organization I mentioned in chapter 8 not only provides a curriculum for teachers and communities to help reduce domestic and school-based violence but also coordinates activities with academic departments of tropical medicine, hygiene, and education. The International Centre for Missing & Exploited Children provides resources and training to schools, communities, and law enforcement, and carries out research to guide policy on a global level. When a child like Albert is left off at the doorstep of an orphanage, there should be an immediate rallying cry among the community to contact child services, law enforcement, doctors, therapists, and teachers, each equipped with the knowledge to begin helping a deprived and abandoned child and to coordinate efforts to provide shelter, care, food, medical treatment, and education. Glimmers of this work are beginning to shine in some countries, but there is a long road forward.

A fourth pathway is to continue our work understanding how a single ACE can lead to further ACEs, potentially piling up the allostatic load, as well as providing distinctive signatures of trauma. Consider, for example, the COVID-19 pandemic, a disease ACE that directly caused death or significant illness among millions across the globe. Because of restrictions imposed by the departments of public health around social distancing, COVID-19 resulted in several more ACEs for millions of other people, including many who were never symptomatic. These ACEs included massive financial hardship that pushed many into poverty; increased mental health problems among children and parents; increased domestic violence; increased cognitive, social, and emotional neglect due to absenteeism from school; and for data coming out of the United States, a significant increase in the number of children killed by guns.[3] These findings highlight the importance of having organizations anticipate and prepare for downstream effects of a single ACE so that they can equip children and their caretakers with the resources to build resilience and aid recovery.

The fifth pathway is making use of our new understanding that children who present with a resilient shell often conceal an epigenetically aged core—they have heightened inflammation, a compromised immune system, a hypercharged stress system, and deteriorating learning and memory. For example, and as I discussed in chapter 7, individuals who seem to be highly self-controlled, able to succeed, may be aging at a much faster pace than individuals who are out of control. It is thus essential to provide screenings and assessments that dig below the surface, focusing on the ways in which childhood adversity injures the autonomic, immune, and nervous systems. This approach will also require the coordination of professionals with different expertise to run and interpret these assays so that they drive effective interventions that build resilience and recovery.

The sixth and final pathway is the many new and promising treatments for people who suffer from trauma, including those who have found little success with medication and therapy. Psychedelic-assisted psychotherapy is on the verge of approval by the FDA. Transcranial magnetic stimulation and neurofeedback are beginning to be used with children and adolescents, and portable devices are getting more traction, enabling scaling and broad dissemination. Investing further in these approaches is necessary so that we may provide vulnerable children with a diversity of treatment options.

Every child is born with vulnerabilities and strengths that are magnified by the experiences of their caretakers, communities, and environments. Adverse experiences, depending on their type, timing, tenure, turbulence, and toxicity, can leave wounds on a child's body and brain—the signatures of trauma. The longer these wounds fester, the longer these children miss out on the opportunity to thrive and create meaningful lives. We owe it to children like Albert to heal their wounds and bring back their smiles. We owe it to children to see them full of possibility and promise.

ACKNOWLEDGMENTS

To all the students that I have worked with, you have taught me so much about what it means to struggle, surmount, and survive. You have welcomed me into your lives, shared personal and difficult experiences, allowed me to teach you, and showed me your gratitude whether with a smile, a fist pump, or even a hug. This book is dedicated to all of you.

For discussion and comments on the book, I thank Jay Belsky, Theresa Betancourt, Alain Brunet, Jean Clinton, Thomas Elbert, Bruce Ellis, Julian Ford, Nathan Fox, James Garbarino, Kathryn Paige Harden, Christine Heim, Charles Nelson, Jennie Noll, Katie McLaughlin, Terrie Moffit, Steven Pinker, Seth Pollak, Roos van der Haer, Jack Shonkoff, and Vincent Felitti.

To my agent, Eric Lupfer, I can't thank you enough for your persistence, encouragement, and brilliant editorial advice in all the stages of the proposal.

To my editor at Avery, Lucia Watson, your enthusiasm for this project inspired my writing at all stages. Your masterful editorial hand beautifully enhanced the clarity and power of my message.

acknowledgments

To my four-legged companions, Odin my large lovable Newfie and JoeJoe my cuddly cat, thank you for pulling me back to reality during my journeys into the universe of writing.

To Lilan, my companion, partner, best friend, and love of my life, you've lived through a few of these book-writing adventures. You know that I disappear into my writing universe. But you graciously and patiently pull me out of it. You listen to my arguments, take in the writing, and always, always provide insights that turn water into wine. Oh how I love thee.

To my two wonderful daughters, Alexandra and Sofia, you give me inspiration and hope every day. You have filled my life with great joy as a father and taught me much about the needs of children.

To my father and mother, Jacques and Bert, you have given me the gifts of compassion, love, and curiosity—positive childhood experiences.

To the school administrators, teachers, clinicians, nurses, doctors, and paraprofessionals that I have had the privilege to work with, thank you for sharing your insights. Thank you for caring for children. Thank you for enriching the lives of children who have struggled with adversity. In particular, I want to thank several educators who brought an outsider in, patiently educated me, and helped to shape a collaboration that has endured: Larry Carroll, Paul Hilton, Melissa Goldstein, Melanie Whipple, Evonne Carvalho, Jim MacMahon, Peter Andrade, Melissa Bissonnette, Sarah Beckner, Phil Nobile, Melissa vanEssendelft, Mike Walsh, Jerry Ouelette, David Heimbecker, Donna Cranshaw-Gabriel, Karen Belenger, Barbara Kutz, Jeannine Audet, Patty Mason, Hank Perrin, Cheryl Jacques, Bill Jacques, Jennie Williams, Rosanna Warwick, Leah Callaghan, Steve Driscoll, John Fosdick, Kara Peterson, Christina Caputo, Anita Woods, Julia Bryant, and Peggy Brookes.

NOTES

INTRODUCTION

1 Part of the policy for treatment is articulated by the *Diagnostic and Statistical Manual of Mental Disorders (DSM)*, created by the American Psychiatric Association and used in the United States, Canada, and a few other countries. This *DSM* sets the criteria for what counts as trauma, and thus, who is eligible for treatment and insurance coverage. The International Classification of Diseases, or ICD, is produced by the World Health Organization and has a much broader international reach and scope for both treatment and insurance.

2 Van der Kolk, Bessel. *The Body Keeps the Score.* New York: Penguin, 2014.

3 Shonkoff, Jack P. "Capitalizing on advances in science to reduce the health consequences of early childhood adversity." *JAMA Pediatrics* 170, no. 10 (2016): 1003–1007.

4 Hauser, Marc D. *Wild Minds: What Animals Really Think.* New York: Henry Holt and Company, 2000; Hauser, Marc D. *Moral Minds: The Nature of Right and Wrong.* New York: HarperCollins, 2006.

5 This book, unlike many excellent ones that are available, is not specifically focused on different therapeutic approaches that have been successfully implemented for people who suffer from trauma. Different therapeutic approaches often accompany the treatment I discuss, and I will mention these approaches where relevant. See: Levine, Peter A. *In an Unspoken Voice: How the Body Releases Trauma and Restores Goodness.* Berkeley, CA: North Atlantic Books, 2010; Levine, Peter A., and Maggie Kline. *Trauma-Proofing Your Kids: A Parents' Guide for Instilling Confidence, Joy and Resilience.* Berkeley, CA: North Atlantic Books, 2008; Maté, Gabor, and Daniel Maté, *The Myth of Normal.* New York: Avery, 2022; Schwartz, Richard C.

Internal Family Systems Therapy. New York: Guilford Press, 2013; Siegel, Daniel J. *The Mindful Therapist.* New York: W. W. Norton & Company, 2010.

6 Perry, Bruce D., and Oprah Winfrey, *What Happened to You?: Conversations on Trauma, Resilience, and Healing.* New York: Flatiron Books, 2021.

PART I

1 Ensler, Eve. "I Am an Emotional Creature," April 21, 2010, https://www.huffpost .com/entry/i-am-an-emotional-creatur_b_468801.

CHAPTER 1

1 Copeland, B. Jack. *The Essential Turing.* New York: Clarendon Press, 2004.

2 To protect the identities of the children and adults that I have worked with, including teachers and clinicians, I have given them different names. In cases where victims of abuse or neglect are named, it is because their stories have already been made public from books, articles, or movies.

3 Bolhuis, Koen, Essi Viding, Ryan L. Muetzel, et al. "Neural profile of callous traits in children: A population-based neuroimaging study." *Biological Psychiatry* 85, no. 5 (2019): 399–407; O'Nions, Elizabeth, César F. Lima, Sophie K. Scott, et al. "Reduced laughter contagion in boys at risk for psychopathy." *Current Biology* 27, no. 19 (2017): 3049–3055; Roberts, Ruth, Eamon McCrory, Geoffrey Bird, et al. "Thinking about others' minds: mental state inference in boys with conduct problems and callous-unemotional traits." *Journal of Abnormal Child Psychology* 48 (2020): 1279–1290; Viding, Essi, and Eamon J. McCrory. "Understanding the development of psychopathy: Progress and challenges." *Psychological Medicine* 48, no. 4 (2018): 566–577.

4 Beebe, Beatrice, Michael M. Myers, Sang Han Lee, et al. "Family nurture intervention for preterm infants facilitates positive mother–infant face-to-face engagement at 4 months." *Developmental Psychology* 54, no. 11 (2018): 2016; Granqvist, Pehr, L. Alan Sroufe, Mary Dozier, et al. "Disorganized attachment in infancy: A review of the phenomenon and its implications for clinicians and policy-makers." *Attachment & Human Development* 19, no. 6 (2017): 534–558; Lyons-Ruth, Karlen, and Laura E. Brumariu. "Emerging child competencies and personality pathology: Toward a developmental cascade model of BPD." *Current Opinion in Psychology* 37 (2021): 32–38.

5 The selection of the original list of ACEs was not based on any quantitative, statistical evidence of prominence or importance.

6 In the original studies, they refer to these as "categories" of ACEs. I use "type" instead, as it dovetails more elegantly with other research in the field.

7 Felitti, Vincent J., Robert F. Anda, Dale Nordenberg, et al. "Relationship of childhood abuse and household dysfunction to many of the leading causes of death in adults: The Adverse Childhood Experiences (ACE) Study." *American Journal of Preventive Medicine* 14, no. 4 (1998): 245–258.

8 Barnett, Miya L., R. Christopher Sheldrick, Sabrina R. Liu, et al. "Implications of adverse childhood experiences screening on behavioral health services: A scoping review and systems modeling analysis." *American Psychologist* 76, no. 2 (2021): 364.

9 Amone-P'Olak, Kennedy, and Nkalosang K. Letswai. "The relationship between adverse childhood experiences and depression: A cross-sectional survey with university students in Botswana." *South African Journal of Psychiatry* 26, no. 1 (2020): 1–8; Ho, Grace W. K., Athena C. Y. Chan, Wai-Tong Chien, et al. "Examining patterns of adversity in Chinese young adults using the Adverse Childhood Experiences—International Questionnaire (ACE-IQ)." *Child Abuse & Neglect* 88 (2019): 179–188; Manyema, Mercy, and Linda M. Richter. "Adverse childhood experiences: Prevalence and associated factors among South African young adults." *Heliyon* 5, no. 12 (2019): e03003.

10 McEwen, Bruce S. "Allostasis and allostatic load: Implications for neuropsychopharmacology." *Neuropsychopharmacology* 22, no. 2 (2000): 108–124.

11 Vincent Felitti lecture to National Congress of American Indians, 2016: https://www.youtube.com/watch?v=-ns8ko9-ljU.

12 Bellis, Mark A., Karen Hughes, Kat Ford, et al. "Life course health consequences and associated annual costs of adverse childhood experiences across Europe and North America: A systematic review and meta-analysis." *Lancet Public Health* 4 no. 10 (2019): e517–e528; Grummitt, Lucinda Rachel, Noah T. Kreski, Stephanie Gyuri Kim, et al. "Association of childhood adversity with morbidity and mortality in US adults: A systematic review." *JAMA Pediatrics* 175, no. 12 (2021): 1269–1278; Hughes, Karen, Mark A. Bellis, Katherine A. Hardcastle, et al. "The effect of multiple adverse childhood experiences on health: A systematic review and meta-analysis." *Lancet Public Health* 2, no. 8 (2017): e356–e366.

13 Bellis et al., "Life course health consequences."

14 Putnam, Frank W., Lisa Amaya-Jackson, Karen T. Putnam, and Ernestine C. Briggs. "Synergistic adversities and behavioral problems in traumatized children and adolescents." *Child Abuse & Neglect* 106 (2020): 104492.

15 Conching, Andie Kealohi Sato, and Zaneta Thayer. "Biological pathways for historical trauma to affect health: A conceptual model focusing on epigenetic modifications." *Social Science & Medicine* 230 (2019): 74–82; Islam, Samiha, Sara R. Jaffee, and Cathy S. Widom. "Breaking the cycle of intergenerational childhood maltreatment: Effects on offspring mental health." *Child Maltreatment* 28, no. 1 (2023): 119–129; Lehrner, Amy, and Rachel Yehuda. "Cultural trauma and epigenetic inheritance." *Development and Psychopathology* 30, no. 5 (2018): 1763–1777; Roubinov, Danielle S., Linda J. Luecken, Sarah G. Curci, et al. "A prenatal programming perspective on the intergenerational transmission of maternal adverse childhood experiences to offspring health problems." *American Psychologist* 76, no. 2 (2021): 337.

16 Aristizabal, Maria J., Ina Anreiter, Thorhildur Halldorsdottir, et al. "Biological embedding of experience: A primer on epigenetics." *Proceedings of the National Academy of Sciences* 117, no. 38 (2020): 23261–23269; Cavalli, Giacomo, and Edith Heard. "Advances in epigenetics link genetics to the environment and disease." *Nature* 571, no. 7766 (2019): 489–499; Howie, Hunter, Chuda M. Rijal, and Kerry J. Ressler. "A review of epigenetic contributions to post-traumatic stress disorder." *Dialogues in Clinical Neuroscience* 21, no. 4 (2019): 417–428.

17 De Rooij, Susanne R., Hans Wouters, Julie E. Yonker, et al. "Prenatal undernutrition and cognitive function in late adulthood." *Proceedings of the National Academy of Sciences* 107, no. 39 (2010): 16881–16886; Hoek, Hans W., Alan S. Brown, and Ezra Susser. "The Dutch famine and schizophrenia spectrum disorders." *Social Psychiatry and Psychiatric Epidemiology* 33 (1998): 373–379; Roseboom, Tessa, Susanne de Rooij, and Rebecca Painter. "The Dutch famine and its long-term consequences for adult health." *Early Human Development* 82, no. 8 (2006): 485–491; Tobi, Elmar W., Jelle J. Goeman, Ramin Monajemi, et al. "DNA methylation signatures link prenatal famine exposure to growth and metabolism." *Nature Communications* 5, no. 1 (2014): 5592.

18 *Jacobellis v. Ohio* (1964), https://mtsu.edu/first-amendment/article/392/jacobellis-v-ohio.

19 Finkelhor, David. "Screening for adverse childhood experiences (ACEs): Cautions and suggestions." *Child Abuse & Neglect* 85 (2018): 174–179; Finkelhor, David, Anne Shattuck, Heather Turner, and Sherry Hamby. "A revised inventory of adverse childhood experiences." *Child Abuse & Neglect* 48 (2015): 13–21.

20 Cuartas, Jorge, David G. Weissman, Margaret A. Sheridan, et al. "Corporal punishment and elevated neural response to threat in children." *Child Development* 92, no. 3 (2021): 821–832; Falcone, Marie, Diana Quintero, and Jon Valant. "Ending Corporal Punishment of Preschool-Age Children." Brookings Institution, 2020, https://www.brookings.edu/blog/brown-center-chalkboard/2020/10/13/ending-corporal-punishment-of-preschool-age-children/; Finkelhor, David, Heather Turner, Brittany Kaye Wormuth, et al. "Corporal punishment: Current rates from a national survey." *Journal of Child and Family Studies* 28 (2019): 1991–1997.

21 McLaughlin, Katie A. "Future directions in childhood adversity and youth psychopathology." *Journal of Clinical Child & Adolescent Psychology* 45, no. 3 (2016): 363. Different terms are sometimes used instead of adversity including, most prominently, toxic stress. There are four reasons why I believe adversity is a more effective term, especially given the broad approach used in this book. First, toxic makes it seem as if the experience must be lethal or extremely deleterious. As we will learn, there is a spectrum of experience and we need to understand how this variation maps onto the responses of the body and brain. Second, labeling something toxic prejudges the response. Those who favor this expression note that toxic stress is the experience, whereas toxic stress response is how the individual's body and brain react to the experience. Third, though our stress response is critical, there are other responses from our immune and nervous

systems that we also wish to understand, while recognizing that the experience may impact all of these systems. Fourth, toxicity is a dimension that I will explore both on its own as well as how it interacts with the type of adversity. See: Burke Harris, Nadine. *Toxic Childhood Stress*. New York: Bluebird, 2020; Nelson, Charles A., Zulfiqar A. Bhutta, Nadine Burke Harris, et al. "Adversity in childhood is linked to mental and physical health throughout life." *Biomedical Journal* 371 (2020): 1–9; Shonkoff, Jack P. "Capitalizing on advances in science to reduce the health consequences of early childhood adversity." *JAMA Pediatrics* 170, no. 10 (2016): 1003–1007.

CHAPTER 2

1 Von Bertalanffy, Ludwig. *General Systems Theory*. New York: George Braziller, 1969; Gunnar, Megan R. "Early adversity, stress, and neurobehavioral development." *Development and Psychopathology* 32, no. 5 (2020): 1555–1562.

2 Birn, Rasmus M., Barbara J. Roeber, and Seth D. Pollak. "Early childhood stress exposure, reward pathways, and adult decision making." *Proceedings of the National Academy of Sciences* 114, no. 51 (2017): 13549–13554.

3 Ellis, Bruce J., JeanMarie Bianchi, Vladas Griskevicius, and Willem E. Frankenhuis. "Beyond risk and protective factors: An adaptation-based approach to resilience." *Perspectives on Psychological Science* 12, no. 4 (2017): 561–587; Ellis, Bruce J., Laura S. Abrams, Ann S. Masten, et al. "Hidden talents in harsh environments." *Development and Psychopathology* 34, no. 1 (2022): 95–113.

4 Pai, Anushka, Alina M. Suris, and Carol S. North. "Posttraumatic stress disorder in the *DSM-5*: Controversy, change, and conceptual considerations." *Behavioral Sciences* 7, no. 1 (2017): 1–7.

5 Bonanno, George A. *The End of Trauma*. New York: Basic Books, 2021; van der Kolk, Bessel. *The Body Keeps the Score*. New York: Penguin Books, 2014; Maté, Gabor, and Daniel Maté, *The Myth of Normal*. New York: Avery, 2022.

6 National Child Traumatic Stress Network: https://www.nctsn.org/.

7 Wakefield, Jerome C. "Psychological justice: *DSM-5*, false positive diagnosis, and fair equality of opportunity." *Public Affairs Quarterly* 29, no. 1 (2015): 32–75. Also see Richard McNally's thoughtful book *What Is Mental Illness?* (Cambridge, MA: Harvard University Press, 2011) for a broad-ranging discussion of mental illness.

8 Ford, Julian D. "Why we need a developmentally appropriate trauma diagnosis for children: A 10-year update on developmental trauma disorder." *Journal of Child & Adolescent Trauma* (2021): 1–16; Ford, Julian D., Damion Grasso, Carolyn Greene, et al. "Clinical significance of a proposed developmental trauma disorder diagnosis: Results of an international survey of clinicians." *Journal of Clinical Psychiatry* 74, no. 8 (2013): 841–849; Spinazzola, Joseph, Bessel van der Kolk, and Julian D. Ford. "Developmental trauma disorder: A legacy of attachment trauma in victimized children." *Journal of Traumatic Stress* 34, no. 4 (2021): 711–720.

9 Frances, Allen. "*DSM-5* is a guide, not a bible: Simply ignore its 10 worst changes."

HuffPost Science Blog, 2012, http://www.huffingtonpost.com/allen-frances/dsm -5_b_2227626.html.

10 Bonanno, *The End of Trauma*; Kalisch, Raffael, Dewleen G. Baker, Ulrike Basten, et al. "The resilience framework as a strategy to combat stress-related disorders." *Nature Human Behaviour* 1, no. 11 (2017): 784–790; Southwick, Steven M., George A. Bonanno, Ann S. Masten, et al. "Resilience definitions, theory, and challenges: Interdisciplinary perspectives." *European Journal of Psychotraumatology* 5, no. 1 (2014): 25338.

11 Belsky, Jay, Marian J. Bakermans-Kranenburg, and Marinus H. Van IJzendoorn. "For better and for worse: Differential susceptibility to environmental influences." *Current Directions in Psychological Science* 16, no. 6 (2007): 300–304; Denckla, Christy A., Dante Cicchetti, Laura D. Kubzansky, et al. "Psychological resilience: An update on definitions, a critical appraisal, and research recommendations." *European Journal of Psychotraumatology* 11, no. 1 (2020): 1822064; Ellis, Bruce J., W. Thomas Boyce, Jay Belsky, et al. "Differential susceptibility to the environment: An evolutionary–neurodevelopmental theory." *Development and Psychopathology* 23, no. 1 (2011): 7–28; Masten, Ann S. *Ordinary Magic: Resilience in Development.* New York: Guilford Press, 2015; Masten, Ann S., Cara M. Lucke, Kayla M. Nelson, and Isabella C. Stallworthy. "Resilience in development and psychopathology: Multisystem perspectives." *Annual Review of Clinical Psychology* 17 (2021): 521–549; Schultebraucks, Katharina, Karmel W. Choi, Isaac R. Galatzer-Levy, and George A. Bonanno. "Discriminating heterogeneous trajectories of resilience and depression after major life stressors using polygenic scores." *JAMA Psychiatry* 78, no. 7 (2021): 744–752.

12 Willmore, Lindsay, Courtney Cameron, John Yang, Ilana B. Witten, and Annegret L. Falkner. "Behavioural and dopaminergic signatures of resilience." *Nature* 611 (2022): 124–132.

13 Bonanno, George A., and Erica D. Diminich. "Annual Research Review: Positive adjustment to adversity—trajectories of minimal–impact resilience and emergent resilience." *Journal of Child Psychology and Psychiatry* 54, no. 4 (2013): 378–401; Halevi, Galit, Amir Djalovski, Adva Vengrober, and Ruth Feldman. "Risk and resilience trajectories in war-exposed children across the first decade of life." *Journal of Child Psychology and Psychiatry* 57, no. 10 (2016): 1183–1193; Hobfoll, Stevan E., Patrick A. Palmieri, Robert J. Johnson, et al. "Trajectories of resilience, resistance, and distress during ongoing terrorism: The case of Jews and Arabs in Israel." *Journal of Consulting and Clinical Psychology* 77, no. 1 (2009): 138; Schultebraucks et al., "Discriminating Heterogeneous Trajectories of Resilience and Depression," 744–752.

14 Anda, Robert F., Laura E. Porter, and David W. Brown. "Inside the adverse childhood experience score: Strengths, limitations, and misapplications." *American Journal of Preventive Medicine* 59, no. 2 (2020): 293–295.

15 Danese, Andrea, and Cathy Spatz Widom. "Objective and subjective experiences

of child maltreatment and their relationships with psychopathology." *Nature Human Behaviour* 4, no. 8 (2020): 811–818; Meehan, Alan J., Jessie R. Baldwin, Stephanie J. Lewis, et al. "Poor individual risk classification from adverse childhood experiences screening." *American Journal of Preventive Medicine* 62, no. 3 (2022): 427–432; Widom, Cathy Spatz. "Are retrospective self-reports accurate representations or existential recollections?" *JAMA Psychiatry* 76, no. 6 (2019): 567–568.

16 Burke Harris, Nadine. *Toxic Childhood Stress*. New York: Bluebird, 2020.

17 Medi-Cal Provider: https://files.medical.ca.gov/pubsdoco/newsroom/newsroom_30091_02.aspx.

18 Aces Aware: https://www.acesaware.org.

19 Finkelhor, David. "Screening for adverse childhood experiences (ACEs): Cautions and suggestions." *Child Abuse & Neglect* 85 (2018): 174–179; See also: Lacey, Rebecca E., and Helen Minnis. "Practitioner review: Twenty years of research with adverse childhood experience scores—advantages, disadvantages and applications to practice." *Journal of Child Psychology and Psychiatry* 61, no. 2 (2020): 116–130; Racine, Nicole, Teresa Killam, and Sheri Madigan. "Trauma-informed care as a universal precaution: Beyond the adverse childhood experiences questionnaire." *JAMA Pediatrics* 174, no. 1 (2020): 5–6; Skar, Ane-Marthe Solheim, Silje Mørup Ormhaug, and Tine K. Jensen. "Reported levels of upset in youth after routine trauma screening at mental health clinics." *JAMA Network Open* 2, no. 5 (2019): e194003.

CHAPTER 3

1 The Adverse T framework proposed here fits with the dimensional model approach by Katie McLaughlin, Margaret Sheridan, and others. It makes clear that type is only one dimension. See: Cohodes, Emily M., Elizabeth R. Kitt, Arielle Baskin-Sommers, and Dylan G. Gee. "Influences of early-life stress on frontolimbic circuitry: Harnessing a dimensional approach to elucidate the effects of heterogeneity in stress exposure." *Developmental Psychobiology* 63, no. 2 (2021): 153–172; McLaughlin, Katie A., Margaret A. Sheridan, Kathryn L. Humphreys, et al. "The value of dimensional models of early experience: Thinking clearly about concepts and categories." *Perspectives on Psychological Science* 16, no. 6 (2021): 1463–1472; Sheridan, Margaret A., and Katie A. McLaughlin. "Dimensions of early experience and neural development: Deprivation and threat." *Trends in Cognitive Sciences* 18, no. 11 (2014): 580–585; Sheridan, Margaret A., Feng Shi, Adam B. Miller, et al. "Network structure reveals clusters of associations between childhood adversities and development outcomes." *Developmental Science* 23, no. 5 (2020): e12934.

2 Clinical and developmental scientists have often discussed some of these dimensions, including especially Katie McLaughlin and Margaret Sheridan (McLaughlin et al. 2021). The terms they use to describe some of these dimensions

occasionally depart from my own, especially terms for turbulence and toxicity. In particular, turbulence is often associated with unpredictability, leaving out the dimension of con-trollability. Toxicity is often referred to as harshness, see: McGinnis, Ellen W., Margaret Sheridan, and William E. Copeland. "Impact of dimensions of early adversity on adult health and functioning: A 2-decade, longitudinal study." *Development and Psychopathology* 34, no. 2 (2022): 527–538.

3 Guessoum, Sélim Benjamin, Jonathan Lachal, Rahmeth Radjack, et al. "Adolescent psychiatric disorders during the COVID-19 pandemic and lockdown." *Psychiatry Research* 291 (2020): 113264; Maurer, Daphne. "Critical periods re-examined: Evidence from children treated for dense cataracts." *Cognitive Development* 42 (2017): 27–36; Racine, Nicole, Jessica E. Cooke, Rachel Eirich, et al. "Child and adolescent mental illness during COVID-19: A rapid review." *Psychiatry Research* 292 (2020): 113307; Racine, Nicole, Brae Anne McArthur, Jessica E. Cooke, et al. "Global prevalence of depressive and anxiety symptoms in children and adolescents during COVID-19: A meta-analysis." *JAMA Pediatrics* 175, no. 11 (2021): 1142–1150.

4 Bergman, Ann-Sofie, Ulf Axberg, and Elizabeth Hanson. "When a parent dies—a systematic review of the effects of support programs for parentally bereaved children and their caregivers." *BMC Palliative Care* 16 (2017): 1–15; Desmond, Chris, Kathryn Watt, Anamika Saha, et al. "Prevalence and number of children living in institutional care: Global, regional, and country estimates." *Lancet Child & Adolescent Health* 4, no. 5 (2020): 370–377; Hillis, Susan D., Alexandra Blenkinsop, Andrés Villaveces, et al. "COVID-19–Associated orphanhood and caregiver death in the United States." *Pediatrics* 148, no. 6 (2021): e2021053760; Hillis, Susan, Joel-Pascal Ntwali N'konzi, William Msemburi, et al. "Orphanhood and caregiver loss among children based on new global excess COVID-19 death estimates." *JAMA Pediatrics* 176, no. 11 (2022): 1145–1148; Owens, Darrell-A. "Recognizing the needs of bereaved children in palliative care." *Journal of Hospice and Palliative Nursing* 10, no. 1 (2008): 14–16; Scherer, Zachary, and Rose M. Kreider. "Exploring the link between socioeconomic factors and parental morality." *SEHSD Working Papers.* Washington, DC: US Census Bureau, 2019.

5 UNHCR: https://data.unhcr.org/en/situations/ukraine/location?secret=unhcrrestricted.

6 Ellis, Bruce J., W. Thomas Boyce, Jay Belsky, et al. "Differential susceptibility to the environment: An evolutionary–neurodevelopmental theory." *Development and Psychopathology* 23, no. 1 (2011): 7–28; Ellis, Bruce J., and Marco Del Giudice. "Developmental adaptation to stress: An evolutionary perspective." *Annual Review of Psychology* 70 (2019): 111–139; Van Lange, Paul A. M., Maria I. Rinderu, and Brad J. Bushman. "Aggression and violence around the world: A model of climate, aggression, and self-control in humans (CLASH)." *Behavioral and Brain Sciences* 40 (2017): 1–58.

7 Malave, Lauren, Milenna T. van Dijk, and Christoph Anacker. "Early life ad-

versity shapes neural circuit function during sensitive postnatal developmental periods." *Translational Psychiatry* 12, no. 1 (2022): 306; Melville, Alysse. "Trauma-exposed infants and toddlers: A review of impacts and evidence-based interventions." *Advances in Social Work* 18, no. 1 (2017): 53–65; Osofsky, Joy D., and Alicia F. Lieberman. "A call for integrating a mental health perspective into systems of care for abused and neglected infants and young children." *American Psychologist* 66, no. 2 (2011): 120; Osofsky, Joy D., Howard J. Osofsky, Andrew L. Frazer, et al. "The importance of adverse childhood experiences during the perinatal period." *American Psychologist* 76, no. 2 (2021): 350–363.

8 Atzl, Victoria M., Angela J. Narayan, Luisa M. Rivera, and Alicia F. Lieberman. "Adverse childhood experiences and prenatal mental health: Type of ACEs and age of maltreatment onset." *Journal of Family Psychology* 33, no. 3 (2019): 304–314; McDonnell, Christina G., and Kristin Valentino. "Intergenerational effects of childhood trauma: Evaluating pathways among maternal ACEs, perinatal depressive symptoms, and infant outcomes." *Child Maltreatment* 21, no. 4 (2016): 317–326; Merrick, Jillian S., Angela J. Narayan, Victoria M. Atzl, et al. "Type versus timing of adverse and benevolent childhood experiences for pregnant women's psychological and reproductive health." *Children and Youth Services Review* 114 (2020): 105056; Sulaiman, Salima, Shahirose Sadrudin Premji, Farideh Tavangar, et al. "Total adverse childhood experiences and preterm birth: A systematic review." *Maternal and Child Health Journal* 25 (2021): 1581–1594.

9 Boyce, W. Thomas, Pat Levitt, Fernando D. Martinez, et al. "Genes, environments, and time: The biology of adversity and resilience." *Pediatrics* 147, no. 2 (2021): e20201651; Cameron, Judy L., Kathie L. Eagleson, Nathan A. Fox, et al. "Social origins of developmental risk for mental and physical illness." *Journal of Neuroscience* 37, no. 45 (2017): 10783–10791; Cowell, Raquel A., Dante Cicchetti, Fred A. Rogosch, and Sheree L. Toth. "Childhood maltreatment and its effect on neurocognitive functioning: Timing and chronicity matter." *Development and Psychopathology* 27, no. 2 (2015): 521–533; Gabard-Durnam, Laurel J., and Katie A. McLaughlin. "Do sensitive periods exist for exposure to adversity?" *Biological Psychiatry* 85, no. 10 (2019): 789–791; Nelson, Charles A., and Laurel J. Gabard-Durnam. "Early adversity and critical periods: Neurodevelopmental consequences of violating the expectable environment." *Trends in Neurosciences* 43, no. 3 (2020): 133–143; Woodard, Kristina, and Seth D. Pollak. "Is there evidence for sensitive periods in emotional development?" *Current Opinion in Behavioral Sciences* 36 (2020): 1–6.

10 Lea, Amanda J., and Stacy Rosebaum. "Understanding how early life effects evolve: Progress, gaps, and future directions." *Current Opinion in Behavioral Sciences* 36 (2020): 29–35; Nelson and Gabard-Durnam, "Early adversity and critical periods," 133–143; Reh, Rebecca K., Brian G. Dias, Charles A. Nelson III, Daniela Kaufer, Janet F. Werker, Bryan Kolb, Joel D. Levine, and Takao K. Hensch.

"Critical period regulation across multiple timescales." *Proceedings of the National Academy of Sciences* 117, no. 38 (2020): 23242–23251.

11 I note here that not all orphanages result in children with poor developmental outcomes, including ones in low- and middle-income countries. The focus here is on those orphanages where, based on decades of evidence, the experiences are so impoverished—the level of deprivation so high—that poor outcomes have been documented. See: Escueta, Maya, Kathryn Whetten, Jan Ostermann. "Adverse childhood experiences, psychosocial well-being and cognitive development among orphans and abandoned children in five low-income countries." *BMC International Health and Human Rights* 14, no. 1 (2014): 1–13; Huynh, Hy V., Susan P. Limber, Christine L. Gray, et al. "Factors affecting the psychosocial well-being of orphan and separated children in five low- and middle-income countries: Which is more important, quality of care or care setting?" *PLOS One* 14, no. 6 (2019): e0218100; Whetten, Kathryn, Jan Ostermann, Brian W. Pence, et al. "Three-year change in the well-being of orphaned and separated children in institutional and family-based care settings in five low- and middle-income countries." *PLOS One* 9, no. 8 (2014): e104872.

12 Dunn, Erin C., Thomas W. Soare, Yiwen Zhu, et al. "Sensitive periods for the effect of childhood adversity on DNA methylation: Results from a prospective, longitudinal study." *Biological Psychiatry* 85, no. 10 (2019): 838–849; Marini, Sandro, Kathryn A. Davis, Thomas W. Soare, et al. "Adversity exposure during sensitive periods predicts accelerated epigenetic aging in children." *Psychoneuroendocrinology* 113 (2020): 104484.

13 Parrott, Dominic J., Miklós B. Halmos, Cynthia A. Stappenbeck, and Kevin Moino. "Intimate partner aggression during the COVID-19 pandemic: Associations with stress and heavy drinking." *Psychology of Violence* 12, no. 2 (2022): 95.

14 United Nations Meeting Coverage and Press, May 20, 2021: https://press.un.org/en/2021/ga12325.doc.htm#:~:text=%E2%80%9CIf%20there%20is%20a%20hell,Nations%2C%20said%20in%20opening%20remarks.

15 https://www.youtube.com/watch?v=Ms4ygeKaXes.

16 Gama, Camila Monteiro Fabricio, Liana Catarina Lima Portugal, Raquel Menezes Gonçalves, et al. "The invisible scars of emotional abuse: A common and highly harmful form of childhood maltreatment." *BMC Psychiatry* 21, no. 1 (2021): 1–14; Lalor, Kevin, and Rosaleen McElvaney. "Child sexual abuse, links to later sexual exploitation/high-risk sexual behavior, and prevention/treatment programs." *Trauma, Violence, & Abuse* 11, no. 4 (2010): 159–177; Ports, Katie A., Derek C. Ford, and Melissa T. Merrick. "Adverse childhood experiences and sexual victimization in adulthood." *Child Abuse & Neglect* 51 (2016): 313–322; Widom, Cathy Spatz, Sally J. Czaja, and Mary Ann Dutton. "Childhood victimization and lifetime revictimization." *Child Abuse & Neglect* 32, no. 8 (2008): 785–796.

17 Porges, Stephen W. *Clinical Applications of the Polyvagal Theory: The Emergence of Polyvagal-Informed Therapies.* New York: W. W. Norton, 2018; Porges, Stephen W.

"Polyvagal theory: A primer." In *Clinical Applications of the Polyvagal Theory: The Emergence of Polyvagal-Informed Therapies*, edited by Porges, S. W., and D. Dana. New York: W. W. Norton, 2018, 50–69.

18 Miller, Gregory E., Edith Chen, Tianyi Yu, and Gene H. Brody. "Metabolic syndrome risks following the great recession in rural black young adults." *Journal of the American Heart Association* 6, no. 9 (2017): e006052.

19 Kunz, Edward. "Henri Laborit and the inhibition of action." *Dialogues in Clinical Neuroscience* 16, no. 1 (2014): 113–117; Maier, Steven F., and Martin E. Seligman. "Learned helplessness: Theory and evidence." *Journal of Experimental Psychology: General* 105, no. 1 (1976): 3–46; Maier, Steven F., and Martin E. P. Seligman. "Learned helplessness at fifty: Insights from neuroscience." *Psychological Review* 123, no. 4 (2016): 349–367; Seligman, Martin E. P. "Learned helplessness." *Annual Review of Medicine* 23, no. 1 (1972): 407–412.

20 Moscarello, Justin M., and Catherine A. Hartley. "Agency and the calibration of motivated behavior." *Trends in Cognitive Sciences* 21, no. 10 (2017): 725–735; Short, Annabel K., and Tallie Z. Baram. "Early-life adversity and neurological disease: Age-old questions and novel answers." *Nature Reviews Neurology* 15, no. 11 (2019): 657–669.

21 Maser, Jack D., and Gordon G. Gallup. "Tonic immobility and related phenomena: A partially annotated, tricentennial bibliography, 1636–1976." *Psychological Record* 27 (1977): 177–217.

22 Ulmer Yaniv, Adi, Roy Salomon, Shani Waidergoren, et al. "Synchronous caregiving from birth to adulthood tunes humans' social brain." *Proceedings of the National Academy of Sciences* 118, no. 14 (2021): e2012900118.

23 Diener, Carol I., and Carol S. Dweck. "An analysis of learned helplessness: Continuous changes in performance, strategy, and achievement cognitions following failure." *Journal of Personality and Social Psychology* 36, no. 5 (1978): 451; Diener, Carol I., and Carol S. Dweck. "An analysis of learned helplessness: II. The processing of success." *Journal of Personality and Social Psychology* 39, no. 5 (1980): 940.

24 Gunnar, Megan R., and Camelia E. Hostinar. "The social buffering of the hypothalamic–pituitary–adrenocortical axis in humans: Developmental and experiential determinants." *Social Neuroscience* 10, no. 5 (2015): 479–488.

25 Schroeder, Allison, Natalie Slopen, and Mona Mittal. "Accumulation, timing, and duration of early childhood adversity and behavior problems at age 9." *Journal of Clinical Child & Adolescent Psychology* 49, no. 1 (2020): 36–49.

26 Frankl, Viktor. *Man's Search for Meaning*. New York: Pocket Books, 1962.

27 Matt Damon interviewed on ABC's *Popcorn with Peter Travers*. https://abcnews .go.com/Entertainment/matt-damon-opens-harvey-weinstein-sexual-harass ment-confidentiality/story?id=51792548.

28 Dunsmoor, Joseph E., Marijn C. W. Kroes, Stephen H. Braren, and Elizabeth A. Phelps. "Threat intensity widens fear generalization gradients." *Behavioral Neuroscience* 131, no. 2 (2017): 168–175.

29 Colich, Natalie L., Maya L. Rosen, Eileen S. Williams, and Katie A. McLaughlin. "Biological aging in childhood and adolescence following experiences of threat and deprivation: A systematic review and meta-analysis." *Psychological Bulletin* 146, no. 9 (2020): 721–764; Martins, Jade, Darina Czamara, Susann Sauer, et al. "Childhood adversity correlates with stable changes in DNA methylation trajectories in children and converges with epigenetic signatures of prenatal stress." *Neurobiology of Stress* 15 (2021): 100336.

PART II

1 Blake, William. "Auguries of Innocence," 1950. Poetry Foundation, https://www.poetryfoundation.org/poems/43650auguries-of-innocence.

CHAPTER 4

1 Ransel, David L. *Mothers of Misery: Child Abandonment in Russia.* Princeton, NJ: Princeton University Press, 1988.

2 Peters, Susan, Peter Marler, and Stephen Nowicki. "Song sparrows learn from limited exposure to song models." *Condor* 94, no. 4 (1992): 1016–1019.

3 Gracia-Rubio, Irene, Maria Moscoso-Castro, Oscar J. Pozo, et al. "Maternal separation induces neuroinflammation and long-lasting emotional alterations in mice." *Progress in Neuro-Psychopharmacology and Biological Psychiatry* 65 (2016): 104–117; Martini, Mariangela, and Olga Valverde. "A single episode of maternal deprivation impairs the motivation for cocaine in adolescent mice." *Psychopharmacology* 219 (2012): 149–158.

4 Sengupta, Pallav. "The laboratory rat: Relating its age with human's." *International Journal of Preventive Medicine* 4, no. 6 (2013): 624–630.

5 Warning to the reader: experiments like these are no longer considered ethical, a change that many, myself included, support. Given the impact of maternal deprivation on rodents, however, one wonders why similar considerations are not applicable.

6 Harlow, Harry F., Robert O. Dodsworth, and Margaret K. Harlow. "Total social isolation in monkeys." *Proceedings of the National Academy of Sciences* 54, no. 1 (1965): 90–97; Novak, Melinda A. "Social recovery of monkeys isolated for the first year of life: II. Long-term assessment." *Developmental Psychology* 15, no. 1 (1979): 50–61; Suomi, Stephen J. "Risk, resilience, and gene-environment interplay in primates." *Journal of the Canadian Academy of Child and Adolescent Psychiatry* 20 no. 4 (2011): 289–297.

7 If interested, there are various internet links to videos of Harlow's experiments: https://www.youtube.com/watch?v=02r3u59FRPU; https://www.youtube.com/watch?v=e5I6d_vq-Cc.

8 Ainsworth, Mary D. Salter. "The Bowlby-Ainsworth Attachment Theory." *Behavioral and Brain Sciences* 1, no. 3 (1978): 436–438; Bowlby, John. "Attachment and

loss: Retrospect and prospect." *American Journal of Orthopsychiatry* 52, no. 4 (1982): 664–678.

9 Cameron, Judy L., Kathie L. Eagleson, Nathan A. Fox, et al. "Social origins of developmental risk for mental and physical illness." *Journal of Neuroscience* 37, no. 45 (2017): 10783–10791; O'Connor, Thomas G., and Judy L. Cameron. "Translating research findings on early experience to prevention: Animal and human evidence on early attachment relationships." *American Journal of Preventive Medicine* 31, no. 6 (2006): 175–181; Sabatini, Michael J., Philip Ebert, David A. Lewis, et al. "Amygdala gene expression correlates of social behavior in monkeys experiencing maternal separation." *Journal of Neuroscience* 27, no. 12 (2007): 3295–3304.

10 This footage from the *20/20* reporting is difficult to watch: https://mn.gov/mnddc /parallels2/one/video/2020shameofthenation.html. For those who do, it is worth noting the parallels between these children and Harlow's socially deprived infant monkeys—rocking, self-stimulation, lethargy, and deadness in their eyes.

11 The Bucharest Early Intervention Project (https://www.bucharestearlyinterven tionproject.org/) and a sample of essential scientific publications discussed here: Bick, Johanna, Nathan Fox, Charles Zeanah, and Charles A. Nelson. "Early deprivation, atypical brain development, and internalizing symptoms in late childhood." *Neuroscience* 342 (2017): 140–153; Bick, Johanna, Rhiannon Luyster, Nathan A. Fox, et al. "Effects of early institutionalization on emotion processing in 12-year-old youth." *Development and Psychopathology* 29, no. 5 (2017): 1749–1761; Bick, Johanna, Charles H. Zeanah, Nathan A. Fox, and Charles A. Nelson. "Memory and executive functioning in 12-year-old children with a history of institutional rearing." *Child Development* 89, no. 2 (2018): 495–508; Colich, Natalie L., Maya L. Rosen, Eileen S. Williams, and Katie A. McLaughlin. "Biological aging in childhood and adolescence following experiences of threat and deprivation: A systematic review and meta-analysis." *Psychological Bulletin* 146, no. 9 (2020): 721–764; Goldman, Philip S., Marian J. Bakermans-Kranenburg, Beth Bradford, et al. "Institutionalisation and deinstitutionalisation of children 2: policy and practice recommendations for global, national, and local actors." *Lancet Child & Adolescent Health* 4, no. 8 (2020): 606–633; Guyon-Harris, Katherine L., Kathryn L. Humphreys, Devi Miron, et al. "Early caregiving quality predicts consistency of competent functioning from middle childhood to adolescence following early psychosocial deprivation." *Development and Psychopathology* 33, no. 1 (2021): 18–28; Humphreys, Kathryn L., Mary Margaret Gleason, et al. "Effects of institutional rearing and foster care on psychopathology at age 12 years in Romania: Follow-up of an open, randomised controlled trial." *Lancet Psychiatry* 2, no. 7 (2015): 625–634; Humphreys, Kathryn L., Kyle Esteves, Charles H. Zeanah, et al. "Accelerated telomere shortening: Tracking the lasting impact of early institutional care at the cellular level." *Psychiatry Research* 246 (2016): 95–100; Humphreys, Kathryn L., Katherine L. Guyon-Harris, Florin Tibu, et al. "Psychiatric

outcomes following severe deprivation in early childhood: Follow-up of a randomized controlled trial at age 16." *Journal of Consulting and Clinical Psychology* 88, no. 12 (2020): 1079–1090; Humphreys, Kathryn L., Charles A. Nelson, Nathan A. Fox, and Charles H. Zeanah. "Signs of reactive attachment disorder and disinhibited social engagement disorder at age 12 years: Effects of institutional care history and high-quality foster care." *Development and Psychopathology* 29, no. 2 (2017): 675–684; Nelson, Charles A., III, Charles H. Zeanah, and Nathan A. Fox. "How early experience shapes human development: The case of psychosocial deprivation." *Neural Plasticity* (2019): 1676285; Nelson, Charles A., III, Charles H. Zeanah, Nathan A. Fox, et al. "Cognitive recovery in socially deprived young children: The Bucharest Early Intervention Project." *Science* 318, no. 5858 (2007): 1937–1940; Sheridan, Margaret A., Katie A. McLaughlin, Warren Winter, et al. "Early deprivation disruption of associative learning is a developmental pathway to depression and social problems." *Nature Communications* 9, no. 1 (2018): 2216; Wade, Mark, Nathan A. Fox, Charles H. Zeanah, and Charles A. Nelson III. "Long-term effects of institutional rearing, foster care, and brain activity on memory and executive functioning." *Proceedings of the National Academy of Sciences* 116, no. 5 (2019): 1808–1813.

12 Huynh, Hy V., Susan P. Limber, Christine L. Gray, et al. "Factors affecting the psychosocial well-being of orphan and separated children in five low- and middle-income countries: Which is more important, quality of care or care setting?" *PLOS One* 14, no. 6 (2019): e0218100; Whetten, Kathryn, Jan Ostermann, Brian W. Pence, et al. "Three-year change in the well-being of orphaned and separated children in institutional and family-based care settings in five low- and middle-income countries." *PLOS One* 9, no. 8 (2014): e104872.

13 Epel, Elissa S., and Aric A. Prather. "Stress, telomeres, and psychopathology: Toward a deeper understanding of a triad of early aging." *Annual Review of Clinical Psychology* 14 (2018): 371–397.

14 Drury, Stacy S., Katherine Theall, Mary M. Gleason, et al. "Telomere length and early severe social deprivation: Linking early adversity and cellular aging." *Molecular Psychiatry* 17, no. 7 (2012): 719–727; Humphreys, Kathryn L., Kyle Esteves, Charles H. Zeanah, et al. "Accelerated telomere shortening: Tracking the lasting impact of early institutional care at the cellular level." *Psychiatry Research* 246 (2016): 95–100; Wade, Mark, Nathan A. Fox, Charles H. Zeanah, et al. "Telomere length and psychopathology: Specificity and direction of effects within the Bucharest Early Intervention Project." *Journal of the American Academy of Child & Adolescent Psychiatry* 59, no. 1 (2020): 140–148.

15 Farah, Martha J. "The neuroscience of socioeconomic status: Correlates, causes, and consequences." *Neuron* 96, no. 1 (2017): 56–71; Farah, Martha J. "Socioeconomic status and the brain: Prospects for neuroscience-informed policy." *Nature Reviews Neuroscience* 19, no. 7 (2018): 428–438; Farah, Martha J., David M. Shera, Jessica H. Savage, et al. "Childhood poverty: Specific associations with neurocognitive development." *Brain Research* 1110, no. 1 (2006): 166–174.

16   Adler, Nancy E., and Judith Stewart. "Health disparities across the lifespan: meaning, methods, and mechanisms." *Annals of the New York Academy of Sciences* 1186, no. 1 (2010): 5–23; Kessler, Ronald C., Patricia Berglund, Olga Demler, et al. "Lifetime prevalence and age-of-onset distributions of *DSM-IV* disorders in the National Comorbidity Survey Replication." *Archives of General Psychiatry* 62, no. 6 (2005): 593–602; Sirin, Selcuk R. "Socioeconomic status and academic achievement: A meta-analytic review of research." *Review of Educational Research* 75, no. 3 (2005): 417–453; von Stumm, Sophie, and Robert Plomin. "Socioeconomic status and the growth of intelligence from infancy through adolescence." *Intelligence* 48 (2015): 30–36.

17   Busso, Daniel S., Katie A. McLaughlin, and Margaret A. Sheridan. "Dimensions of adversity, physiological reactivity, and externalizing psychopathology in adolescence: Deprivation and threat." *Psychosomatic Medicine* 79, no. 2 (2017): 162; Dennison, Meg J., Maya L. Rosen, Kelly A. Sambrook, et al. "Differential associations of distinct forms of childhood adversity with neurobehavioral measures of reward processing: A developmental pathway to depression." *Child Development* 90, no. 1 (2019): e96–e113; Holz, Nathalie E., Regina Boecker, Erika Hohm, et al. "The long-term impact of early life poverty on orbitofrontal cortex volume in adulthood: Results from a prospective study over 25 years." *Neuropsychopharmacology* 40, no. 4 (2015): 996–1004; Lurie, Lucy A., McKenzie P. Hagen, Katie A. McLaughlin, et al. "Mechanisms linking socioeconomic status and academic achievement in early childhood: Cognitive stimulation and language." *Cognitive Development* 58 (2021): 101045; Rosen, Maya L., Margaret A. Sheridan, Kelly A. Sambrook, et al. "Socioeconomic disparities in academic achievement: A multimodal investigation of neural mechanisms in children and adolescents." *NeuroImage* 173 (2018): 298–310; Sarsour, Khaled, Margaret Sheridan, Douglas Jutte, et al. "Family socioeconomic status and child executive functions: The roles of language, home environment, and single parenthood." *Journal of the International Neuropsychological Society* 17, no. 1 (2011): 120–132; White, Stuart F., Joel L. Voss, Jessica J. Chiang, et al. "Exposure to violence and low family income are associated with heightened amygdala responsiveness to threat among adolescents." *Developmental Cognitive Neuroscience* 40 (2019): 100709.

18   UNICEF report. https://www.unicef.org/lac/en/impact-covid-19-mental-health-adolescents-and-youth; Stephenson, J. "Children and teens struggling with mental health during COVID-19 pandemic." *Jama Health Forum* 2 (2021): e211701.

19   Dickerson, Caitlin. "The Secret History of the U.S. Government's Family-Separation Policy," *Atlantic*, August 2022.

20   Blakemore, Sarah-Jayne, and Kathryn L. Mills. "Is adolescence a sensitive period for sociocultural processing?" *Annual Review of Psychology* 65 (2014): 187–207; Breaux, Rosanna, Melissa R. Dvorsky, Nicholas P. Marsh, et al. "Prospective impact of COVID-19 on mental health functioning in adolescents with and without ADHD: Protective role of emotion regulation abilities." *Journal of Child Psychol-*

ogy and Psychiatry 62, no. 9 (2021): 1132–1139; Fuhrmann, Delia, Lisa J. Knoll, and Sarah-Jayne Blakemore. "Adolescence as a sensitive period of brain development." *Trends in Cognitive Sciences* 19, no. 10 (2015): 558–566; Jones, Elizabeth A. K., Amal K. Mitra, and Azad R. Bhuiyan. "Impact of COVID-19 on mental health in adolescents: A systematic review." *International Journal of Environmental Research and Public Health* 18, no. 5 (2021): 2470; Kolacz, Jacek, Lourdes P. Dale, Evan J. Nix, et al. "Adversity history predicts self-reported autonomic reactivity and mental health in US residents during the COVID-19 pandemic." *Frontiers in Psychiatry* 11 (2020): 1119; Magson, Natasha R., Justin Y. A. Freeman, Ronald M. Rapee, et al. "Risk and protective factors for prospective changes in adolescent mental health during the COVID-19 pandemic." *Journal of Youth and Adolescence* 50 (2021): 44–57; Orben, Amy, Livia Tomova, and Sarah-Jayne Blakemore. "The effects of social deprivation on adolescent development and mental health." *Lancet Child & Adolescent Health* 4, no. 8 (2020): 634–640; Racine, Nicole, Jessica E. Cooke, Rachel Eirich, et al. "Child and adolescent mental illness during COVID-19: A rapid review." *Psychiatry Research* 292 (2020): 113307; Racine, Nicole, Brae Anne McArthur, Jessica E. Cooke, et al. "Global prevalence of depressive and anxiety symptoms in children and adolescents during COVID-19: a meta-analysis." *JAMA Pediatrics* 175, no. 11 (2021): 1142–1150.

CHAPTER 5

1 De Gelder, Beatrice, Josh Snyder, Doug Greve, et al. "Fear fosters flight: A mechanism for fear contagion when perceiving emotion expressed by a whole body." *Proceedings of the National Academy of Sciences* 101, no. 47 (2004): 16701–16706; Mihov, Yoan, Keith M. Kendrick, Benjamin Becker, et al. "Mirroring fear in the absence of a functional amygdala." *Biological Psychiatry* 73, no. 7 (2013): e9–e11.

2 Hutchinson, Lisa, and David Mueller. "Sticks and stones and broken bones: The influence of parental verbal abuse on peer related victimization." *Western Criminology Review* 9 no. 1 (2008): 17–30; Post, Robert M., Lori L. Altshuler, Ralph Kupka, et al. "Verbal abuse, like physical and sexual abuse, in childhood is associated with an earlier onset and more difficult course of bipolar disorder." *Bipolar Disorders* 17, no. 3 (2015): 323–330; Wang, Ming-Te, and Sarah Kenny. "Longitudinal links between fathers' and mothers' harsh verbal discipline and adolescents' conduct problems and depressive symptoms." *Child Development* 85, no. 3 (2014): 908–923.

3 Shonkoff, Jack P., Natalie Slopen, and David R. Williams. "Early childhood adversity, toxic stress, and the impacts of racism on the foundations of health." *Annual Review of Public Health* 42 (2021): 115–134.

4 Hankerson, Sidney H., Nathalie Moise, Diane Wilson, et al. "The intergenerational impact of structural racism and cumulative trauma on depression." *American Journal of Psychiatry* 179, no. 6 (2022): 434–440; Rosenthal, Lisa, Valerie A. Earnshaw, Joan M. Moore, et al. "Intergenerational consequences: Women's experiences of discrimination in pregnancy predict infant social-emotional

development at six months and one year." *Journal of Developmental and Behavioral Pediatrics* 39, no. 3 (2018); 228–237; Wildeman, Christopher, Alyssa W. Goldman, and Kristin Turney. "Parental incarceration and child health in the United States." *Epidemiologic Reviews* 40, no. 1 (2018): 146–156; Williams, David R., and Selina A. Mohammed. "Racism and health I: Pathways and scientific evidence." *American Behavioral Scientist* 57, no. 8 (2013): 1152–1173.

5 Choi, Jeewook, Bumseok Jeong, Michael L. Rohan, Ann M. Polcari, and Martin H. Teicher. "Preliminary evidence for white matter tract abnormalities in young adults exposed to parental verbal abuse." *Biological Psychiatry* 65, no. 3 (2009): 227–234; Lee, Sang Won, Jae Hyun Yoo, Ko Woon Kim, et al. "Hippocampal subfields volume reduction in high schoolers with previous verbal abuse experiences." *Clinical Psychopharmacology and Neuroscience* 16, no. 1 (2018): 46–56; Teicher, Martin H., Jacqueline A. Samson, Ann Polcari, and Cynthia E. McGreenery. "Sticks, stones, and hurtful words: Relative effects of various forms of childhood maltreatment." *American Journal of Psychiatry* 163, no. 6 (2006): 993–1000; Teicher, Martin H., Jacqueline A. Samson, Yi-Shin Sheu, et al. "Hurtful words: Association of exposure to peer verbal abuse with elevated psychiatric symptom scores and corpus callosum abnormalities." *American Journal of Psychiatry* 167, no. 12 (2010): 1464–1471; Tomoda, Akemi, Yi-Shin Sheu, Keren Rabi, et al. "Exposure to parental verbal abuse is associated with increased gray matter volume in superior temporal gyrus." *Neuroimage* 54 (2011): S280–S286.

6 Choi et al., "Preliminary evidence for white matter," 232.

7 Shuhada interview with Dr. Phil: https://www.youtube.com/watch?v=h6-sgG mRcxU.

8 Hess, Amanda. "Sinead O'Connor Remembers Things Differently." *New York Times*, May 18, 2021, https://www.nytimes.com/2021/05/18/arts/music/sinead -oconnor-rememberings.html.

9 Nelson, Charles A., Alissa Westerlund, Jennifer Martin McDermott, et al. "Emotion recognition following early psychosocial deprivation." *Development and Psychopathology* 25, no. 2 (2013): 517–525; Pears, Katherine C., and Philip A. Fisher. "Emotion understanding and theory of mind among maltreated children in foster care: Evidence of deficits." *Development and Psychopathology* 17, no. 1 (2005): 47–65; Perlman, Susan B., Charles W. Kalish, and Seth D. Pollak. "The role of maltreatment experience in children's understanding of the antecedents of emotion." *Cognition & Emotion* 22, no. 4 (2008): 651–670; Pollak, Seth D., Dante Cicchetti, Katherine Hornung, and Alex Reed. "Recognizing emotion in faces: Developmental effects of child abuse and neglect." *Developmental Psychology* 36, no. 5 (2000): 679–688; Pollak, Seth D., and Doris J. Kistler. "Early experience is associated with the development of categorical representations for facial expressions of emotion." *Proceedings of the National Academy of Sciences* 99, no. 13 (2002): 9072–9076; Pollak, Seth D., Rafael Klorman, Joan E. Thatcher, and Dante Cicchetti. "P3b reflects maltreated children's reactions to facial displays of

emotion." *Psychophysiology* 38, no. 2 (2001): 267–274; Pollak, Seth D., and Stephanie A. Tolley-Schell. "Selective attention to facial emotion in physically abused children." *Journal of Abnormal Psychology* 112, no. 3 (2003): 323–338; Ruba, Ashley L., and Seth D. Pollak. "The development of emotion reasoning in infancy and early childhood." *Annual Review of Developmental Psychology* 2 (2020): 503–531; Turgeon, Jessica, Annie Bérubé, Caroline Blais, et al. "Recognition of children's emotional facial expressions among mothers reporting a history of childhood maltreatment." *PLOS One* 15, no. 12 (2020): e0243083; Young, Audrey, Rhiannon J. Luyster, Nathan A. Fox, et al. "The effects of early institutionalization on emotional face processing: Evidence for sparing via an experience-dependent mechanism." *British Journal of Developmental Psychology* 35, no. 3 (2017): 439–453.

10 Lambert, Hilary K., Kevin M. King, Kathryn C. Monahan, and Katie A. McLaughlin. "Differential associations of threat and deprivation with emotion regulation and cognitive control in adolescence." *Development and Psychopathology* 29, no. 3 (2017): 929–940; McLaughlin, Katie A., Margaret A. Sheridan, Andrea L. Gold, et al. "Maltreatment exposure, brain structure, and fear conditioning in children and adolescents." *Neuropsychopharmacology* 41, no. 8 (2016): 1956–1964.

11 Bounoua, Nadia, Rickie Miglin, Jeffrey M. Spielberg, and Naomi Sadeh. "Childhood assaultive trauma and physical aggression: Links with cortical thickness in prefrontal and occipital cortices." *Neuroimage: Clinical* 27 (2020): 102321; Colich, Natalie L., Maya L. Rosen, Eileen S. Williams, and Katie A. McLaughlin. "Biological aging in childhood and adolescence following experiences of threat and deprivation: A systematic review and meta-analysis." *Psychological Bulletin* 146, no. 9 (2020): 721–764; Cuartas, Jorge, David G. Weissman, Margaret A. Sheridan, et al. "Corporal punishment and elevated neural response to threat in children." *Child Development* 92, no. 3 (2021): 821–832; Jenness, Jessica L., Matthew Peverill, Adam Bryant Miller, et al. "Alterations in neural circuits underlying emotion regulation following child maltreatment: A mechanism underlying trauma-related psychopathology." *Psychological Medicine* 51, no. 11 (2021): 1880–1889; Weissman, David G., Jessica L. Jenness, Natalie L. Colich, et al. "Altered neural processing of threat-related information in children and adolescents exposed to violence: A transdiagnostic mechanism contributing to the emergence of psychopathology." *Journal of the American Academy of Child & Adolescent Psychiatry* 59, no. 11 (2020): 1274–1284.

12 https://coloradosun.com/2020/02/19/lawrence-st-peter-colorado-priest-abuse -story/.

13 Goldstein, Joseph. "U.S. Soldiers Told to Ignore Sexual Abuse of Boys by Afghan Allies." *New York Times*, September 20, 2015. https://www.nytimes.com/2015/09/21 /world/asia/us-soldiers-told-to-ignore-afghan-allies-abuse-of-boys.html.

14 Proudfoot, Ben. "He Blew the Whistle on the Catholic Church in 1985. Why Didn't We Listen?" *New York Times*, Aug. 24, 2021, https://www.nytimes.com/2021/08 /24/opinion/catholic-church-abuse-jason-berry-first-report.html.

15 Gbahabo, Dooshima Dorothy, and Sinegugu Evidence Duma. "I just became like a log of wood . . . I was paralyzed all over my body": Women's lived experiences of tonic immobility following rape." *Heliyon* 7, no. 7 (2021): e07471; Kalaf, Juliana, Evandro Silva Freire Coutinho, Liliane Maria Pereira Vilete, et al. "Sexual trauma is more strongly associated with tonic immobility than other types of trauma—A population based study." *Journal of Affective Disorders* 215 (2017): 71–76.

16 Noll, Jennie G. "Child sexual abuse as a unique risk factor for the development of psychopathology: The compounded convergence of mechanisms." *Annual Review of Clinical Psychology* 17 (2021): 439–464; Noll, Jennie G., Penelope K. Trickett, Jeffrey D. Long, et al. "Childhood sexual abuse and early timing of puberty." *Journal of Adolescent Health* 60, no. 1 (2017): 65–71.

17 Because these results come from cross-sectional, as opposed to longitudinal, data, we must be cautious in our interpretation of the association between adversity and impact on the brain. Andersen, Susan L., Akemi Tomada, Evelyn S. Vincow, et al. "Preliminary evidence for sensitive periods in the effect of childhood sexual abuse on regional brain development." *Journal of Neuropsychiatry and Clinical Neurosciences* 20, no. 3 (2008): 292–301.

18 Guiney, Hayley, Avshalom Caspi, Antony Ambler, et al. "Childhood sexual abuse and pervasive problems across multiple life domains: Findings from a five-decade study." *Development and Psychopathology* (2022): 1–17.

19 Kendler, Kenneth S., Cynthia M. Bulik, Judy Silberg, et al. "Childhood sexual abuse and adult psychiatric and substance use disorders in women: An epidemiological and cotwin control analysis." *Archives of General Psychiatry* 57, no. 10 (2000): 953–959.

20 Pulverman, Carey S., Chelsea D. Kilimnik, and Cindy M. Meston. "The impact of childhood sexual abuse on women's sexual health: A comprehensive review." *Sexual Medicine Reviews* 6, no. 2 (2018): 188–200; Trickett, Penelope K., Jennie G. Noll, Elizabeth J. Susman, et al. "Attenuation of cortisol across development for victims of sexual abuse." *Development and Psychopathology* 22, no. 1 (2010): 165–175; Trickett, Penelope K., Jennie G. Noll, and Frank W. Putnam. "The impact of sexual abuse on female development: Lessons from a multigenerational, longitudinal research study." *Development and Psychopathology* 23, no. 2 (2011): 453–476.

21 Heim, Christine M., Helen S. Mayberg, Tanja Mletzko, et al. "Decreased cortical representation of genital somatosensory field after childhood sexual abuse." *American Journal of Psychiatry* 170, no. 6 (2013): 616–623.

22 Danese, Andrea, and Bruce S. McEwen. "Adverse childhood experiences, allostasis, allostatic load, and age-related disease." *Physiology & Behavior* 106, no. 1 (2012): 29–39; Evans, Gary W. "A multimethodological analysis of cumulative risk and allostatic load among rural children." *Developmental Psychology* 39, no. 5 (2003): 924; Evans, Gary W. "Childhood poverty and adult psychological well-being." *Proceedings of the National Academy of Sciences* 113, no. 52 (2016): 14949–14952; Evans,

Gary W., and Michelle A. Schamberg. "Childhood poverty, chronic stress, and adult working memory." *Proceedings of the National Academy of Sciences* 106, no. 16 (2009): 6545–6549.

23 Busso, Daniel S., Katie A. McLaughlin, and Margaret A. Sheridan. "Dimensions of adversity, physiological reactivity, and externalizing psychopathology in ado-lescence: Deprivation and threat." *Psychosomatic Medicine* 79, no. 2 (2017): 162; Entringer, Sonja, Karin De Punder, Judith Overfeld, et al. "Immediate and longitudinal effects of maltreatment on systemic inflammation in young children." *Development and Psychopathology* 32, no. 5 (2020): 1725–1731; Hamlat, Elissa J., Aric A. Prather, Steve Horvath, et al. "Early life adversity, pubertal timing, and epigenetic age acceleration in adulthood." *Developmental Psychobiology* 63, no. 5 (2021): 890–902; Jenness, Jessica L., Matthew Peverill, Adam Bryant Miller, et al. "Alterations in neural circuits underlying emotion regulation following child maltreatment: A mechanism underlying trauma-related psychopathology." *Psychological Medicine* 51, no. 11 (2021): 1880–1889; Lambert, Hilary K., Matthew Peverill, Kelly A. Sambrook, et al. "Altered development of hippocampus-dependent associative learning following early-life adversity." *Developmental Cognitive Neuroscience* 38 (2019): 100666; Lambert, Hilary K., Margaret A. Sheridan, Kelly A. Sambrook, et al. "Hippocampal contribution to context encoding across development is disrupted following early-life adversity." *Journal of Neuroscience* 37, no. 7 (2017): 1925–1934; Osborn, Max, and Cathy Spatz Widom. "Do documented records and retrospective reports of childhood maltreatment similarly predict chronic inflammation?" *Psychological Medicine* 50, no. 14 (2020): 2406–2415; Renna, Megan E., Juan Peng, M. Rosie Shrout, et al. "Childhood abuse histories predict steeper inflammatory trajectories across time." *Brain, Behavior, and Immunity* 91 (2021): 541–545; Centers for Disease Control. "Preventing Child Abuse & Neglect" (2019). https://www.cdc.gov/violenceprevention/pdf/CAN-factsheet.pdf.

24 Briggs, Ernestine C., Lisa Amaya-Jackson, Karen T. Putnam, and Frank W. Putnam. "All adverse childhood experiences are not equal: The contribution of synergy to adverse childhood experience scores." *American Psychologist* 76, no. 2 (2021): 243; Putnam, Frank W., Lisa Amaya-Jackson, Karen T. Putnam, and Ernestine C. Briggs. "Synergistic adversities and behavioral problems in traumatized children and adolescents." *Child Abuse & Neglect* 106 (2020): 104492.

CHAPTER 6

1 Eichstaedt, Peter. *First Kill Your Family: Child Soldiers of Uganda and the Lord's Resistance Army*. Chicago: Chicago Review Press, 2009; Garbarino, James, Amy Governale, and Danielle Nesi. "Vulnerable children: Protection and social reintegration of child soldiers and youth members of gangs." *Child Abuse & Neglect* 110 (2020): 104415; Kerig, Patricia K., and Cecilia Wainryb. *Trauma and Resilience among Former Child Soldiers around the World*. Abingdon, UK: Routledge, 2014.

2 Pyrooz, David C., and Gary Sweeten. "Gang membership between ages 5 and 17

years in the United States." *Journal of Adolescent Health* 56, no. 4 (2015): 414–419; Coalition to Stop the Use of Child Soldiers. "Child Soldiers: Global Report 2008." London: Coalition to Stop the Use of Child Soldiers, 2008.

3 Pyrooz and Sweeten, "Gang Membership between Ages 5 and 17."

4 Paris Principles and Guidelines on Children Associated with Armed Forces or Armed Groups, February 2007. Machel Report: https://childrenandarmedcon flict.un.org/1996/08/1996-graca-machel-report-impact-armed-conflict-children/. In part because of the Paris principles and guidelines, many experts refer to children associated with armed forces, as opposed to child soldiers, to capture the fact that many children engaged with rogue armies or rebel groups are not involved at all with killing others, whether proactively or in self-defense.

5 Converting children to jihad: https://www.thetimes.co.uk/article/generation -jihad-the-british-children-brutalised-by-terror-dbjgkxkqx.

6 Brooks, Nathan, Vaishnavi Honnavalli, and Briar Jacobson-Lang. "Children of ISIS: Considerations regarding trauma, treatment and risk." *Psychiatry, Psychology and Law* 29, no. 1 (2022): 107–133.

7 Crombach, Anselm, and Thomas Elbert. "The benefits of aggressive traits: A study with current and former street children in Burundi." *Child Abuse & Neglect* 38, no. 6 (2014): 1041–1050; Crombach, Anselm, Roland Weierstall, Tobias Hecker, et al. "Social status and the desire to resort to violence: Using the example of Uganda's former child soldiers." *Journal of Aggression, Maltreatment & Trauma* 22, no. 5 (2013): 559–575; Hermenau, Katharin, Tobias Hecker, Anna Maedl, et al. "Growing up in armed groups: Trauma and aggression among child soldiers in DR Congo." *European Journal of Psychotraumatology* 4, no. 1 (2013): 21408–21417; Robjant, Katy, Anke Koebach, Sabine Schmitt, et al. "The treatment of posttraumatic stress symptoms and aggression in female former child soldiers using adapted narrative exposure therapy—A RCT in Eastern Democratic Republic of Congo." *Behaviour Research and Therapy* 123 (2019): 103482.

8 Crombach and Elbert, "The benefits of aggressive traits,"

9 Umiltà, Maria Allessandra, Rachel Wood, Francesca Loffredo, et al. "Impact of civil war on emotion recognition: The denial of sadness in Sierra Leone." *Frontiers in Psychology* 4 (2013): 523.

10 Kohrt, Brandon A. "The role of traditional rituals for reintegration and psychosocial well-being of child soldiers in Nepal," 369–387. In *Genocide and Mass Violence: Memory, Symptom, and Recovery*, edited by Devon E. Hinton and Alexander L. Hinton. Cambridge, UK: Cambridge University Press, 2014; Kohrt, Brandon A., Mark J. D. Jordans, Wietse A. Tol, et al. "Comparison of mental health between former child soldiers and children never conscripted by armed groups in Nepal." *JAMA* 300, no. 6 (2008): 691–702; Kohrt, Brandon A., Mark J. D. Jordans, Suraj Koirala, and Carol M. Worthman. "Designing mental health interventions informed by child development and human biology theory: A social ecology intervention for child soldiers in Nepal." *American Journal of Human Biology* 27, no. 1 (2015): 27–40;

Kohrt, Brandon A., Carol M. Worthman, Ramesh P. Adhikari, et al. "Psychological resilience and the gene regulatory impact of posttraumatic stress in Nepali child soldiers." *Proceedings of the National Academy of Sciences* 113, no. 29 (2016): 8156–8161.

11 Kerig, Patricia K., and Cecilia Wainryb (eds). *Trauma and Resilience Among Former Child Soldiers Around the World.* New York: Routledge, 2014; Kerig, Patricia K. "Linking childhood trauma exposure to adolescent justice involvement: The concept of posttraumatic risk-seeking." *Clinical Psychology: Science and Practice* 26, no. 3 (2019): e12280; Kerig, Patricia K., Shannon D. Chaplo, Diana C. Bennett, and Crosby A. Modrowski: "'Harm as harm'—Gang membership, perpetration trauma, and posttraumatic stress symptoms among youth in the juvenile justice system." *Criminal Justice and Behavior* 43, no. 5 (2016): 635–652; Mendez, Lucybel, Michaela M. Mozley, and Patricia K. Kerig. "Associations among trauma exposure, callous-unemotionality, race or ethnicity, and gang involvement in justice-involved youth." *Criminal Justice and Behavior* 47, no. 4 (2020): 457–469; Mendez, Lucybel, Michaela M. Mozley, and Patricia K. Kerig. "Beyond trauma exposure: Discrimination and posttraumatic stress, internalizing, and externalizing problems among detained youth." *Journal of Interpersonal Violence* 37, no. 3–4 (2022): 1825–1851.

12 Alleyne, Emma, and Jane L. Wood. "Gang involvement: Psychological and behavioral characteristics of gang members, peripheral youth and non-gang youth." *Aggressive Behavior* 36 (2010): 423–436; Alleyne, Emma, and Jane L. Wood. "Gang-Related Crime: The Social, Psychological and Behavioral Correlates." *Psychology, Crime & Law* 19, no. 7 (2013): 611–627. DeLisi, Matt, Alan J. Drury, and Michael J. Elbert. "Do behavioral disorders render gang status spurious? New insights." *International Journal of Law and Psychiatry* 62 (2019): 117–124; Frisby-Osman, Sarah, and Jane L. Wood. "Rethinking how we view gang members: An examination into affective, behavioral, and mental health predictors of UK gang-involved youth." *Youth Justice* 20, no. 1–2 (2020): 93–112; Katz, Charles M., Vincent J. Webb, Kate Fox, and Jennifer N. Shaffer. "Understanding the relationship between violent victimization and gang membership." *Journal of Criminal Justice* 39, no. 1 (2011): 48–59; Niebieszczanski, Rebecca, Leigh Harkins, Sian Judson, et al. "The role of moral disengagement in street gang offending." *Psychology, Crime & Law* 21, no. 6 (2015): 589–605.

13 Fang, Jie, Xingchao Wang, Ke-Hai Yuan, and Zhonglin Wen. "Childhood psychological maltreatment and moral disengagement: A moderated mediation model of callous-unemotional traits and empathy." *Personality and Individual Differences* 157 (2020): 109814; Niebieszczanski, et al. "The role of moral disengagement in street gang offending." 589–605; Van Noorden, Tirza H. J., Gerbert J. T. Haselager, Antonius H. N. Cillessen, and William M. Bukowski. "Dehumanization in children: The link with moral disengagement in bullying and victimization." *Aggressive Behavior* 40, no. 4 (2014): 320–328.

14 Gerson, Michael. "There's a Reason Russian Soldiers Can't Look Their Victims in the Face." *Washington Post*, April 22, 2022. https://www.washingtonpost.com /opinions/2022/04/22/russia-ukraine-mass-killings-dehumanize-civilians/.

15 Crombach and Elbert, "The benefits of aggressive traits," 1041–1050.

16 Garbarino, James, Amy Governale, and Danielle Nesi. "Vulnerable children: Protection and social reintegration of child soldiers and youth members of gangs." *Child Abuse & Neglect* 110 (2020): 104415.

17 Hunter, Jack, Alexandra Fouché, and Angy Ghannam. "Israel-Gaza Violence: The Children Who Have Died in the Conflict." BBC News, May 19, 2021. https://www .bbc.com/news/world-middle-east-57142627.

18 Kadir, Ayesha, Sherry Shenoda, and Jeffrey Goldhagen. "Effects of armed conflict on child health and development: a systematic review." *PLOS One* 14, no. 1 (2019): e0210071; Kadir, Ayesha, Sherry Shenoda, Jeffrey Goldhagen, et al. "The effects of armed conflict on children." *Pediatrics* 142 no. 6 (2018): e20182586; Østby, Gudrun, Siri Aas Rustad, and Andreas Forø Tollefsen. "Children affected by armed conflict, 1990–2019." *Conflict Trends* 6. Oslo: PRIO, 2020. https://www. prio.org/publi cations/12527.

19 Feldman, Ruth, Adva Vengrober, Moranne Eidelman-Rothman, and Orna Zagoory-Sharon. "Stress reactivity in war-exposed young children with and without posttraumatic stress disorder: relations to maternal stress hormones, parenting, and child emotionality and regulation." *Development and Psychopathology* 25, no. 4 (2013): 943–955; Halevi, Galit, Amir Djalovski, Yaniv Kanat-Maymon, et al. "The social transmission of risk: Maternal stress physiology, synchronous parenting, and well-being mediate the effects of war exposure on child psychopathology." *Journal of Abnormal Psychology* 126, no. 8 (2017): 1087–1103; Halevi, Galit, Amir Djalovski, Adva Vengrober, and Ruth Feldman. "Risk and resilience trajectories in war-exposed children across the first decade of life." *Journal of Child Psychology and Psychiatry* 57, no. 10 (2016): 1183–1193; Levy, Jonathan, Abraham Goldstein, Moran Influs, et al. "Adolescents growing up amidst intractable conflict attenuate brain response to pain of outgroup." *Proceedings of the National Academy of Sciences* 113, no. 48 (2016): 13696–13701; Levy, Jonathan, Abraham Goldstein, Maayan Pratt, and Ruth Feldman. "Maturation of pain empathy from child to adult shifts from single to multiple neural rhythms to support interoceptive representations." *Scientific Reports* 8, no. 1 (2018): 1810; Levy, Jonathan, Karen Yirmiya, Abraham Goldstein, and Ruth Feldman. "Chronic trauma impairs the neural basis of empathy in mothers: Relations to parenting and children's empathic abilities." *Developmental Cognitive Neuroscience* 38 (2019): 100658; Motsan, Shai, Karen Yirmiya, and Ruth Feldman. "Chronic early trauma impairs emotion recognition and executive functions in youth; specifying biobehavioral precursors of risk and resilience." *Development and Psychopathology* 34, no. 4 (2022): 1339–1352; Zeev-Wolf, Maor, Jonathan Levy, Richard P.

Ebstein, and Ruth Feldman. "Cumulative risk on oxytocin-pathway genes impairs default mode network connectivity in trauma-exposed youth." *Frontiers in Endocrinology* 11 (2020): 335.

20 Though the discussion here has been on the intergenerational relay from mothers to their children, fathers are often part of the relay team, with evidence that a father's stress can leave an imprint of stress on his offspring: Bale, Tracy L., Tallie Z. Baram, Alan S. Brown, et al. "Early life programming and neurodevelopmental disorders." *Biological Psychiatry* 68, no. 4 (2010): 314–319; Dietz, David M., Quincey LaPlant, Emily L. Watts, et al. "Paternal transmission of stress-induced pathologies." *Biological Psychiatry* 70, no. 5 (2011): 408–414; Dietz, David M., and Eric J. Nestler. "From father to offspring: Paternal transmission of depressive-like behaviors." *Neuropsychopharmacology* 37, no. 1 (2012): 311; Short, A. K., K. A. Fennell, Victoria M. Perreau, et al. "Elevated paternal glucocorticoid exposure alters the small noncoding RNA profile in sperm and modifies anxiety and depressive phenotypes in the offspring." *Translational Psychiatry* 6, no. 6 (2016): e837.

21 Ducke, Emily. "The Children of War." *New York Times,* August 6, 2022, https://www.nytimes.com/live/2022/08/06/world/ukraine-russia-war-children; "Ukraine: At least two children killed in war every day, says UNICEF." United Nations, June 1, 2022. https://news.un.org/en/story/2022/06/1119432.

PART III

1 Hemingway, Ernest. *A Farewell to Arms.* 1929; New York: Scribner, 1995, 249.

CHAPTER 7

1 Dantzer, Robert, Sheldon Cohen, Scott Russo, and Timothy Dinan. "Resilience and Immunity." *Brain, Behavior, and Immunity* 74 (2018): 28–42; Flajnik, Martin F., and Masanori Kasahara. "Origin and evolution of the adaptive immune system: Genetic events and selective pressures." *Nature Reviews Genetics* 11, no. 1 (2010): 47–59; Gaebler, Christian, Zijun Wang, Julio CC Lorenzi, et al. "Evolution of antibody immunity to SARS-CoV-2." *Nature* 591, no. 7851 (2021): 639–644.

2 Karlsson Linnér, Richard, Pietro Biroli, Edward Kong, et al. "Genome-wide association analyses of risk tolerance and risky behaviors in over 1 million individuals identify hundreds of loci and shared genetic influences." *Nature Genetics* 51, no. 2 (2019): 245–257.

3 Kennedy, Bryan V., Jamie L. Hanson, Nicholas J. Buser, et al. "Accumbofrontal tract integrity is related to early life adversity and feedback learning." *Neuropsychopharmacology* 46, no. 13 (2021): 2288–2294.

4 Chey, Mary, and Antony M. Jose. "Heritable epigenetic changes at single genes: Challenges and opportunities in *Caenorhabditis elegans.*" *Trends in Genetics* 38, no. 2 (2022): 116–119.

5 Chen, Stephen H., Emily Cohodes, Nicole R. Bush, and Alicia F. Lieberman. "Child and caregiver executive function in trauma-exposed families: Relations with

children's behavioral and cognitive functioning." *Journal of Experimental Child Psychology* 200 (2020): 104946; Lange, Brittany C. L., Eileen M. Condon, and Frances Gardner. "A systematic review of the association between the childhood sexual abuse experiences of mothers and the abuse status of their children: Protection strategies, intergenerational transmission, and reactions to the abuse of their children." *Social Science & Medicine* 233 (2019): 113–137; Roubinov, Danielle S., Linda J. Luecken, Sarah G. Curci, et al. "A prenatal programming perspective on the intergenerational transmission of maternal adverse childhood experiences to offspring health problems." *American Psychologist* 76, no. 2 (2021): 337; Warmingham, Jennifer M., Fred A. Rogosch, and Dante Cicchetti. "Intergenerational maltreatment and child emotion dysregulation." *Child Abuse & Neglect* 102 (2020): 104377.

6 Vågerö, Denny, Pia R. Pinger, Vanda Aronsson, and Gerard J. van den Berg. "Paternal grandfather's access to food predicts all-cause and cancer mortality in grandsons." *Nature Communications* 9, no. 1 (2018): 5124–5130.

7 Boyce, Thomas. "How to nurture an orchid child." *Psyche,* October 2020; Boyce, W. Thomas, Pat Levitt, Fernando D. Martinez, et al. "Genes, environments, and time: the biology of adversity and resilience." *Pediatrics* 147, no. 2 (2021): e20201651; Layfield, Savannah Dee, Lucie Anne Duffy, Karlye Allison Phillips, et al. "Multiomic biological approaches to the study of child abuse and neglect." *Pharmacology Biochemistry and Behavior* 210 (2021): 173271; Shonkoff, Jack P., W. Thomas Boyce, Pat Levitt, et al. "Leveraging the biology of adversity and resilience to transform pediatric practice." *Pediatrics* 147, no. 2 (2021): e20193845; Shonkoff, Jack P., Natalie Slopen, and David R. Williams. "Early childhood adversity, toxic stress, and the impacts of racism on the foundations of health." *Annual Review of Public Health* 42 (2021): 115–134.

8 Scott, Anna L., Marco Bortolato, Kevin Chen, and Jean C. Shih. "Novel monoamine oxidase A knock out mice with human-like spontaneous mutation." *Neuroreport* 19, no. 7 (2008): 739–743.

9 Brunner, Han G., M. Nelen, Xandra O. Breakefield, et al. "Abnormal behavior associated with a point mutation in the structural gene for monoamine oxidase A." *Science* 262, no. 5133 (1993): 578–580.

10 Brunner et al., "Abnormal behavior associated with a point mutation"; Eccles, David A., Donia Macartney-Coxson, Geoffrey K. Chambers, and Rodney A. Lea. "A unique demographic history exists for the MAO-A gene in Polynesians." *Journal of Human Genetics* 57, no. 5 (2012): 294–300.

11 Gibbons, Ann. "Tracking the evolutionary history of a 'warrior' gene." *Science* 304 no. 5672 (2004): 818a; *Born to Rage* documentary (https://vimeo.com/24659039); Mackenzie, Deborah. "People with 'warrior gene' better at risky decisions." *New Scientist,* December 9, 2010.

12 McSwiggan, Sally, Bernice Elger, and Paul S. Appelbaum. "The forensic use of behavioral genetics in criminal proceedings: Case of the MAOA-L genotype." *International Journal of Law and Psychiatry* 50 (2017): 17–23.

13 Buckholtz, Joshua W., and Andreas Meyer-Lindenberg. "MAOA and the neurogenetic architecture of human aggression." *Trends in Neurosciences* 31, no. 3 (2008): 120–129; Dorfman, Hayley M., Andreas Meyer-Lindenberg, and Joshua W. Buckholtz. "Neurobiological Mechanisms for Impulsive-Aggression: The Role of MAOA," 297–313. In *Neuroscience of Aggression: Current Topics in Behavioral Neurosciences,* vol. 17, edited by K. Miczek and A. Meyer-Lindenberg. Berlin: Springer-Verlag, 2013.

14 Boyce et al., "Genes, environments, and time."

15 Henry, Jeffrey, J-B. Pingault, Michel Boivin, et al. "Genetic and environmental aetiology of the dimensions of Callous-Unemotional traits." *Psychological Medicine* 46, no. 2 (2016): 405–414; Linnér, Richard Karlsson, Pietro Biroli, Edward Kong, et al. "Genome-wide association analyses of risk tolerance and risky behaviors in over 1 million individuals identify hundreds of loci and shared genetic influences." *Nature Genetics* 51, no. 2 (2019): 245–257.

16 Silveira, Patricia P., Hélène Gaudreau, Leslie Atkinson, et al. "Genetic differential susceptibility to socioeconomic status and childhood obesogenic behavior: Why targeted prevention may be the best societal investment." *JAMA Pediatrics* 170, no. 4 (2016): 359–364.

17 Boparai, Sukhdip K. Purewal, Vanessa Au, Kadiatou Koita, et al. "Ameliorating the biological impacts of childhood adversity: A review of intervention programs." *Child Abuse & Neglect* 81 (2018): 82–105; Boyce, "How to nurture an orchid child"; Boyce et al., "Genes, environments, and time"; Ellis, Bruce J., W. Thomas Boyce, Jay Belsky, et al. "Differential susceptibility to the environment: An evolutionary–neurodevelopmental theory." *Development and Psychopathology* 23, no. 1 (2011): 7–28; Rith-Najarian, Leslie R., Noah S. Triplett, John R. Weisz, and Katie A. McLaughlin. "Identifying intervention strategies for preventing the mental health consequences of childhood adversity: A modified Delphi study." *Development and Psychopathology* 33, no. 2 (2021): 748–765.

18 Caspi, Avshalom, Ahmad R. Hariri, Andrew Holmes, et al. "Genetic sensitivity to the environment: The case of the serotonin transporter gene and its implications for studying complex diseases and traits." *American Journal of Psychiatry* 167, no. 5 (2010): 509–527.

19 Byrd, Amy L., and Stephen B. Manuck. "MAOA, childhood maltreatment, and antisocial behavior: Meta-analysis of a gene-environment interaction." *Biological Psychiatry* 75, no. 1 (2014): 9–17; Mentis, Alexios-Fotios A., Efthimios Dardiotis, Eleni Katsouni, and George P. Chrousos. "From warrior genes to translational solutions: Novel insights into monoamine oxidases (MAOs) and aggression." *Translational Psychiatry* 11, no. 1 (2021): 130.

20 Belsky, Daniel W., Avshalom Caspi, Renate Houts, et al. "Quantification of biological aging in young adults." *Proceedings of the National Academy of Sciences* 112, no. 30 (2015): e4104–e4110; Belsky, Jay, Avshalom Caspi, Terrie E. Moffitt, and Richie Poulton, *The Origins of You: How Childhood Shapes Later Life.* Cambridge,

MA: Harvard University Press, 2020; Caspi, Avshalom, Renate M. Houts, Antony Ambler, et al. "Longitudinal assessment of mental health disorders and comorbidities across 4 decades among participants in the Dunedin birth cohort study." *JAMA Network Open* 3, no. 4 (2020): e203221; Caspi, Avshalom, Renate M. Houts, Daniel W. Belsky, et al. "Childhood forecasting of a small segment of the population with large economic burden." *Nature Human Behaviour* 1, no. 1 (2016): 0005; Gehred, Maria Z., Annchen R. Knodt, Antony Ambler, et al. "Long-term neural embedding of childhood adversity in a population-representative birth cohort followed for 5 decades." *Biological Psychiatry* 90, no. 3 (2021): 182–193; Moffitt, Terrie E., Richie Poulton, and Avshalom Caspi. "Lifelong impact of early self-control." *American Scientist* 101, no. 5 (2013): 352–359; Moffitt, Terrie E., Louise Arseneault, Daniel Belsky, et al. "A gradient of childhood self-control predicts health, wealth, and public safety." *Proceedings of the National Academy of Sciences* 108, no. 7 (2011): 2693–2698; Rasmussen, Line Jee Hartmann, Terrie E. Moffitt, Jesper Eugen-Olsen, et al. "Cumulative childhood risk is associated with a new measure of chronic inflammation in adulthood." *Journal of Child Psychology and Psychiatry* 60, no. 2 (2019): 199–208; Richmond-Rakerd, Leah S., Avshalom Caspi, Antony Ambler, et al. "Childhood self-control forecasts the pace of midlife aging and preparedness for old age." *Proceedings of the National Academy of Sciences* 118, no. 3 (2021): e2010211118; Shalev, Idan, Terrie E. Moffitt, et al. "Exposure to violence during childhood is associated with telomere erosion from 5 to 10 years of age: A longitudinal study." *Molecular Psychiatry* 18, no. 5 (2013): 576–581.

21 Miller, Gregory E., Tianyi Yu, Edith Chen, and Gene H. Brody. "Self-control forecasts better psychosocial outcomes but faster epigenetic aging in low-SES youth." *Proceedings of the National Academy of Sciences* 112, no. 33 (2015): 10325–10330.

22 Nardou, Romain, Eastman M. Lewis, Rebecca Rothhaas, et al. "Oxytocin-dependent reopening of a social reward learning critical period with MDMA." *Nature* 569, no. 7754 (2019): 116–120.

23 Gunnar, Megan R., Carrie E. DePasquale, Brie M. Reid, et al. "Pubertal stress recalibration reverses the effects of early life stress in postinstitutionalized children." *Proceedings of the National Academy of Sciences* 116, no. 48 (2019): 23984–23988; Reid, Brie M., Carrie E. DePasquale, Bonny Donzella, et al. "Pubertal transition with current life stress and support alters longitudinal diurnal cortisol patterns in adolescents exposed to early life adversity." *Developmental Psychobiology* 63, no. 6 (2021): e22146.

24 King, Lucy S., Natalie L. Colich, Joelle LeMoult, et al. "The impact of the severity of early life stress on diurnal cortisol: The role of puberty." *Psychoneuroendocrinology* 77 (2017): 68–74; Reid et al., "Pubertal transition with current life stress"; Wade, Mark, Margaret A. Sheridan, Charles H. Zeanah, et al. "Environmental determinants of physiological reactivity to stress: The interacting effects of early life deprivation, caregiving quality, and stressful life events." *Development and Psychopathology* 32, no. 5 (2020): 1732–1742.

25 Ellis, Bruce J., Laura S. Abrams, Ann S. Masten, et al. "Hidden talents in harsh environments." *Development and Psychopathology* 34, no. 1 (2022): 95–113; Ellis, Bruce J., Margaret A. Sheridan, Jay Belsky, and Katie A. McLaughlin. "Why and how does early adversity influence development? Toward an integrated model of dimensions of environmental experience." *Development and Psychopathology* 34, no. 2 (2022): 447–471; Frankenhuis, Willem E., and Daniel Nettle. "Integration of plasticity research across disciplines." *Current Opinion in Behavioral Sciences* 36 (2020): 157–162; Frankenhuis, Willem E., Karthik Panchanathan, and Daniel Nettle. "Cognition in harsh and unpredictable environments." *Current Opinion in Psychology* 7 (2016): 76–80.

26 Frankenhuis, Willem E., and Dorsa Amir. "What is the expected human childhood? Insights from evolutionary anthropology." *Development and Psychopathology* 34, no. 2 (2022): 473–497; Frankenhuis, W. E. and N. Walasek. "Modeling the evolution of sensitive periods." *Developmental Cognitive Neuroscience*, 41 (2020): 100715.

27 Mackes, Nuria K., Dennis Golm, Sagari Sarkar, et al. "Early childhood deprivation is associated with alterations in adult brain structure despite subsequent environmental enrichment." *Proceedings of the National Academy of Sciences* 117, no. 1 (2020): 641–649.

28 Ohashi, Kyoko, Carl M. Anderson, Elizabeth A. Bolger, et al. "Susceptibility or resilience to maltreatment can be explained by specific differences in brain network architecture." *Biological Psychiatry* 85, no. 8 (2019): 690–702; Teicher, Martin H., Jeoffry B. Gordon, and Charles B. Nemeroff. "Recognizing the importance of childhood maltreatment as a critical factor in psychiatric diagnoses, treatment, research, prevention, and education." *Molecular Psychiatry* 27, no. 3 (2022): 1331–1338.

29 Roeckner, Alyssa R., Katelyn I. Oliver, Lauren A. M. Lebois, et al. "Neural contributors to trauma resilience: A review of longitudinal neuroimaging studies." *Translational Psychiatry* 11, no. 1 (2021): 508.

30 Ellis, Bruce J., Laura S. Abrams, Ann S. Masten, et al. "Hidden talents in harsh environments." *Development and Psychopathology* 34, no. 1 (2022): 95–113; Ellis, Bruce J., JeanMarie Bianchi, Vladas Griskevicius, and Willem E. Frankenhuis. "Beyond risk and protective factors: An adaptation-based approach to resilience." *Perspectives on Psychological Science* 12, no. 4 (2017): 561–587; Ellis, Bruce J., W. Thomas Boyce, Jay Belsky, et al. "Differential susceptibility to the environment: An evolutionary–neurodevelopmental theory." *Development and Psychopathology* 23, no. 1 (2011): 7–28; Ellis, Bruce J., and Marco Del Giudice. "Developmental adaptation to stress: An evolutionary perspective." *Annual Review of Psychology* 70 (2019): 111–139; Ellis, Bruce J., Alexander J. Horn, C. Sue Carter, et al. "Developmental programming of oxytocin through variation in early-life stress: Four meta-analyses and a theoretical reinterpretation." *Clinical Psychology Review* 86 (2021): 101985; Ellis et al. "Why and how does early adversity influence development?," 447–471;

Frankenhuis et al. "Integration of plasticity research across disciplines," 157–162; Frankenhuis et al. "Cognition in harsh and unpredictable environments," 76–80.

CHAPTER 8

1 The thousand or so monkeys on Cayo Santiago are named by initials and numbers. The name is mine.

2 Novak, Melinda A. "Social recovery of monkeys isolated for the first year of life: II. Long-term assessment." *Developmental Psychology* 15, no. 1 (1979): 50–61; Novak, Melinda A., and H. F. Harlow. "Social recovery of monkeys isolated for the first year of life: I. Rehabilitation and therapy." *Developmental Psychology* 11, no. 4 (1975): 453–465.

3 Abraham, Eyal, and Ruth Feldman. "The neurobiology of human allomaternal care: Implications for fathering, coparenting, and children's social development." *Physiology & Behavior* 193 (2018): 25–34; Hrdy, Sarah Blaffer, and Judith M. Burkart. "The emergence of emotionally modern humans: Implications for language and learning." *Philosophical Transactions of the Royal Society B* 375, no. 1803 (2020): 20190499.

4 Caramazza, Alfonso, and Argye E. Hillis. "Lexical organization of nouns and verbs in the brain." *Nature* 349, no. 6312 (1991): 788–790; Hart, John, Jr., Rita Sloan Berndt, and Alfonso Caramazza. "Category-specific naming deficit following cerebral infarction." *Nature* 316, no. 6027 (1985): 439–440.

5 Conflict recurrence is 18 percent higher with than without child soldiers, and conflicts lasting more than two thousand days are 40 percent higher with child soldiers and 3 percent without. Haer, Roos, and Tobias Böhmelt. "Child soldiers as time bombs? Adolescents' participation in rebel groups and the recurrence of armed conflict." *European Journal of International Relations* 22, no. 2 (2016): 408–436; Haer, Roos, and Tobias Böhmelt. "Could rebel child soldiers prolong civil wars?" *Cooperation and Conflict* 52, no. 3 (2017): 332–359.

6 Kohrt, Brandon A. "The role of traditional rituals for reintegration and psychosocial well-being of child soldiers in Nepal," 369–387. In *Genocide and Mass Violence: Memory, Symptom, and Recovery*, edited by Devon E. Hinton and Alexander L. Hinton. New York: Cambridge University Press, 2014.

7 Carleial, Samuel, Daniel Nätt, Eva Unternährer, et al. "DNA methylation changes following narrative exposure therapy in a randomized controlled trial with female former child soldiers." *Scientific Reports* 11, no. 1 (2021): 18493; Crombach, Anselm, and Thomas Elbert. "Controlling offensive behavior using narrative exposure therapy: A randomized controlled trial of former street children." *Clinical Psychological Science* 3, no. 2 (2015): 270–282; Ertl, Verena, Anett Pfeiffer, Elisabeth Schauer, et al. "Community-implemented trauma therapy for former child soldiers in Northern Uganda: A randomized controlled trial." *JAMA* 306, no. 5 (2011): 503–512; Koebach, Anke, Samuel Carleial, Thomas Elbert, et al. "Treating

trauma and aggression with narrative exposure therapy in former child and adult soldiers: A randomized controlled trial in Eastern DR Congo." *Journal of Consulting and Clinical Psychology* 89, no. 3 (2021): 143–155; Robjant, Katy, Anke Koebach, Sabine Schmitt, et al. "The treatment of posttraumatic stress symptoms and aggression in female former child soldiers using adapted Narrative Exposure therapy—A RCT in Eastern Democratic Republic of Congo." *Behaviour Research and Therapy* 123 (2019): 103482.

8 Drury, Flora. "'My Father the Rapist': Hidden Victims of Rwanda's Genocide." BBC, June 19, 2019. https://www.bbc.com/news/world-africa-48673713.

9 Yaffa, Joshua. "The Psychologists Treating Rape Victims in Ukraine." *New Yorker*, July 14, 2022, https://www.newyorker.com/news/dispatch/the-psychologists -treating-rape-victims-in-ukraine.

10 Feldman, Ruth, Adva Vengrober, Moranne Eidelman-Rothman, and Orna Zagoory-Sharon. "Stress reactivity in war-exposed young children with and without posttraumatic stress disorder: Relations to maternal stress hormones, parenting, and child emotionality and regulation." *Development and Psychopathology* 25, no. 4 (2013): 943–955; Halevi, Galit, Amir Djalovski, Yaniv Kanat-Maymon, et al. "The social transmission of risk: Maternal stress physiology, synchronous parenting, and well-being mediate the effects of war exposure on child psychopathology." *Journal of Abnormal Psychology* 126, no. 8 (2017): 1087–1103; Levy, Jonathan, Abraham Goldstein, and Ruth Feldman. "The neural development of empathy is sensitive to caregiving and early trauma." *Nature Communications* 10, no. 1 (2019): 1905; Levy, Jonathan, Abraham Goldstein, Moran Influs, et al. "Adolescents growing up amidst intractable conflict attenuate brain response to pain of outgroup." *Proceedings of the National Academy of Sciences* 113, no. 48 (2016): 13696–13701; Ulmer Yaniv, Adi, Roy Salomon, Shani Waidergoren, et al. "Synchronous caregiving from birth to adulthood tunes humans' social brain." *Proceedings of the National Academy of Sciences* 118, no. 14 (2021): e2012900118; Zeev-Wolf, Maor, Jonathan Levy, Richard P. Ebstein, and Ruth Feldman. "Cumulative risk on oxytocin-pathway genes impairs default mode network connectivity in trauma-exposed youth." *Frontiers in Endocrinology* 11 (2020): 335.

11 Betancourt, Theresa S., Sarah K. G. Jensen, Dale A. Barnhart, et al. "Promoting parent-child relationships and preventing violence via home-visiting: A pre-post cluster randomised trial among Rwandan families linked to social protection programmes." *BMC Public Health* 20 (2020): 1–11.

12 Global Trauma Project: https://www.globaltraumaproject.com.

13 Cheadle, Jacob E., Bridget J. Goosby, Joseph C. Jochman, et al. "Race and ethnic variation in college students' allostatic regulation of racism-related stress." *Proceedings of the National Academy of Sciences* 117, no. 49 (2020): 31053–31062; Mendez, Lucybel, Michaela M. Mozley, and Patricia K. Kerig. "Beyond trauma exposure: Discrimination and posttraumatic stress, internalizing, and externalizing problems among detained youth." *Journal of Interpersonal Violence* 37, no. 3–4 (2022): 1825–1851; Mulligan, Connie J. "Systemic racism can get under our skin and into our genes." *American Journal of Physical Anthropology* 175, no. 2 (2021): 399–405; Sue, Derald Wing, Sarah Alsaidi, Michael N. Awad, et al. "Disarming racial microaggressions: Microintervention strategies for targets, White allies, and bystanders." *American Psychologist* 74, no. 1 (2019): 128–142.

14 Shonkoff, Jack, Natalie Slopen, and David R. Williams. "Early childhood adversity, toxic stress, and the impacts of racism on the foundations of health." *Annual Review of Public Health* 42 (2021): 1–20; Lui, Priscilla P., and Lucia Quezada. "Associations between microaggression and adjustment outcomes: A meta-analytic and narrative review." *Psychological Bulletin* 145 (2019), 45–78.

15 Hwang, Hyesung G., Ranjan Debnath, Marlene Meyer, et al. "Neighborhood racial demographics predict infants' neural responses to people of different races." *Developmental Science* 24, no. 4 (2021): e13070; Perszyk, Danielle R., Ryan F. Lei, Galen V. Bodenhausen, et al. "Bias at the intersection of race and gender: Evidence from preschool-aged children." *Developmental Science* 22, no. 3 (2019): e12788; Quinn, Paul C., Kang Lee, and Olivier Pascalis. "Face processing in infancy and beyond: The case of social categories." *Annual Review of Psychology* 70 (2019): 165–189; Shonkoff et al., "Early childhood adversity, toxic stress, and the impacts of racism on the foundations of health," 115–134.

16 Murphy, Mary C., Maithreyi Gopalan, Evelyn R. Carter, et al. "A customized belonging intervention improves retention of socially disadvantaged students at a broad-access university." *Science Advances* 6, no. 29 (2020): eaba4677; Walton, Gregory M., Jason A. Okonofua, Kathleen Remington Cunningham, et al. "Lifting the bar: A relationship-orienting intervention reduces recidivism among children reentering school from juvenile detention." *Psychological Science* 32, no. 11 (2021): 1747–1767.

17 Forster, Myriam, Amy L. Gower, Barbara J. McMorris, and Iris W. Borowsky. "Adverse childhood experiences and school-based victimization and perpetration." *Journal of Interpersonal Violence* 35, no. 3–4 (2020): 662–681.

18 Brunzell, Tom, Helen Stokes, and Lea Waters. "Trauma-informed positive education: Using positive psychology to strengthen vulnerable students." *Contemporary School Psychology* 20 (2016): 63–83; Garay, Beatriz, Gema Lasarte, Irune Corres-Medrano, and Imanol Santamaría-Goicuria. "Why should educators receive training in childhood trauma?" *Trends in Psychology* (2022): 1–28; Herrenkohl, Todd I., Sunghyun Hong, and Bethany Verbrugge. "Trauma-informed programs based in schools: Linking concepts to practices and assessing the evidence." *American Journal of Community Psychology* 64, no. 3–4 (2019): 373–388; Maddox, Robert Paul, James Rujimora, Lindsey M. Nichols, et al. "Trauma-informed schools: Implications for special education and school counseling." *TEACHING*

Exceptional Children (2022): 00400599221107142; O'Toole, Catriona. "When trauma comes to school: Toward a socially just trauma-informed praxis." *International Journal of School Social Work* 6, no. 2 (2022): 4; Overstreet, Stacy, and Sandra M. Chafouleas. "Trauma-informed schools: Introduction to the special issue." *School Mental Health* 8 (2016): 1-6; Scott, Jesse, Lindsey S. Jaber, and Christina M. Rinaldi. "Trauma-informed school strategies for SEL and ACE concerns during COVID-19." *Education Sciences* 11, no. 12 (2021): 796; Thomas, M. Shelley, Shantel Crosby, and Judi Vanderhaar. "Trauma-informed practices in schools across two decades: An interdisciplinary review of research." *Review of Research in Education* 43, no. 1 (2019): 422–452.

19 Hecker, Tobias, Katharin Hermenau, Dorothea Isele, and Thomas Elbert. "Corporal punishment and children's externalizing problems: A cross-sectional study of Tanzanian primary school aged children." *Child Abuse & Neglect* 38, no. 5 (2014): 884–892; Hillis, Susan D., Alexandra Blenkinsop, Andrés Villaveces, et al. "COVID-19—Associated orphanhood and caregiver death in the United States." *Pediatrics* 148, no. 6 (2021): e2021053760; Pace, Cecilia Serena, Stefania Muzi, Guyonne Rogier, et al. "The Adverse Childhood Experiences—International Questionnaire (ACE-IQ) in community samples around the world: A systematic review (part I)." *Child Abuse & Neglect* 129 (2022): 105640.

20 End Violence Against Children: https://tinyurl.com/2kgj5fgj; Raising Voices: https://raisingvoices.org/.

21 Bartlett, Jessica Dym, and Kate Steber. "How to implement trauma-informed care to build resilience to childhood trauma—Child trends." *Child Welfare*, May 2019, 1–13; Burdick, Lynn S., and Catherine Corr. "Helping teach-ers understand and mitigate trauma in their classrooms." *TEACHING Exceptional Children* (2021): 00400599211061870. Also see the National Child Traumatic Stress Network's statement on the essential ingredients of trauma-informed schools, along with several excellent resources: https://www.nctsn.org/trauma-informed-care/creating-trauma-informed-systems/schools.

22 Ainslie, George. "Willpower with and without effort." *Behavioral and Brain Sciences* 44 (2020): e30; Duckworth, Angela Lee, Heidi Grant, Benjamin Loew, et al. "Self-regulation strategies improve self-discipline in adolescents: Benefits of mental contrasting and implementation intentions." *Educational Psychology* 31, no. 1 (2011): 17–26; Duckworth, Angela L., Jamie L. Taxer, Lauren Eskreis-Winkler, et al. "Self-control and academic achievement." *Annual Review of Psychology* 70 (2019): 373–399; Duckworth, Angela L., Katherine L. Milkman, and David Laibson. "Beyond willpower: Strategies for reducing failures of self-control." *Psychological Science in the Public Interest* 19, no. 3 (2018): 102–129; Friese, Malte, David D. Loschelder, Karolin Gieseler, et al. "Is ego depletion real? An analysis of arguments." *Personality and Social Psychology Review* 23, no. 2 (2019): 107–131; Inzlicht, Michael, Brandon J. Schmeichel, K. Vohs, and R. Baumeister. "Beyond limited resources: Self-control failure as the product of shifting priorities," 165–181. In

The Handbook of Self-Regulation, 3rd ed., edited by Vohs, K., & R. Baumeister. New York: Guilford Press, 2016; Inzlicht, Michael, and Elliot Berkman. "Six questions for the resource model of control (and some answers)." *Social and Personality Psychology Compass* 9, no. 10 (2015): 511–524; Inzlicht, Michael, Kaitlyn M. Werner, Julia L. Briskin, and Brent W. Roberts. "Integrating models of self-regulation." *Annual Review of Psychology* 72 (2021): 319–345.

23 Duckworth, Angela Lee, Teri A. Kirby, Anton Gollwitzer, and Gabriele Oettingen. "From fantasy to action: Mental contrasting with implementation intentions (MCII) improves academic performance in children." *Social Psychological and Personality Science* 4, no. 6 (2013): 745–753; Gollwitzer, Anton, Gabriele Oettingen, Teri A. Kirby, et al. "Mental contrasting facilitates academic performance in school children." *Motivation and Emotion* 35 (2011): 403–412; Gollwitzer, Peter M. "Implementation intentions: Strong effects of simple plans." *American Psychologist* 54, no. 7 (1999): 493–503; Gollwitzer, Peter M., and Gabriele Oettingen. "From studying the determinants of action to analysing its regulation: A commentary on Sniehotta, Presseau and Araújo-Soares." *Health Psychology Review* 9, no. 2 (2015): 146–150; Hauser, Marc D. "How early life adversity transforms the learning brain." *Mind, Brain, and Education* 15, no. 1 (2021): 35–47; Oettingen, G., and Peter M. Gollwitzer. "Self-regulation: Principles and tools," 3–29. In *Self-Regulation in Adolescence*, edited by Oettingen, G., and P. M. Gollwitzer. New York: Cambridge University Press, 2015; Oettingen, Gabriele. "Future thought and behaviour change." *European Review of Social Psychology* 23, no. 1 (2012): 1–63; Oettingen, Gabriele, and Bettina Schwörer. "Mind wandering via mental contrasting as a tool for behavior change." *Frontiers in Psychology* 4 (2013): 562; Oettingen, Gabriele, Heather Barry Kappes, Katie B. Guttenberg, and Peter M. Gollwitzer. "Self-regulation of time management: Mental contrasting with implementation intentions." *European Journal of Social Psychology* 45, no. 2 (2015): 218–229; Oettingen, Gabriele, Doris Mayer, A. Timur Sevincer, et al. "Mental contrasting and goal commitment: The mediating role of energization." *Personality and Social Psychology Bulletin* 35, no. 5 (2009): 608–622.

24 Gawrilow, Caterina, Katrin Morgenroth, Regina Schultz, et al. "Mental contrasting with implementation intentions enhances self-regulation of goal pursuit in schoolchildren at risk for ADHD." *Motivation and Emotion* 37 (2013): 134–145.

25 There is no evidence that children have distinctive learning styles, though children may have preferences for learning in different modalities, and instruction that includes different modalities is helpful for maintaining engagement. Pashler, Harold, Mark McDaniel, Doug Rohrer, and Robert Bjork. "Learning styles: Concepts and evidence." *Psychological Science in the Public Interest* 9, no. 3 (2008): 105–119.

26 Heissel, Jennifer A., Patrick T. Sharkey, Gerard Torrats-Espinosa, et al. "Violence and vigilance: The acute effects of community violent crime on sleep and cortisol." *Child Development* 89, no. 4 (2018): e323–e331; McCoy, Dana Charles, C.

Cybele Raver, and Patrick Sharkey. "Children's cognitive performance and selective attention following recent community violence." *Journal of Health and Social Behavior* 56, no. 1 (2015): 19–36; Obradovic, Jelena, and Emma Armstrong-Carter. "Addressing educational inequalities and promoting learning through studies of stress physiology in elementary school students." *Development and Psychopathology* 32, no. 5 (2020): 1899–1913; Sharkey, Patrick, Amy Ellen Schwartz, Ingrid Gould Ellen, and Johanna Lacoe. "High stakes in the classroom, high stakes on the street: The effects of community violence on student's standardized test performance." *Sociological Science* 1 (2014): 199–220.

27 Bornemann, Boris, Peter Kovacs, and Tania Singer. "Voluntary upregulation of heart rate variability through biofeedback is improved by mental contemplative training." *Scientific Reports* 9, no. 1 (2019): 7860; Engert, Veronika, Bethany E. Kok, Ioannis Papassotiriou, et al. "Specific reduction in cortisol stress reactivity after social but not attention-based mental training." *Science Advances* 3, no. 10 (2017): e1700495; Engert, Veronika, Roman Linz, and Joshua A. Grant. "Embodied stress: The physiological resonance of psychosocial stress." *Psychoneuroendocrinology* 105 (2019): 138–146; Puhlmann, Lara, Veronika Engert, Filia Apostolakou, et al. "Only vulnerable adults show change in chronic low-grade inflammation after contemplative mental training: evidence from a randomized clinical trial." *Scientific Reports* 9, no. 1 (2019): 1–12.

28 Boyd, Jenna E., Ruth A. Lanius, and Margaret C. McKinnon. "Mindfulness-based treatments for posttraumatic stress disorder: A review of the treatment literature and neurobiological evidence." *Journal of Psychiatry and Neuroscience* 43, no. 1 (2018): 7–25; Carsley, Dana, Bassam Khoury, and Nancy L. Heath. "Effectiveness of mindfulness interventions for mental health in schools: A comprehensive meta-analysis." *Mindfulness* 9 (2018): 693–707; Dunning, Darren L., Kirsty Griffiths, Willem Kuyken, et al. "Research review: The effects of mindfulness-based interventions on cognition and mental health in children and adolescents—A meta-analysis of randomized controlled trials." *Journal of Child Psychology and Psychiatry* 60, no. 3 (2019): 244–258; Schonert-Reichl, Kimberly A., Eva Oberle, Molly Stewart Lawlor, et al. "Enhancing cognitive and social–emotional development through a simple-to-administer mindfulness-based school program for elementary school children: A randomized controlled trial." *Developmental Psychology* 51, no. 1 (2015): 52–66; Zelazo, Philip David, Jessica L. Forston, Ann S. Masten, and Stephanie M. Carlson. "Mindfulness plus reflection training: Effects on executive function in early childhood." *Frontiers in Psychology* 9 (2018): 208; Zeller, Mordechai, Kim Yuval, Yaara Nitzan-Assayag, and Amit Bernstein. "Self-compassion in recovery following potentially traumatic stress: Longitudinal study of at-risk youth." *Journal of Abnormal Child Psychology* 43 (2015): 645–653.

29 In this conversation between clinical scientists Rachel Yehuda and Bessel van der Kolk, they discuss the role of imagination in individuals with trauma, includ-

ing the ways in which psychedelics and therapy opens the mind up to imagining a more positive future: https://www.youtube.com/watch?v=3c84KdHVZVI. Studies by cognitive neuroscientist Danielle Schiller and colleagues shows that even imagining prior adverse experiences can help reduce their pathological impact on body and brain as much as actually experiencing the adverse events: Reddan, Marianne Cumella, Tor Dessart Wager, and Daniela Schiller. "Attenuating neural threat expression with imagination." *Neuron* 100, no. 4 (2018): 994–1005.

30 Caplan, Barbara, Melanie Feldman, Abbey Eisenhower, and Jan Blacher. "Student-teacher relationships for young children with autism spectrum disorder: Risk and protective factors." *Journal of Autism and Developmental Disorders* 46 (2016): 3653–3666; Pakarinen, Eija, Gintautas Silinskas, Bridget K. Hamre, et al. "Cross-lagged associations between problem behaviors and teacher-student relationships in early adolescence." *Journal of Early Adolescence* 38, no. 8 (2018): 1100–1141.

31 Creswell, Cathy, Adrienne Shum, Samantha Pearcey, et al. "Young people's mental health during the COVID-19 pandemic." *Lancet Child & Adolescent Health* 5, no. 8 (2021): 535–537; Guessoum, Sélim Benjamin, Jonathan Lachal, Rahmeth Radjack, et al. "Adolescent psychiatric disorders during the COVID-19 pandemic and lockdown." *Psychiatry Research* 291 (2020): 113264; Jones, Elizabeth A. K., Amal K. Mitra, and Azad R. Bhuiyan. "Impact of COVID-19 on mental health in adolescents: A systematic review." *International Journal of Environmental Research and Public Health* 18, no. 5 (2021): 2470; Racine, Nicole, Jessica E. Cooke, Rachel Eirich, et al. "Child and adolescent mental illness during COVID-19: A rapid review." *Psychiatry Research* 292 (2020): 113307; Racine, Nicole, Brae Anne McArthur, Jessica E. Cooke, et al. "Global prevalence of depressive and anxiety symptoms in children and adolescents during COVID-19: A meta-analysis." *JAMA Pediatrics* 175, no. 11 (2021): 1142–1150.

32 Herrenkohl, Todd I., Sunghyun Hong, and Bethany Verbrugge. "Trauma-informed programs based in schools: Linking concepts to practices and assessing the evidence." *American Journal of Community Psychology* 64, no. 3–4 (2019): 373–388; Maynard, Brandy R., Anne Farina, Nathaniel A. Dell, and Michael S. Kelly. "Effects of trauma-informed approaches in schools: A systematic review." *Campbell Systematic Reviews* 15, no. 1–2 (2019): 1–18; Thomas, M. Shelley, Shantel Crosby, and Judi Vanderhaar. "Trauma-informed practices in schools across two decades: An interdisciplinary review of research." *Review of Research in Education* 43, no. 1 (2019): 422–452.

CHAPTER 9

1 Frewen, Paul, Jenney Zhu, and Ruth Lanius. "Lifetime traumatic stressors and adverse childhood experiences uniquely predict concurrent PTSD, complex PTSD, and dissociative subtype of PTSD symptoms whereas recent adult non-traumatic stressors do not: Results from an online survey study." *European*

Journal of Psychotraumatology 10, no. 1 (2019): 1606625; Harricharan, Sherain, Margaret C. McKinnon, and Ruth A. Lanius. "How processing of sensory information from the internal and external worlds shape the perception and engagement with the world in the aftermath of trauma: Implications for PTSD." *Frontiers in Neuroscience* 15 (2021): 625490; Harricharan, Sherain, Andrew A. Nicholson, Maria Densmore, et al. "Sensory overload and imbalance: Resting-state vestibular connectivity in PTSD and its dissociative subtype." *Neuropsychologia* 106 (2017): 169–178; Lanius, Ruth A. "Trauma-related dissociation and altered states of consciousness: A call for clinical, treatment, and neuroscience research." *European Journal of Psychotraumatology* 6, no. 1 (2015): 27905; Lanius, Ruth A., Braeden A. Terpou, and Margaret C. McKinnon. "The sense of self in the aftermath of trauma: Lessons from the default mode network in posttraumatic stress disorder." *European Journal of Psychotraumatology* 11, no. 1 (2020): 1807703.

2 Nummenmaa, Lauri, Enrico Glerean, Riitta Hari, and Jari K. Hietanen. "Bodily maps of emotions." *Proceedings of the National Academy of Sciences* 111, no. 2 (2014): 646–651; Nummenmaa, Lauri, Riitta Hari, Jari K. Hietanen, and Enrico Glerean. "Maps of subjective feelings." *Proceedings of the National Academy of Sciences* 115, no. 37 (2018): 9198–9203; Volynets, Sofia, Enrico Glerean, Jari K. Hietanen, et al. "Bodily maps of emotions are culturally universal." *Emotion* 20, no. 7 (2020): 1127.

3 Zoldbrod, Aline P. "Sexual issues in treating trauma survivors." *Current Sexual Health Reports* 7, no. 1 (2015): 3–11.

4 Barlow, M. R., and J. J. Freyd. "Adaptive dissociation: Information processing and response to betrayal," 93–105. In *Dissociation and the Dissociative Disorders: DSM-V and Beyond,* edited by Dell, P. F., and J. A. O'Neil. New York: Routledge, 2009; Dimitrova, Lora I., Sophie L. Dean, Yolanda R. Schlumpf, et al. "A neurostructural biomarker of dissociative amnesia: A hippocampal study in dissociative identity disorder." *Psychological Medicine* (2021): 1–9; Harricharan et al., "Sensory overload and imbalance," 169–178; Lanius, Ruth A. "Trauma-related dissociation and altered states of consciousness: A call for clinical, treatment, and neuroscience research." *European Journal of Psychotraumatology* 6, no. 1 (2015): 27905; Terpou, Braeden A., Maria Densmore, Jean Théberge, et al. "The hijacked self: Disrupted functional connectivity between the periaqueductal gray and the default mode network in posttraumatic stress disorder using dynamic causal modeling." *NeuroImage: Clinical* 27 (2020): 102345.

5 Rogel, Ainat, Alysse M. Loomis, Ed Hamlin, et al. "The impact of neurofeed-back training on children with developmental trauma: A randomized controlled study." *Psychological Trauma: Theory, Research, Practice, and Policy* 12, no. 8 (2020): 918.

6 Thaler, Richard H., and Cass R. Sunstein. *Nudge: Improving Decisions about Health, Wealth, and Happiness.* New York: Penguin Books, 2009.

7 Groeneveld, Kayleah M., Anna M. Mennenga, Robert C. Heidelberg, et al. "Z-score neurofeedback and heart rate variability training for adults and children

with symptoms of attention-deficit/hyperactivity disorder: A retrospective study." *Applied Psychophysiology and Biofeedback* 44 (2019): 291–308; Lehrer, Paul, Karenjot Kaur, Agratta Sharma, et al. "Heart rate variability biofeedback improves emotional and physical health and performance: A systematic review and meta analysis." *Applied Psychophysiology and Biofeedback* 45 (2020): 109–129; Petrocchi, Nicola, and Simone Cheli. "The social brain and heart rate variability: Implications for psychotherapy." *Psychology and Psychotherapy: Theory, Research and Practice* 92, no. 2 (2019): 208–223; Porges, Stephen W., and Jacek Kolacz. "Neurocardiology through the lens of the polyvagal theory." In *Neurocardiology: Pathophysiological Aspects and Clinical Implications*, edited by Gelpi, R. J., and B. Buchholz. Spain: Elsevier, 2018.

8 As in many commercial tools that build off basic research, one has to be cautious in choosing an accurate device. Stone, Jason D., Hana K. Ulman, Kaylee Tran, et al. "Assessing the accuracy of popular commercial technologies that measure resting heart rate and heart rate variability." *Frontiers in Sports and Active Living* 3 (2021): 585870.

9 Bornemann, Boris, Peter Kovacs, and Tania Singer. "Voluntary upregulation of heart rate variability through biofeedback is improved by mental contemplative training." *Scientific Reports* 9, no. 1 (2019): 7860.

10 Singer looked at the oxytocin receptor gene polymorphism rs53576 and, in particular, compared individuals carrying the A variant of this gene (AA or AG)—who appear to be less social—with individuals who are homozygous for the G variant (GG).

11 Ellis, Bruce J., Alexander J. Horn, C. Sue Carter, et al. "Developmental programming of oxytocin through variation in early-life stress: Four meta-analyses and a theoretical reinterpretation." *Clinical Psychology Review* 86 (2021): 101985.

12 Silva-Filho, Edson, Giuseppina Pilloni, Leigh E. Charvet, et al. "Factors supporting availability of home-based neuromodulation using remote supervision in middle-income countries: Brazil experience." *Brain Stimulation: Basic, Translational, and Clinical Research in Neuromodulation* 15, no. 2 (2022): 385–387.

13 Frewen, Paul A., Claire Pain, David J. A. Dozois, and Ruth A. Lanius. "Alexithymia in PTSD: Psychometric and fMRI studies." *Annals of the New York Academy of Sciences* 1071, no. 1 (2006): 397–400.

14 Keynan, Jackob N., Avihay Cohen, Gilan Jackont, et al. "Electrical fingerprint of the amygdala guides neurofeedback training for stress resilience." *Nature Human Behaviour* 3, no. 1 (2019): 63–73.

15 Fruchtman-Steinbok, Tom, Jackob N. Keynan, Avihay Cohen, et al. "Amygdala electrical-finger-print (AmygEFP) NeuroFeedback guided by individually-tailored Trauma script for post-traumatic stress disorder: Proof-of-concept." *NeuroImage: Clinical* 32 (2021): 102859.

16 Riesco-Matías, Pablo, José Ramón Yela-Bernabé, Antonio Crego, and Elena Sánchez-Zaballos. "What do meta-analyses have to say about the efficacy of

neurofeedback applied to children with ADHD? Review of previous meta-analyses and a new meta-analysis." *Journal of Attention Disorders* 25, no. 4 (2021): 473–485.

17 Stern, Adi, Jessica Agnew-Blais, Andrea Danese, et al. "Associations between abuse/neglect and ADHD from childhood to young adulthood: A prospective nationally representative twin study." *Child Abuse & Neglect* 81 (2018): 274–285.

18 Rogel et al., "The impact of neurofeedback training on children with developmental trauma," 918.

19 Fleischman, Matthew J. "Documenting the impact of infra low frequency neurofeedback on underserved populations with complex clinical presentations." *Frontiers in Human Neuroscience* (2022): 329.

20 Young, Liane, Joan Albert Camprodon, Marc Hauser, et al. "Disruption of the right temporoparietal junction with transcranial magnetic stimulation reduces the role of beliefs in moral judgments." *Proceedings of the National Academy of Sciences* 107, no. 15 (2010): 6753–6758.

21 I focus on magnetic over electrical stimulation in part because there has been FDA approval for TMS, an official recognition of the significance and applicability of the method for treatment.

22 Borgomaneri, Sara, Simone Battaglia, Sara Garofalo, et al. "State-dependent TMS over prefrontal cortex disrupts fear-memory reconsolidation and prevents the return of fear." *Current Biology* 30, no. 18 (2020): 3672–3679.

23 Herz, Noa, Yair Bar-Haim, Ido Tavor, et al. "Neuromodulation of visual cortex reduces the intensity of intrusive memories." *Cerebral Cortex* 32, no. 2 (2022): 408–417.

24 Beynel, Lysianne, Ethan Campbell, Maria Naclerio, et al. "The effects of functionally guided, connectivity-based rTMS on amygdala activation." *Brain Sciences* 11, no. 4 (2021): 494; Oathes, Desmond J., Jared P. Zimmerman, Romain Duprat, et al. "Resting fMRI-guided TMS results in subcortical and brain network modulation indexed by interleaved TMS/fMRI." *Experimental Brain Research* 239 (2021): 1165–1178; Philip, Noah S., Ryan A. Doherty, Christiana Faucher, et al. "Transcranial magnetic stimulation for posttraumatic stress disorder and major depression: Comparing commonly used clinical protocols." *Journal of Traumatic Stress* 35, no. 1 (2022): 101–108; Tambini, Arielle, Derek Evan Nee, and Mark D'Esposito. "Hippocampal-targeted theta-burst stimulation enhances associative memory formation." *Journal of Cognitive Neuroscience* 30, no. 10 (2018): 1452–1472; Thakral, Preston P., Kevin P. Madore, Sarah E. Kalinowski, and Daniel L. Schacter. "Modulation of hippocampal brain networks produces changes in episodic simulation and divergent thinking." *Proceedings of the National Academy of Sciences* 117, no. 23 (2020): 12729–12740.

25 Sokhadze, Guela, Manuel F. Casanova, Desmond Kelly, et al. "Neuromodulation based on rTMS affects behavioral measures and autonomic nervous system activity in children with autism." *NeuroRegulation* 4, no. 2 (2017): 65–65; Wang,

Yao, Marie K. Hensley, Allan Tasman, et al. "Heart rate variability and skin conductance during repetitive TMS course in children with autism." *Applied Psychophysiology and Biofeedback* 41 (2016): 47–60; Zewdie, E., P. Ciechanski, H. C. Kuo, et al. "Safety and tolerability of transcranial magnetic and direct current stimulation in children: Prospective single center evidence from 3.5 million stimulations." *Brain Stimulation* 13, no. 3 (2020): 565–575; Zhang, TianHong, JunJuan Zhu, LiHua Xu, et al. "Add-on rTMS for the acute treatment of depressive symptoms is probably more effective in adolescents than in adults: Evidence from real-world clinical practice." *Brain Stimulation* 12, no. 1 (2019): 103–109.

26 Kosakowski, Heather L., Michael A. Cohen, Atsushi Takahshi, Boris Keil, Nancy Kanwisher, and Rebecca Saxe. "Selective responses to faces, scenes, and bodies in the ventral visual pathway of infants." *Current Biology* 32, no. 2 (2021): 265–274.

27 Experimental studies of fear conditioning and propranolol in mice—results and ambiguities regarding mechanisms: Dębiec, Jacek, David E. A. Bush, and Joseph E. LeDoux. "Noradrenergic enhancement of reconsolidation in the amygdala impairs extinction of conditioned fear in rats—A possible mechanism for the persistence of traumatic memories in PTSD." *Depression and Anxiety* 28, no. 3 (2011): 186–193; Giustino, Thomas F., Paul J. Fitzgerald, and Stephen Maren. "Revisiting propranolol and PTSD: Memory erasure or extinction enhancement?" *Neurobiology of Learning and Memory* 130 (2016): 26–33; Muravieva, Elizaveta V., and Cristina M. Alberini. "Limited efficacy of propranolol on the reconsolidation of fear memories." *Learning & Memory* 17, no. 6 (2010): 306–313; Przybyslawski, Jean, Pascal Roullet, and Susan J. Sara. "Attenuation of emotional and nonemotional memories after their reactivation: Role of β adrenergic receptors." *Journal of Neuroscience* 19, no. 15 (1999): 6623–6628.

28 Brunet, Alain, Daniel Saumier, Aihua Liu, et al. "Reduction of PTSD symptoms with pre-reactivation propranolol therapy: A randomized controlled trial." *American Journal of Psychiatry* 175, no. 5 (2018): 427–433; Thierrée, Sarah, Sami Richa, Alain Brunet, et al. "Trauma reactivation under propranolol among traumatized Syrian refugee children: Preliminary evidence regarding efficacy." *European Journal of Psychotraumatology* 11, no. 1 (2020): 1733248; Thomas, Émilie, Daniel Saumier, Roger K. Pitman, et al. "Consolidation and reconsolidation are impaired by oral propranolol administered before but not after memory (re)activation in humans." *Neurobiology of Learning and Memory* 142 (2017): 118–125.

29 Elsey, James W. B., Vanessa A. Van Ast, and Merel Kindt. "Human memory reconsolidation: A guiding framework and critical review of the evidence." *Psychological Bulletin* 144, no. 8 (2018): 797; Elsey, James W. B., Tamar A. Bekker, Alice M. De Bree, and Merel Kindt. "Encoding or consolidation? The effects of pre- and post-learning propranolol on the impact of an emotional scene." *Journal of Behavior Therapy and Experimental Psychiatry* 67 (2020): 101480; Giustino, Thomas F., Paul J. Fitzgerald, and Stephen Maren. "Revisiting propranolol and PTSD: Memory erasure or extinction enhancement?" *Neurobiology of Learning and Memory* 130

(2016): 26–33; Kamboj, Sunjeev K., An Tong Gong, ZhiHui Sim, et al. "Reduction in the occurrence of distressing involuntary memories following propranolol or hydrocortisone in healthy women." *Psychological Medicine* 50, no. 7 (2020): 1148–1155; Kindt, Merel, and Arnold van Emmerik. "New avenues for treating emotional memory disorders: Towards a reconsolidation intervention for post-traumatic stress disorder." *Therapeutic Advances in Psychopharmacology* 6, no. 4 (2016): 283–295.

30 Carrigan, Matthew A., Oleg Uryasev, Carole B. Frye, et al. "Hominids adapted to metabolize ethanol long before human-directed fermentation." *Proceedings of the National Academy of Sciences* 112, no. 2 (2015): 458–463.

31 Hockings, Kimberley J., Nicola Bryson-Morrison, Susana Carvalho, et al. "Tools to tipple: Ethanol ingestion by wild chimpanzees using leaf-sponges." *Royal Society Open Science* 2, no. 6 (2015): 150150.

32 Huffman, Michael A. "Folklore, animal self-medication, and phytotherapy—Something old, something new, something borrowed, some things true." *Planta Medica* 88 no. 3–4 (2021): 187–199.

33 Despite the absence of scientific evidence that psychedelics such as LSD, mescaline, or magic mushrooms were either harmful or addictive, they were classified in 1967 as Schedule 1 drugs under the United Nations convention, effectively taking them out of the research arena for forty years, living an underground existence as illegal recreational toys. Nutt, David J., and Harriet de Wit. "Putting the MD back into MDMA." *Nature Medicine* 27, no. 6 (2021): 950–951; Pollan, Michael, *How to Change Your Mind.* New York: Penguin, 2019; Pollan, Michael, *This Is Your Mind on Plants.* New York: Penguin, 2022.

34 Miller, Melanie J., Juan Albarracin-Jordan, Christine Moore, and José M. Capriles. "Chemical evidence for the use of multiple psychotropic plants in a 1,000-year-old ritual bundle from South America." *Proceedings of the National Academy of Sciences* 116, no. 23 (2019): 11207–11212.

35 David E. Carpenter, "Saved by Psychedelics: After traditional methods fail, ayahuasca heals a deep emotional trauma," *Forbes,* January 27, 2020.

36 Palhano-Fontes, Fernanda, Dayanna Barreto, Heloisa Onias, et al. "Rapid antidepressant effects of the psychedelic ayahuasca in treatment-resistant depression: A randomized placebo-controlled trial." *Psychological Medicine* 49, no. 4 (2019): 655–663.

37 Araujo, Draulio B. de, Sidarta Ribeiro, Guillermo A. Cecchi, et al. "Seeing with the eyes shut: Neural basis of enhanced imagery following ayahuasca ingestion." *Human Brain Mapping* 33, no. 11 (2012): 2550–2560; James, Edward, Joachim Keppler, Thomas L Robertshaw, and Ben Sessa. "N, N-dimethyltryptamine and Amazonian ayahuasca plant medicine." *Human Psychopharmacology: Clinical and Experimental* 37, no. 3 (2022): e2835; Jiménez-Garrido, Daniel F., María Gómez-Sousa, Genís Ona, et al. "Effects of ayahuasca on mental health and quality of life

in naïve users: A longitudinal and cross-sectional study combination." *Scientific Reports* 10, no. 1 (2020): 4075; Mendes Rocha, Juliana, Giordano Novak Rossi, Flávia L. Osório, et al. "Effects of ayahuasca on personality: Results of two randomized, placebo-controlled trials in healthy volunteers." *Frontiers in Psychiatry* 12 (2021): 1359; Pasquini, Lorenzo, Fernanda Palhano-Fontes, and Draulio B. Araujo. "Subacute effects of the psychedelic ayahuasca on the salience and default mode networks." *Journal of Psychopharmacology* 34, no. 6 (2020): 623–635; Ruffell, Simon, Nige Netzband, Catherine Bird, et al. "The pharmacological interaction of compounds in ayahuasca: A systematic review." *Brazilian Journal of Psychiatry* 42 (2020): 646–656; Viol, Aline, Fernanda Palhano-Fontes, Heloisa Onias, et al. "Characterizing complex networks using entropy-degree diagrams: Unveiling changes in functional brain connectivity induced by Ayahuasca." *Entropy* 21, no. 2 (2019): 128; Zeifman, Richard J., Nikhita Singhal, Rafael G. Dos Santos, "Rapid and sustained decreases in suicidality following a single dose of ayahuasca among individuals with recurrent major depressive disorder: Results from an open-label trial." *Psychopharmacology* 238 (2021): 453–459.

38 The Goop Lab: https://www.netflix.com/title/80244690; *Rolling Stone*: https://www.rollingstone.com/culture/culture-news/psilocybin-legal-therapy-mdma-753946/; *New York Times*: https://www.nytimes.com/2021/05/09/health/psychedelics-mdma-psilocybin-molly-mental-health.html.

39 Daws, Richard E., Christopher Timmermann, Bruna Giribaldi, et al. "Increased global integration in the brain after psilocybin therapy for depression." *Nature Medicine* 28, no. 4 (2022): 844–851.

40 Mitchell, Jennifer M., Michael Bogenschutz, Alia Lilienstein, et al. "MDMA-assisted therapy for severe PTSD: A randomized, double-blind, placebo-controlled phase 3 study." *Nature Medicine* 27, no. 6 (2021): 1025–1033.

41 Burke, Matthew J., and Daniel M. Blumberger. "Caution at psychiatry's psychedelic frontier." *Nature Medicine* 27, no. 10 (2021): 1687–1688; Halvorsen, Joar Øveraas, Florian Naudet, and Ioana A. Cristea. "Challenges with benchmarking of MDMA-assisted psychotherapy." *Nature Medicine* 27, no. 10 (2021): 1689–1690; Marek, Scott, Brenden Tervo-Clemmens, Finnegan J. Calabro, et al. "Reproducible brain-wide association studies require thousands of individuals." *Nature* 603, no. 7902 (2022): 654–660; Marks, Mason, and I. Glenn Cohen. "Psychedelic therapy: A roadmap for wider acceptance and utilization." *Nature Medicine* 27, no. 10 (2021): 1669–1671; Noorani, Tehseen, and Jonny Martell. "New frontiers or a bursting bubble? Psychedelic therapy beyond the dichotomy." *Frontiers in Psychiatry* 12 (2021): 727050; Nutt and de Wit, "Putting the MD back into MDMA," 950–951; Pantoni, Madeline M., Jinah L. Kim, Kaitlin R. Van Alstyne, and Stephan G. Anagnostaras. "MDMA and memory, addiction, and depression: Dose-effect analysis." *Psychopharmacology* 239, no. 3 (2022): 935–949.

notes

AFTERWORD

1 Shimkhada, Riti, Jacqueline Miller, Elizabeth Magnan, et al. "Policy considerations for routine screening for adverse childhood events (ACEs)." *Journal of the American Board of Family Medicine* 35, no. 4 (2022): 862–866.

2 McGinty, Emma E., and Matthew D. Eisenberg. "Mental health treatment gap—The implementation problem as a research problem." *JAMA Psychiatry* 79, no. 8 (2022): 746–747.

3 Peña, Pablo A., and Anupam Jena. "Child deaths by gun violence in the US during the COVID-19 pandemic." *JAMA Network Open* 5, no. 8 (2022): e2225339.

abandonment, 10–12, 71, 84
abuse. *See* child abuse
ACE scores. *See also* adverse childhood
    experiences
  adversity characteristics, 20–21
  famine and, 21–22
  impact on government policy, 241
  limitations of, 43–45, 241
  modifying, 48–49
  sexual abuse disproportionately
      contributing to, 20
  timing of events and, 20–21
Aces Aware, 44
acquired immune system, 145–46
acute stress, 62–63, 200
adaptive functioning, 147
adaptive responses, 69, 97, 119–20, 125, 162
ADHD (attention deficit hyperactivity
    disorder), 197–98, 216–17
adverse childhood experiences (ACEs).
    See also ACE scores
  allostatic load, 18–19
  annual cost of, 19–20
  cumulative burden of, 17–20, 240–41,
    243–44
  demographics, 16
  effects on adults, xiii
  enhancing plasticity, 162

impact of, 19
international translation, 16
odds ratio, 19
origins of, 12–17
prevalence rates, 16–17
questionnaire, 14–16, 42–45
resilience to (*See* RACEs)
synergistic effects of, 120–21
traumatic reactions to (*See* TRACEs)
Adverse Ts framework
  critical tests of, 88–89
  described, 49–51
  tenure dimension, 50, 62–67, 86, 92
  timing dimension, 50, 56–61, 86, 89,
    116, 162–63
  toxicity dimension, 50, 66, 73–77,
    88–89
  turbulence dimension, 50, 67–73, 94
  type dimension, 50, 51–56, 86, 116
adversity. *See also* adverse childhood
    experiences; Adverse Ts framework;
    early adversity
  abandonment threats and, 10–12
  allostatic load modified by, 119–20
  chronic component of, 27
  closing gap between scientific
      understanding and practice, 242
  communities as cause of, 167–68

adversity (*cont.*)
    coordination of organizations and
        professionals, 242–43
    cross-cultural differences in
        perception of, 25
    cross-pollinating disciplines with, xv
    cumulative, 19, 79
    defined, 25–27
    delayed pathology path, 40–41
    discrimination as form of, 187–88
    early-occurring experiences of, 56
    erasing pathological responses to, xiv
    example of, xi–xii
    intergenerational effects on, xii
    neglect as type of, 60
    oppression as form of, 187–88
    resistant path, 40–41
    sensitive period for, 61
    seriousness of, 27
    toxicity as dimension of, 76–77
    types of, xii, 25, 51
    universality of, 16–17
    war as type of, 66
Afghanistan, 114
African Americans, 108
aggression, 25, 38, 55–56, 134–35,
        150, 154. *See also* microaggressions;
        violence
aging marker, 21–23, 61, 79, 96, 112, 120,
        158, 188, 244
Ainsworth, Mary, 89–90, 93
Albert (case subject), 239–40, 241
alcohol consumption, 228–29
alcohol dehydrogenase, 229
alexithymia, 214–15
al-Hadidi children, 136
Aliya (case subject), 54–55, 162, 220
allomothers, 170–73, 185, 240
allostasis, 17–18
allostatic load, 18–19, 31, 119–20
Amber (case subject), 232–33
Amboseli National Park, Kenya, 78
American Psychological Association, 35
Amin, Idi, 124
amygdala
    abuse affecting size of, 112, 116–17, 120
    calming of, 215–16
    described, 11
    fear conditioning and, 75–77

    frontal lobe connectivity with, 100
    mental health and, 163
    neurofeedback and, 214–16
    stimulation of, 223
    visual cortex connection, 222–23
amygdala electrical fingerprinting
    feedback, 215–16
Anda, Robert, xiii, 13–14, 42
anger recognition, 111–12
animal hypnosis, 68–69
anti-inflammatories, 157
anxiety
    in adulthood, 140
    benzodiazepine receptors, 11
    COVID-19 and, 52
    eating and, 13
    escitalopram, 235
    heat map, 208
    as overreaction to pain, 109
    physiological level, 72
    propranolol treatment, 226–27
    psychological level, 72
    separation and, 87, 108
    turbulence dimension, 68, 72
appetitive aggression, 134
appetitive violence, 134–35, 183
associative learning, 94–95
asynchronous brain prints, 140
attachment
    to caregivers, 139, 177
    critical period for, 59–60
    developmental signatures, 9–12
    disorganized, 10–12, 70, 93–94
    erasing signature of, 9–12
    as healthy, 70
    in mother-child relationships, 112
    secure, 9–10, 101, 177
    social, 148
    styles, 137–38
attachment bonds, 60
attachment signatures, 9–12
attention deficit hyperactivity disorder
    (ADHD), 197–98, 216–17
attentional focus, 111
autism, 35, 157, 174, 211
Automatic Computing Engine, 3
autonomic nervous system, 77, 153,
        176, 211, 244
ayahuasca, 231–35

bacha bazi (boy play), 114
Badrick (case subject), 149, 158, 220
Balanites fruit, 228
Beasts of No Nation (film), 125
A Beautiful Mind (film), 219
Bellis, Mark, 19
Belsky, Jay, 116
benzodiazepine receptors, 11
Berry, Jason, 114
beta-blockers, 224
Betancourt, Theresa, 185
biases, 188, 189
biofeedback, 211–14, 217–18. *See also*
    neurofeedback
Birn, Rasmus, 30–31, 146
Blackburn, Elizabeth, 96
Böhmelt, Tobias, 179
Bolondemu (case subject), 124–25, 158,
    162, 220, 222
Bonanno, George, 40, 41
borderline personality disorder, 11–12
Bossou region, Guinea, West
    Africa, 229
Boston Globe, 114
Bowlby, John, 89–90
boy play (*bacha bazi*), 114
brain development
    parasympathetic nervous system,
        65, 138–39, 211, 224
    sexual abuse and, 115–16
    vagus nerve, 64, 138, 211–12, 213
    war exposure and, 139–40
brain maturation, 56, 116, 127, 135
brain prints, 140
brain regions, synchrony of, 140
brain stimulation, 218–23
breathing awareness, 201–2
Brookwood, Marilyn, 171
Brunet, Alain, 224–25
Bucharest Early Intervention Project
    (BEIP), 91–93, 172–73
Burke Harris, Nadine, 44

Caenorhabditis elegans, 147–48
callous-unemotional traits, 8–9, 42
calming techniques, 198–203, 215–16
Cameron, Judy, 90
Caramazza, Alfonso, 176
caregivers. *See also* allomothers;
    mother-child relationships;
    parent-reared children
    as buffer to stress, 71
    developmental trauma disorder and, 139
    frayed bond with, 101
    instability with, 99
    positive stress and, 63
    reliance on, 60
    secure attachment to, 139, 177
    serve-and-return relationships, 84, 101
    understanding of early childhood
        development, 185
    verbal abuse from, 107–8
caretaker loss, 48, 52, 54, 131
Carine (case subject), 184
Caspi, Avshalom, 116, 153–54, 155–56
Catherine the Great, Russia, 83
Catholic priests, 113, 114
Ceaușescu, Nicolae, 90
celibacy tax, 90
Centers for Disease Control and
    Prevention (CDC), 13, 16, 120
central nervous system, 211
Charlie (case subject), 195–98
child abuse. *See also* emotional abuse;
    physical abuse; sexual abuse; verbal
    abuse
    amygdala size affected by, 112,
        116–17, 120
    in East Africa, 192
    as an identity crisis, 109
    neglect, 216–17
    triggers, 119–20
child development. *See also* developmental
    programs
    cognitive control, 176–77
    developmental periods of, 173
    foster care interventions and,
        173–79
    heart rate variability response, 176
    language expression and
        comprehension, 174–76
    of orphanage-reared children, 173–79
    physical and motor growth, 173–74
    social skills, 176–77
    tenure dimension's impact on, 67
    toxic deprivation halting growth
        in, 90–95
    turbulent adversity's impact on, 72–73

child soldiers. *See also* children in gangs
case story, 124–25
civilian children compared to, 131–32
cubs of the caliphate, 128–29
defining, 126–28
emotional development of, 130–31
feeling stigmatized, 182
impact of the trauma on, 130
interventions designed for, 180–82
mental health recovery, 182
of Nepal, 131, 180
recruitment of, 128–29
rehabilitation of, 129–30
reintegration process, 180–81
as resistant to change, 179–80
therapeutic treatment, 182–83
transformation of, 129
childhood
adversity (*See* adversity)
age cutoff for, 127, 135
with callous-unemotional traits, 8–9
defined, 24
with emotional disabilities, 7–9
later life outcomes, 155–56
children in gangs, 125–26, 132–33. *See also*
child soldiers
chimpanzee community, 123–24, 228–29
chlorpromazine, 68
chronic pathology, 40–41
chronic physical abuse, 38–39
chronic stress. *See* stress
chronic traumatic encephalopathy
(CTE), 17
cognitive behavioral therapy, 209
cognitive control, 176–77
cognitive development, 94
cognitive neglect, 51–52
Communist Party of Nepal, 131
communities, as cause of adversity, 167–68
community violence, 199
complex trauma, 217
conduct problems, 8
conflict zones, 136–40
consolidation, 200, 224–25
control deprivation, 69–71
corporal punishment in schools, 192–93
cortisol stress response, 176
Cosby, Bill, 74
COVID-19, 52, 145, 204, 243

Crisis Childhood (documentary), 125
critical periods, defined, 59
critical thinking, 198–99
Crombach, Anselm, 134
cubs of the caliphate, 128–29
cultural dysfunction, 53
culture change, 194
cumulative adversity, 19, 79

Dahl, Roald, 107
Dalai Lama, 218–19
Damon, Matt, 74
Dare, Isa, 128
Daws, Richard, 235
default mode network (DMN), 140, 234
delayed pathology, 40–41
Democratic Republic of the Congo,
129, 182–83
depression, treatment-resistant, 108,
230–31, 233–36. *See also* post-traumatic
stress disorder
deprivation
in animals, 85–86
brain volume, 162–63
child development and, 90–95
cortisol stress response in, 176
deficits in reward learning and, 146–47
impact of, 83–84, 95
of maternal care, 87–90, 170–71
rhesus monkeys experiment, 169–71
socioeconomic status and, 99–101
timing dimension, 162–63
toxic, 96–98
developmental programs
alterations to, 55–56
animals and, 3–4
creating executive functioning,
176–77
as damaged, 4
environment's role in, 4
experience-expectant, 5–7
gene-environment interactions and,
153–54
opportunity windows in, 58–59
plasticity in, 161–62
reliance on unconscious processes, 5
for survival, 4–5
developmental signatures
of attachment, 9–12

emotional awareness and, 7–9
of success, 4–7
of toxic deprivation, 96–98
developmental trauma disorder (DTD),
35–37, 134, 139, 210, 217, 227
di Pellegrino, Giuseppe, 221
*Diagnostic and Statistical Manual of
Mental Disorders* (*DSM-5*)
limited prosocial emotions, 8–9
on PTSD, 35–36
rejecting developmental trauma
disorder, 37
trauma, defined, 33
dialectical behavioral therapy, 209
Dickerson, Caitlin, 100
diffusion tensor imaging, 108
dimethyltryptamine (DMT), 231–33
disabilities, students with, 190
discrimination, 108, 187–90
discrimination bias, 123
disorganized attachment, 10–12, 70, 93–94
dissociation, 29, 139–40, 186, 202,
207–9, 227
DNA methylation, 22–23, 61, 153, 158
Doblin, Rick, 236–37
dopamine, 38–39
dorsal (back) vagal state, 65
dorsolateral prefrontal cortex, 221
Duckworth, Angela, 197
Dunn, Erin, 61
Dunsmoor, Joseph, 76–77
Dutch famine study, 23, 67, 137

early adversity, xi–xii, xiii–xv. *See also*
adversity
East Africa, 192
eating, anxiety and, 13
Ebert, Roger, 67
ecological threats, 53
economics, 19–20
ecstasy. *See* MDMA
EEG (electroencephalogram)
readings, 97–98
Eid al-Fitr, 136
Elbert, Thomas, 134, 182
electroconvulsive shock therapy, 219
Ellis, Bruce, 32
emotion blindness, 214–15
emotion recognition, 138, 146, 177–78

emotional abuse, 20, 36–37, 74–75, 104,
117, 192–93
emotional awareness, 7–9
emotional dysregulation
abuse triggering, 119–20
brain wiring and, 163
developmental trauma disorder and, 36
meditation and, 201
reactive violence leading to, 134
reducing, 221
self-control and, 194
source of, 195–98
therapeutic intervention and, 186
emotional neglect, 20, 48–49, 51,
64, 243–44
empathy mindset intervention, 189–90
encoding, 200
engineered expectations, 5
environmentally regulating conditions,
152–53
environmentally triggering
conditions, 152
environment-gene interactions, 152–54
epigenetics, 21–23, 67, 148–49, 244.
See also aging marker;
intergenerational effects
escitalopram, 235
Ethan (case subject), 84, 98
Evans, Gary, 120
evolutionary programming, 3–4
executive functioning, 138–39, 148, 163,
172–73, 176–77, 207
expected experience, 5
experience, defined, 24–25
experience-expectant developmental
programs, 5–7

face recognition deficit, 35
Family Strengthening (Sugira Muryango)
intervention, 185–86
famine, 21–23, 78, 137. *See also* Dutch
famine study
fear
acquiring, 106
capacity for, 105
consolidation, 200, 224–25
overgeneralizing response to, 77
reactions to, 106–7
triggering, 105–7

index

fear conditioning, 75–77, 106, 221.
  See also learning by association
Feldman, Ruth, 137–40, 185
Felitti, Vincent, xiii, 12–13, 18
Finkelhor, David, 44
Fionna (case study), 207, 209, 218, 220
Food and Drug Administration, 228
Ford, Julian, 35–36
Forensic Offender Rehabilitation through
  Narrative Exposure Therapy
  (FORNET), 182–83
foster care interventions
  Bucharest Early Intervention Project
    (BEIP), 172–73
  child development and, 173–79
  cognitive control, 176–77
  developing, 172
  effectiveness of, 161
  language acquisition, 174
  reducing risk of psychiatric
    disorders, 177–78
  social skills, 176–77
foundling homes, 83–84
Fox, Nathan, 91, 172
Frances, Allen, 36
Frank (case subject), 198–200, 202–3
Frankl, Viktor, 73
free will, 67–68
frontal lobes, 24, 66, 72, 100, 112, 127, 155,
  163, 214–16, 221

gangs. *See* children in gangs
Garbarino, James, 135
Gawrilow, Caterina, 197
gene-environment interactions, 152–54
genetically altering conditions, 152
Global Trauma Project, 186
Gollwitzer, Peter, 196
Good School Toolkit (GST), 192–94
government policies, ACE scores'
  impact on, 241
Greider, Carol, 96
guided interventions, xii
Gunnar, Megan, 160
Guterres, António, 62

habits of mind, 195–98
Haer, Roos, 179
Harlow, Harry, 88–89, 169–71

harmaline, 231
healthy attachment, 70
heart rate variability, 176, 187–88, 201,
  211–14, 217
heat map scale, 208–9
Heim, Christine, 118
helplessness, learned, 68–70
heritability of a trait, 42–43
hermaphrodites, 147–48
Herz, Noa, 222–23
Hess, Amanda, 109
hibernation, as response to stress, 97
hidden talents, 32, 111–12, 164–65, 195
high-frequency heart rate variability
  (HFHRV), 211–13
hippocampus, 69, 72, 98, 100, 109, 112,
  116–17, 120, 163, 223
Hobfoll, Stevan, 40, 41
Hoffman, Wendell, 171–72
Holy Family School, 113
home displacement, 52–53
home visit interventions, 185–86
household dysfunction, 14–15, 25, 51, 52, 54
HPA system. *See* hypothalamic-
  pituitary-adrenal (HPA) system
Hughes, Karen, 19
human cruelty, 104
Hutu tribe, 184
hypothalamic-pituitary-adrenal (HPA)
  system, 69, 72, 97, 117, 160–61

identity crisis, 109, 110
IF-THEN plans, 196–98
imaginary play, 208
immobility, as adaptive response, 68–69
immune system, 145–46
imprinting, 59–60, 97–98
inflammation, 157
innate immune system, 145
institutionalized children. *See also*
  orphanage-reared children
  cognitive development, 94
  disorganized attachment in, 93–94
  parent-reared children vs., 93–97
  pediatric measures of, 93
  social-emotional development, 94
insulin shock therapy, 219
intergenerational effects.
  See also epigenetics

adversities as pathway of, xii
of famine, 137
of neglect, 60
of physical abuse, 112
of structural racism, 108
timing and, 56
of violent norms, 149
of war, 137–38
International Centre for Missing &
    Exploited Children, 243
International Organization for
    Migration, 53
intrusive memories, 220–23
Islamic State of Iraq and Syria (ISIS),
    128–29
isolation. *See* social isolation
Israeli-Palestinian conflict, 62

Jacobellis, Nico, 23
Jacobellis v. Ohio, 23
Jacques (case subject), 164–65
James, LeBron, xi–xii
Jarriel, Tom, 91

Kendler, Kenneth, 117
Kenya, 192
Kevin, 103–5, 220, 222
Keynan, Jackob, 215–16
Kibale Forest, Uganda, 123, 228
Kohrt, Brandon, 131–32, 180, 182

language, 6
language acquisition, 57–58, 174–75, 241
language delay, 57–58, 175–76
language expression and comprehension,
    174–76
Leah (case subject), 47–49, 220
learned helplessness, 68–70,
    94, 106, 129
learning
    associative, 94–95
    critical moments for, 85–90
    songbird study, 85–86
    stress as help to, 200
learning by association, 68–69, 94–95, 106.
    See also fear conditioning
limited prosocial emotions, 8–9
Lord's Resistance Army (LRA), 124–25, 158
Lorenz, Konrad, 59–60

The Lovers (film), 23
Lyons-Ruth, Karlen, 10

Machel, Graça, 126
Mackes, Nuria, 162–63
magic mushrooms, 234–36
Mai-Mai rebel group, 129
Malle, Louis, 23
maltreatment, 12
MAOA mutations, 150–51
MAOA-H variant, 153–54
MAOA-L variant, 151, 154
Marler, Peter, 86
maternal care, 87–90
maternal deprivation, 87–90, 170–71
McEwen, Bruce, 18
McLaughlin, Katie, 26, 120
MDMA, 213, 236–37. *See also* psychedelics
Medi-Cal, 44
medications, 224–28. *See also* psychedelics
meditative practices, 201–2
memories
    erasing, 224–27
    intrusiveness of, 220–23
    propranolol's affect on, 225–26
mental contrasting with implementation
        intentions, 196–98
mental disorder, defined, 36
mental health
    amygdala and, 163
    electrical treatments for, 220–21
    sexual abuse and, 115–17
microaggressions, 187–88
migration. *See* home displacement
Milgram, Stanley, 75
Miller, Gregory, 158
Miller, Melanie, 231
mirror neurons, 106
Mittal, Mona, 72
Moffitt, Terrie, 116, 153–54, 155–56
molly. *See* MDMA
Mon Oncle d'Amérique (film), 67–68, 75
monoamine oxidase A (MAOA)
    gene, 150–54
monoamine oxidase (MAO)
    enzymes, 231–32
moral disengagement, 133
mother-child relationships.
        See also caregivers

mother-child relationships (*cont.*)
attachment and, 112
bond in, 9–12
deprivation of care, 87–90, 170–71
intergenerational legacy (*See*
intergenerational effects)
serve-and-return, 70–71, 101, 107–8,
148, 185
motor development, 173–74
Mulligan, Connie, 39
Multidisciplinary Association for
Psychedelic Studies (MAPS), 236–37
mushrooms, 234–36
My American Uncle (film), 67–68, 75

Nadine (case subject), 62–63, 66, 222
Nardou, Romain, 159–60, 236
Nassar, Larry, 114
National Child Traumatic Stress
Network, 33, 243
neglect
abuse associated with, 216–17
COVID-19 and, 204
described, 14–15
emotional, 20, 48–49, 64, 243–44
intergenerational effects of, 60
physical, 22, 51
teacher-student relationships, 216–17
as type of adversity, 60
types of, 51–54
Neil (case subject), 113
Nelson, Charles, 91, 172
Nepal government, 131
neurofeedback, 214–17, 244
neuroplasticity, 115
New York Times, 109, 114, 140
Novak, Melinda, 171
nucleus accumbens, 159–60, 213
nudging
biofeedback as form of, 211–14, 217–18
to make the right choice, 210–11
vagus nerve and, 212–13
numbers model, 61
Nummenmaa, Lauri, 208

obedience, 75–76
obesity, sexual abuse connected with, 13
observational learning. *See* learning by
association

odds ratio, 19
Oettingen, Gabriele, 196
Omalu, Bennet, 17
Omar (case subject), 136–37
One Flew Over the Cuckoo's Nest (film), 219
opportunity windows, 58–59, 214, 217
oppression, 108, 187–90
orphanage-reared children, 84, 173–79. *See
also* Bucharest Early Intervention
Project; institutionalized children;
Romanian orphans
The Orphans of Davenport
(Brookwood), 171
overgeneralization, 77
own-race bias, 188
oxytocin hormone, 159–60, 213

pain, anxiety as overreaction to, 109
parasympathetic nervous system, 65,
138–39, 211, 224
parental verbal abuse, 109
parent-reared children, 93–97. *See also*
mother-child relationships
Pavlov, Ivan, 68
physical abuse
anger recognition and, 111
Shuhada (Sinéad O'Connor), 110
results of, 112
physical aggression, 135
physical neglect, 22, 51
plasticity
adverse childhood experiences
enhancing, 243–44
in the brain, 116, 118–19
in developmental systems, 161–62
enhancing, 162
hidden talents as form of, 164–65
of nucleus accumbens, 159–60
potential in puberty, 159–61
self-control and, 157
in sensitive periods, 59
of somatosensory cortex, 117–18
pleasure
in harming others, 130
sexual abuse and, 118
Pollak, Seth, 111, 146
Pollan, Michael, 230
polyvagal theory, 64–66, 211
Porges, Stephen, 64–65, 211

positive stress, 63
post-traumatic stress disorder (PTSD), 33, 35–37, 131–32, 139, 216–17, 223, 225–27, 236–37
proactive violence, 133–34
propranolol, 224–28
prosopagnosia, 35
psilocin, 234
psilocybin, 234–36
psychedelics
    ayahuasca, 231–35
    described, 230
    dimethyltryptamine (DMT), 231–33
    as exhilarating, 230
    as frightening, 230
    harmaline, 231
    as helpful therapy, 157
    as liberating, 230
    magic mushrooms, 234–36
    MDMA, 213, 236–37
    psilocybin, 234–36
    self-medicating with, 229–30
    therapy-assisted treatment, 236–38, 244
    transformative impact of, 230–31
psychiatric disorders, 95, 96, 157, 163, 177–78. See also anxiety; post-traumatic stress disorder
psychopathology, 121
psychopathy, 9
puberty, plasticity potential of, 159–61
Putnam, Frank, 120

RACEs (resilient responses to adverse childhood experiences), 30–32
racial inequities, 188–89
Raising Voices organization, 192–94, 243
Ramachandran, Vilayanur, 118
rape. See sexual abuse
reactive aggression, 134
reactive violence, 133–34
reconsolidation, 224–25
rehabilitation, 129–30
reintegration, 180–81
relentless stress, 68–69
Rememberings (Shuhada), 110
repetitive transcranial magnetic stimulation (rTMS), 218–19, 221–23, 227–28

resilience, 38, 74–75, 162–63
resilience signatures, 38–39
Resnais, Alain, 67–68
resourcefulness, 32
revictimization, 64, 115
reward, 39
reward learning, 146–47
reward processing, 31, 146, 159–60
rewards, 38–39, 159, 178
rhesus monkeys, 169–71
risky behaviors, 31–32, 146–47
rodent research, 86–88
Romania, 90–93
Romanian orphans. See also institutionalized children
    associative learning, 94–95
    Bucharest Early Intervention Project (BEIP), 91–93
    deficient children, 91
    learning by association, 94
    parent-reared children vs., 93–97
    productive children, 91
    stereotyped behaviors of, 174
    telomeres, measurement of, 96–97
    toxic deprivation of, 97–98, 160
Rwanda, 184

safe schools, 190–94
Sandusky, Jerry, 114
Sasha (case subject), 190–91
schools
    corporal punishment in, 192–93
    empathy mindset intervention, 189–90
    empowering trauma-sensitive teachers, 203–4
    Good School Toolkit (GST), 192–94
    racial inequities in, 188–89
    Raising Voices, 192–94
    safe schools, 190–94
    students with disabilities, 190
    teacher-student relationships, 190, 192–93, 203–4, 216–17
    trauma-informed, 191–94, 199–200
Schroeder, Allison, 72
secure attachment, 9–10, 101, 177
self, sense of, 110, 148, 209, 234
self-control, 155–59, 194, 196
self-medication, 229–30
self-regulation, 39

Seligman, Martin, 68
sense of agency, 210
sense of self, 110, 148, 209, 234
sensitive periods, 59, 61
separation, 87, 100, 108
Serena (case subject), 78–79
serve-and-return relationships, 70–71,
    101, 107–8, 148, 185
sex trafficking, 114
sexual abuse
    ACE scores and, 20
    bacha bazi (boy play), 114
    brain development and, 115–16
    by Catholic priests, 113, 114
    effects on women's bodies, 118–19
    emotional response to, 208–9
    impact of, 115–17
    later-life heath linked to, 13
    mental health and, 115–17
    obesity connected with, 13
    paired with other ACEs, 121
    as part of culture, 114
    physical health and, 115–18
    prevalence rates, 192
    before puberty, 118–19
    pubescent adolescence and, 115
    recovery from, 74
    revictimization, risk of, 64, 115
    scars of, 114–15
    subtypes, 26
    systemic cover-up of, 113–14
    toxicity of, 117
    Victoria's experience of, 73–74
sexual maturation, 87
Sheridan, Margaret, 94–95, 120, 178
Shonkoff, Jack, xii
Shuhada (Sinéad O'Connor), 110
signatures. *See* developmental signatures
Silva, Phil, 155–56
Singer, Tania, 212–13
skin conductance, 77
Slopen, Natalie, 72
social attachments, 148
social isolation, 63, 88, 89, 100, 171, 175–76
social neglect, 51–52
social relationships, 8
social skills, 176–78
social-emotional development, 94
socializing, 159

socioeconomic status, impact of, 99–101
Sofia (case subject), 56–58, 98, 210
somatosensory cortex, 117–18, 208
songbird learning, 85–86
Spinazzola, Joseph, 35–36, 209–10, 217
spiritual cleansing, 181
St. Peter, Lawrence, 113
Stewart, Potter, 23
stress
    acute, 62–63, 200
    calming techniques, 198–203
    caregivers and, 63
    health impact of, 185
    as help to learning, 200
    hibernation as response to, 97
    physical experience of, 64–66
    positive, 63
    relentless, 68–69
    as subjective experience, 64
    tolerable, 63
    toxic, 63
    in war zones, 185
stress system, 62–63
structural racism, 108
students with disabilities, 190
Sudan, 186
Sugira Muryango (Family Strengthening)
    intervention, 185–86
Sunstein, Cass, 210–11
support network, 63. *See also* caregivers
Supreme Court, 23
sympathetic nervous system, 65, 224
synchronous brain prints, 140
synergistic effect, 120–21
Syrian refugees, 39, 226–27
Szostak, Jack, 96

Tanzania, 192
teacher-student relationships, 190, 192–93,
    203–4, 216–17
Teicher, Martin, 108–9, 163
telomeres, 96–97
Tenure dimension of ACEs, 50,
    62–67, 86, 92
Thaler, Richard, 210–11
therapy-assisted treatment, 236–38, 244
Think It class, 198, 202
threats, response to, 105–6, 134.
    See also fear

Timing dimension of ACEs, 50, 56–61, 86, 89, 116
tolerable stress, 63
Tommy (case subject), 111, 220, 222
tonic immobility, 68–69
toxic deprivation, 96–98
toxic stress, 63
Toxicity dimension of ACEs, 50, 66, 73–77, 88–89
TRACEs (traumatic reactions to adverse childhood experiences), 30–32, 41, 63, 67, 104, 115, 117, 140, 186
transcranial direct current stimulation (TDCS), 220
transcranial magnetic stimulation (TMS), 220, 223, 227–28, 244
trauma
    complex, 217
    defining, 33–34
    DSM-5 defining, 33
    signatures, 34–37
    stress reactions, 33–34
trauma-informed care, 191–92, 199
Trauma-Informed Community Empowerment, 186
trauma-informed schools, 191–94
trauma-sensitive teachers, 203–4
treatment-resistant depression, 108, 230–31, 233–36
Trier Social Stress Test, 160
Turbulence dimension of ACEs, 50, 67–73, 94
Turing, Alan, 3
Tutsi tribe, 184
20/20 (television program), 91
Type dimension of ACEs, 50, 51–56, 86, 116

Uganda, 123–24, 182–83, 192
Ukraine, 140, 184–85
Umiltà, Maria, 130
UN Convention on the Rights of Children, xii, 135
UNICEF, 100, 140

vagus nerve, 64, 138, 211–13
van der Kolk, Bessel, 35–36, 209–10, 217, 223
ventral (front) vagal state, 65
verbal abuse

    from caregivers, 107–8
    in children's books, 107
    consequences of, 108
    forms of, 107–8
    impact of, 108–9
    parental, 109
    psychological results of, 109
    signatures, 108–9
Victoria (case subject), 73–74
Viding, Essi, 9
violence
    appetitive, 134–35, 183
    exposure to, 135
    monoamine oxidase A (MAOA) gene, 150–52
    as normalized, 133
    proactive vs. reactive, 133–34
    witnessing, 104
visceromotor cortex, 138
visual cortex, 222–23
visual imagery, 222–23

Wakefield, Jerome, 35
Walton, Greg, 189–90
war/war zones
    allomothers, 185
    brain development and, 139–40
    childhood exposure to, 184–85
    chronic stress and, 185
    home visit interventions, 185–86
    imprint of, 136–37
    intergenerational effects from, 137–38
    recovery from, 185–86
    as type of adversity, 66
Weinstein, Harvey, 74
Williamson, David, 13
Willmore, Lindsay, 38–39
windows of opportunity. *See* opportunity windows
WOOP (Wish-Outcome-Obstacle-Plan), 196–98
World Health Organization, xiii, 16
World Migration Report 2020, 53

Young, Liane, 218–19

Zeanah, Charles, 91, 172
Zoldbrod, Aline, 209